Journal of Semitic Studies Supplement 40

Statistics, Linguistics and the 'Biblical' Dead Sea Scrolls

by

Jarod Jacobs

Published by Oxford University Press
on behalf of the University of Manchester
2018

UNIVERSITY PRESS

Great Clarendon Street, Oxford OX2 6DP

Oxford University Press is a department of the University of Oxford.
It furthers the University's objective of excellence in research, scholarship,
and education by publishing worldwide in

Oxford New York

Athens Auckland Bangkok Bogotá Buenos Aires Cape Town
Chennai Dar es Salaam Delhi Florence Hong Kong Istanbul Karachi
Kolkata Kuala Lumpur Madrid Melbourne Mexico City Mumbai Nairobi
Paris São Paulo Shanghai Singapore Taipei Tokyo Toronto Warsaw

with associated companies in Berlin Ibadan

Oxford is a registered trade mark of Oxford University Press in the UK
and in certain other countries

Published in the United Kingdom
by Oxford University Press, Oxford

© The University of Manchester, 2018

The moral rights of the author have been asserted
Database right Oxford University Press (maker)

First published 2018

All rights reserved. No part of this publication may be reproduced,
stored in a retrieval system, or transmitted, in any form or by any means,
without the prior permission in writing of Oxford University Press,
or as expressly permitted by law, or under terms agreed with the appropriate
reprographics rights organization. Enquiries concerning reproduction
outside the scope of the above should be sent to the Rights Department, Journals
Division, Oxford University Press, at the address above

You must not circulate this book in any other binding or cover and
you must impose this same condition on any acquirer

A catalogue for this book is available from the British Library

Library of Congress Cataloguing in Publication Data
(Data available)

ISSN 0022-4480
ISBN 978-0-19-882937-9

Subscription information for the Journal of Semitic Studies is available at the journal website:
jss.oxfordjournals.org

Printed in Great Britain by Bell & Bain Ltd, Glasgow

Table of Contents

List of Figures	vii
List of Tables	viii
Abbreviations	x
Acknowledgements	xi
Chapter I Introduction	1
A. Aims and Objectives	6
B. Terminology	9
1. Qumran	9
2. 'Biblical'	9
3. Plus and Minus	11
C. Linguistic Issues	11
D. Nature of the Corpus and Justification of Its Use	14
Chapter II History of Linguistic Studies on the 'Biblical' Scrolls	17
A. Burrows	18
B. Mansoor	20
C. Kutscher	21
D. Qimron	24
E. Tov	24
F. Muraoka	26
G. Abegg	27
H. Fassberg	28
I. Reymond	29
J. Hornkohl	30
K. Rezetko and Young	32
1. Unprincipled Corpus	33
2. Lack of Linguistic Theoretical Foundation	34
3. Deficient Data or Rigorous Analytical Analysis of the Data	34
4. MT-Centred Comparisons	35
5. Neglected Syntactic Variations	35

Chapter III Methodology 37
   A. Grammatical Variable Analysis 37
      1. Cross-Textual Variable Analysis and the
         'Biblical' Dead Sea Scrolls 38
      2. Inter-Textual Variable Analysis and the
         'Biblical' Dead Sea Scrolls 39
   B. Corpus Linguistics 40
      1. Empirical Analysis 40
      2. Corpus Design 41
      3. Data Collection 60
      4. Quantitative Analysis 61
   C. Conclusion 69

Chapter IV Global Analysis of the Linguistic Character of the 'Biblical'
Dead Sea Scrolls 73
   A. Global Analysis of the Particle System 73
      1. Directive *he* 76
      2. מאדה 80
      3. The Definite Article 83
      4. Direct Object Marker 90
      5. Interchange Between אל – על 93
      6. The Inseparable Prepositions – ב, כ and ל 96
      7. The Conjunction *Vav* 98
      8. Conclusions 100
   B. Global Analysis of the Verbal System 101
      1. The Role of 1QIsa[a] and its Influence on the Data 103
      2. Distinctive Readings in the Qumran 'Biblical' Manuscripts 104
      3. *Vav* plus Imperfect 105
      4. Preterite 109
      5. Infinitives 111
      6. Conclusions 112
   C. Global Analysis of the Nominal System 113
      1. Shifts in Number 114
      2. Pluses and Minuses of Suffixes 117
      3. Shifts in Gender 119

4. Names for God	120
5. Conclusions	121
D. General Conclusions	121
Chapter V The Linguistic Character of Individual Scrolls	125
A. 1QIsa[a]	126
1. Orthography	127
2. Textual Character	128
3. One Text or Two	128
4. Verbal System	130
5. QH Characteristics and the Verbal System of 1QIsa[a]	132
6. Nominal System	135
7. Particles	136
B. 1QIsa[b]	142
1. Orthography	143
2. Textual Character	143
3. Verbal System	143
4. Nominal System	144
5. Particle System	144
6. Conclusion	144
C. 4QNum[b]	145
1. Orthography	145
2. Textual Character	145
3. Verbal System	146
4. Nominal System	146
5. Particles	148
6. Conclusion	152
D. 4QSam[a]	152
1. Orthography	153
2. Textual Character	153
3. Verbal System	153
4. Nominal System	155
5. Particles	157
6. Conclusion	160

Chapter VI Qualitative Analysis of the Linguistic Character of the 'Biblical'
Dead Sea Scrolls: Some Broader Implications 161
- A. Antilanguage 161
- B. Secondary Socialization 163
- C. Linguistic Stability and Textual Authority 167
- D. Conclusions 170

Chapter VII Conclusion 171
- A. Addressing the Problems with Past Research 171
- B. Review of Conclusions 173
- C. Steps Toward a Comprehensive Picture of the Linguistic Character of the Dead Sea Scrolls 174

Bibliography 177

Appendices 183
- A. Pluses and Minuses of the Directive *he* 183
- B. מאדה 190
- C. Definite Article 191
- D. Direct Object Marker 198
- E. על and אל Interchange 205
- F. Particles ב, כ, ל 212
- G. Conjunction *Vav* 219
- H. Shifts to *Vav* Plus Imperfect 227
- I. Preterite 234
- J. Infinitive Absolute 241
- K. Suffix - Plus 248

Indices 255

List of Figures

Figure 1. Variation Rate of 1QIsa^a I	49
Figure 2. Variation Rate of 1QIsa^a II	51
Figure 3. Variation Rate of 1QIsa^b	52
Figure 4. Variation Rate of 11QPs^a	53
Figure 5. Variation Rate of 4QpaleoExod^m	54
Figure 6. Histogram of Variation Rates for All 'Biblical' DSS	56
Figure 7. Histogram of 'Biblical' Scrolls Over 100 Words	57
Figure 8. Histogram of 'Biblical' Scrolls Over 200 Words	57
Figure 9. Gaussian Curve and Standard Deviations	68
Figure 10. Variation Rates for Particles	75
Figure 11. Variation Rates for 1QIsa^a I and II	129

List of Tables

Table 1. 'Biblical' DSS Corpus for Statistical Analysis	59
Table 2. Hypothetical Comparison Between EBH and LBH	63
Table 3. Variations Involving Particles	74
Table 4. Directive *he*s	77
Table 5. T-Test Applied to the Directive *he* (Pluses) Data	78
Table 6. T-Test Applied to the Directive *he* (Minuses) Data	78
Table 7. Directive *he* and שם	79
Table 8. מאד and מאדה Data	81
Table 9. Definite Article Data	83
Table 10. T-Test Applied to the Definite Article (Pluses) Data	83
Table 11. T-Test Applied to the Definite Article (Minuses) Data	84
Table 12. Definite Article and *Aleph, He, Khet* and *Ayin*: Pluses and Minuses (1QIsa^a)	86
Table 13. Definite Article and *Aleph, He, Khet* and *Ayin*: by Letter (1QIsa^a)	86
Table 14. Definite Article and *Aleph, He, Khet* and *Ayin*: Pluses and Minuses ('Biblical' Dead Sea Scrolls)	87
Table 15. Definite Article and *Aleph, He, Khet* and *Ayin*: Rate of Occurrence	87
Table 16. Definite Article and *Nomen Regens*	88
Table 17. Definite Article and Proclitic Prepositions	89
Table 18. Direct Object Marker (Pluses and Minuses) Data	90
Table 19. T-Test Applied to the Direct Object Marker (Pluses) Data	91
Table 20. T-Test Applied to the Direct Object Marker (Minuses) Data	91
Table 21. Variations Involving Particles	92
Table 22. Overall Variation Rate	92
Table 23. Interchange Between אל – על	93
Table 24. T-Test Applied to the MT = אל, Scroll = על Variations Data	94
Table 25. T-Test Applied to the MT = על, Scroll = אל Variations Data	94
Table 26. T-Test Applied to the MT = אל, Scroll = על Variations Data (Distinctive Readings)	95
Table 27. Interchange Between אל and על by Corpus	96
Table 28. The Inseparable Prepositions – ל, כ, ב	97

Table 29. The Conjunction *Vav*	98
Table 30. T-Test Applied to the Conjunction *Vav* (Pluses) Data	99
Table 31. T-Test Applied to the Conjunction *Vav* (Minuses) Data	99
Table 32. Verbal System Variations	102
Table 33. Verbal System Variations Excluding 1QIsa[a]	103
Table 34. Verbal System Variations 1QIsa[a]	104
Table 35. Distinctive Verbal System Variations in the 'Biblical' DSS	105
Table 36. Shifts to *Vav* Plus Imperfect	105
Table 37. T-Test Applied to the Shifts Towards *Vav* Plus Imperfect Data	106
Table 38. Pluses and Minuses of the Preterite	109
Table 39. Verbal System Variations	110
Table 40. Preterite Variations and Orthographic Style	110
Table 41. T-Test Applied to the Preterite (Minuses) Data	111
Table 42. Infinitive Absolute Data	112
Table 43. Nominal Variations	113
Table 44. Shifts in Number Data	114
Table 45. T-Test Applied to the Shifts from S to P/D Data	114
Table 46. T-Test Applied to the Shifts from P/D to S Data	115
Table 47. Comparison of the Use of די and ידי in Hebrew Corpora	116
Table 48. Suffix Pluses Data	117
Table 49. T-Test Applied to the Suffix (Pluses) Data	118
Table 50. T-Test Applied to the Suffix (Minuses) Data	118
Table 51. Shifts in Gender Data	119
Table 52. Shifts in Gender Compared with Orthographic Style	119
Table 53. T-Test Applied to Variation Rates of the Two Halves of 1QIsa[a]	130
Table 54. The Use of אל and ל in the Phrase 'and He Said to Him'	139
Table 55. The Use of אל and לא in Hebrew Corpora	150

Abbreviations

ARPH	*Annual Review of Public Health*
BibOr	Biblica et Orientalia
CahRB	Cahiers de la Revue biblique
DJD	Discoveries in the Judaean Desert
DSD	*Dead Sea Discoveries*
EHB	*Economics and Human Biology*
EHLL	Encyclopedia of Hebrew Language and Linguistics
EncJud	Encyclopaedia Judaica
ErIsr	Eretz-Israel
HS	Hebrew Studies
HSM	Harvard Semitic Monographs
IEJ	*Israel Exploration Journal*
JAOS	Journal of the American Oriental Society
JBL	Journal of Biblical Literature
JHS	Journal of Hebrew Scriptures
JSOTSup	Journal for the Study of the Old Testament Supplement Series
JSS	*Journal of Semitic Studies*
LLC	Literary and Linguistic Computing
LNTS	Library of New Testament Studies
LS	*Language in Society*
LSAWS	Linguistic Studies in Ancient West Semitic
SBLANEM	Society of Biblical Literature Ancient Near Eastern Monographs
SBLEJL	Society of Biblical Literature Early Judaism and Its Literature
SBLRBS	Society of Biblical Literature Resources for Biblical Study
ScrHier	Scripta Hierosolymitana
STDJ	Studies on the Text of the Desert of Judah
VT	*Vetus Testamentum*
VTSup	Supplements to Vetus Testamentum
ZAW	*Zeitschrift für die alttestamentliche Wissenschaft*

Acknowledgements

The present book had its beginnings as my PhD thesis for the University of Manchester. I am grateful for the expert guidance provided by my advisors, George Brooke and Todd Klutz. I am also deeply indebted to Robert Rezetko, who provided many helpful suggestions as I modified my thesis into this book. Lastly, and most importantly, I would like to thank my wife, Alma, for her endless encouragement as I have attempted to complete this project.

I would like to dedicate this work to the memory of my mother, Lori Dunross, who sacrificed so much as she raised my brothers and me. I most definitely would not have been able to accomplish the things that I have if it were not for her endless love.

Chapter I

Introduction

The language of the Dead Sea Scrolls (DSS) has played an important role in the field of Hebrew linguistics. This is especially true in studies of the diachronic development of this ancient language. In order to place this project in the larger context of Hebrew linguistics and the study of its development over time, I will begin by discussing the current state of the field.

Until recently, Hebrew scholars have been in broad agreement about the development of Hebrew over time. Most scholars have used essentially the same methodology, based mainly on A. Hurvitz's work,[1] to explore the diachronic development of Hebrew. However, over the past decade a dissenting view, proposed by R. Rezetko and I. Young, has challenged the majority view.[2] Traditionally, linguistic data was considered with textual and historical information to date texts. This linguistic research presented a diachronic picture of the Hebrew language that contained three basic phases: Archaic Biblical Hebrew (ABH), Early/Classical/Standard Biblical Hebrew[3] (EBH) and Late Biblical Hebrew[4] (LBH). Rezetko et al. have agreed that there are different styles of Hebrew represented in biblical literature, but they argue that the differences between the various forms of Hebrew should not be understood as a diachronic development. Instead, they claim that multiple styles of Hebrew were used during the Second Temple period (and possibly even before) and differences in style reflect an author's preference.[5] Never-

---

1 See for example, A. Hurvitz, *A Linguistic Study of the Relationship between the Priestly Source and the Book of Ezekiel: A New Approach to an Old Problem* (CahRB 20, Paris 1982), 2. And Idem, 'Can Biblical Texts Be Dated Linguistically? Chronological Perspectives in the Historical Study of Biblical Hebrew', in A. Lemaire and M. Saebø (eds), *Congress Volume, Oslo 1998* (VTSup 80, Leiden 2000), 154.
2 See I. Young, 'Late Biblical Hebrew and Hebrew Inscriptions', in I. Young (ed.), *Biblical Hebrew: Studies in Chronology and Typology* (JSOTSup 369, London 2003), 276–311. Idem, 'Biblical Texts Cannot be Dated Linguistically', *HS* 46 (2005), 341–51. I. Young, R. Rezetko and M. Ehrensvärd, *Linguistic Dating of Biblical Texts*, 2 vols. (London 2008). M. Ehrensvärd, 'Why Biblical Texts Cannot Be Dated Linguistically', *HS* 47 (2006), 177–89.
3 While various books and passages have been included in this corpus by different scholars, I will utilize the following for EBH: Genesis; Exodus 1–19, 23:20–4:18, 31–5, 40; Leviticus 8–10, 24:10–23; Numbers 10–25, 31–6; Deuteronomy 1–11, 26–34; Joshua–2 Kings.
4 I will use the following texts for LBH: 1 Chronicles, 2 Chronicles, Esther, Ezra, Nehemiah, Daniel.
5 Young, Rezetko and Ehrensvärd, *Linguistic Dating of Biblical Texts*, 2, 96.

theless, Rezetko and Young hardly hold to a 'non-chronological model' of ancient Hebrew as is sometimes claimed by others.[6]

The methodology of the traditional scholars has undergone some development over time. In an attempt to refine the diachronic approach, R. Polzin compared 1 and 2 Samuel (used as a representative of EBH) with 1 and 2 Chronicles (representative of LBH) in order to identify linguistic differences.[7] From this study Polzin gathered nineteen non-lexical features he considered distinctive of LBH. Shortly after Polzin, Hurvitz refined this approach further by developing three criteria for a specific linguistic feature to be considered useful for diachronic studies: 1) the feature must be found almost exclusively in the LBH corpus, 2) EBH must have a contrasting feature and 3) the feature must be used widely in extra-biblical texts from the Second Temple period.[8] Hurvitz's methodology gave the diachronic enterprise a scientific quality, but the traditional approach did not engage with the science of modern linguistic theory until the recent work of scholars such as J.A. Cook[9] and R.D. Holmstedt.[10] Cook and Holmstedt intentionally engaged current historical linguistic theories as a foundation for their arguments. One of their primary historical linguistic tools is the Sigmoid Curve (S-curve). C.-J. N. Bailey, who was one of the first scholars to use this tool in historical linguistics, defines the S-curve as follows: 'A given change begins quite gradually; after reaching a certain point (say, twenty percent), it picks up momentum and proceeds at a much faster rate; and finally tails off slowly before reaching completion. The result is an S-curve'.[11] Both Cook and Holmstedt use the S-curve to plot the development from an 'early' feature to a 'late' feature within a selected corpus of texts. The foundational work of Polzin, the basic criteria of Hurvitz, and the interaction with modern historical linguistic theory by Cook and Holmstedt has all resulted in the traditional diachronic approach being accepted as the consensus paradigm for understanding the different variations of Biblical Hebrew.

The dissenting viewpoint (developed by Young et al.) challenges the tradi-

---

6   See, for example, Rezetko and Young, *Historical Linguistics* 5, 400, 594–6.
7   R. Polzin, *Late Biblical Hebrew: Toward an Historical Typology of Biblical Hebrew Prose* (HSM 12, Missoula, MT 1976).
8   Hurvitz, *A Linguistic Study*.
9   J.A. Cook, 'Detecting Development in Biblical Hebrew Using Diachronic Typology', in C. Miller-Naudé and Z. Ziony (eds), *Diachrony in Biblical Hebrew* (LSAWS 8, Winona Lake, IN 2012), 83–95.
10 R.D. Holmstedt, 'Historical Linguistics and Biblical Hebrew', in *Diachrony*, 97–124.
11 C.-J.N. Bailey, *Variation and Linguistic Theory* (Arlington, TX 1973), 77.

tional model at every point. Their arguments are developed in three monographs and a number of articles (see note 2 above). In response to scholars such as Polzin and Hurvitz, whom I have characterized as representative of the early stages of the traditional view, the 'challengers' (as they have become known)[12] have provided a critique that can be summarized with three points. First, they argue scholars too quickly interpret typological differences between EBH and LBH as chronological, instead of considering other alternatives. Second, they claim the traditional paradigm favours linguistic evidence over non-linguistic evidence, such as archaeology, without a solid basis for doing so. Finally, Rezetko and Young see circular reasoning at play where the literary evidence of two corpora within the Hebrew Bible supports the linguistic evidence of two phases of Hebrew and vice-versa.[13]

Rezetko and Young also challenge more recent developments to the traditional paradigm. For instance, they[14] along with others such as A.D. Forbes[15] argue that Cook and Holmstedt are using the S-curve incorrectly. Rezetko and Young point out that the S-curve is a descriptive tool, based on the observation that many linguistic features that go through diachronic change follow an S-curve in their diffusion and innovation. Yet this is not always the case. Many features of a language begin to change, aligning with the early phase of an S-curve, but as time passes, some features may fail to completely diffuse. If the data for such a feature were plotted on a graph, it would look more like a bell-shaped curve than an S-curve. In fact, languages change in so many different ways that the data can take any shape. Because of this 'the shape of the adopter distribution for a particular innovation ought to be regarded as an open question, to be determined empirically'.[16] That is to say, all aspects of the chronological development of a linguistic feature (rate of change, texts with the change and date of the texts) need to be established independently. Yet Cook and Holmstedt gather their linguistic data for individual texts and lay it over an S-curve in order to establish the relative date for the authorship of each text. They are therefore

---

12 A. Hurvitz, 'The Recent Debate on Late Biblical Hebrew: Solid Data, Experts' Opinions, and Inconclusive Arguments', *HS* 47 (2006), 201.
13 R. Rezetko and I. Young, *Historical Linguistics and Biblical Hebrew: Steps Toward an Integrated Approach* (ANEM 9, Atlanta 2014), 55.
14 For their full discussion, see Ibid., 223–6.
15 A.D. Forbes calls Holmstedt's use of the s-curve 'Naïve' stating '[t]he reality of fluctuating data makes untrustworthy the s-curve for ש-diffusion produced by Holmstedt'. (Paper presented at the Annual Meeting of the SBL, Atlanta, GA, 20–4 November 2015).
16 W. Labov, *Social Change* (Malden, MA 2001), 75.

using the S-curve as a predictive rather than a descriptive tool.

Another critique that Rezetko and Young make of the traditional diachronic approach to the Hebrew language is the comparison of dissimilar texts. Relying on arguments from O. Fischer,[17] Rezetko and Young critique recent developments in the traditional paradigm for comparing the language of texts written in different genres.[18] The problem they see is that any differences between the texts could be due to either the difference in genre or the different times that they were written (along with other potential factors). However, Holmstedt and J. Screnock argue that a diachronic explanation should always be considered first. If a diachronic factor is found, then other factors are not considered, thus allowing them to compare the language of texts of different genres because they have developed a hierarchy of possible causes of linguistic difference. They explain their reason as follows:

> In his discussion of stylistics, Crystal asserts that before 'style' can be discussed, all historical and dialectal factors must be eliminated… We thus begin with a diachronic analysis, assuming that if the variation between two features aligns with the S-curve of diffusion, it is unlikely to be coincidental. We move beyond diachrony only if the tokens are too few for statistically-valid analysis or if the pattern of variation does not fit the S-curve model of diffusion.[19]

The first problem with this approach, as outlined above, is the assumption that all linguistic change follows an S-curve. In fact, linguistic changes can follow any pattern, although research has shown the S-curve to be common. D. Crystal cites another problem: 'Regional, social, and historical variations in a use of language have to be eliminated before we can get down to some serious study of what we consider to be "style"'.[20] Holmstedt and Screnock focus on diachronic change based on Crystal's comments, while pushing all other types of language variation aside. However, Crystal is only advocating pushing aside issues of style until all other types of variation are ruled out. Instead of ranking diachronic change above all others, questions of dialect, register and genre as well as diachrony (and eventually style) need to be carefully balanced. Part of the problem here is the definition of style. Holmstedt and Screnock seem to be defining style very broadly to include all variation types except diachronic and dialectal (style

---

17 O. Fischer, *Morphosyntactic Change: Functional and Formal Perspectives* (Oxford 2007), 12–15.
18 Rezetko and Young, *Historical Linguistics*, 6.
19 R.D. Holmstedt and J. Screnock, 'Whither Esther? A Linguistic Profile of the Book of Esther' (Paper presented at the Annual Meeting of the SBL, Baltimore, 24 November 2013).
20 D. Crystal, 'Style: The Varieties of English', in W.F. Bolton and D. Crystal (eds), *The English Language* (London 1987), 206.

then would include differences in genre). However, Crystal is focusing upon two very specific types of style, authorial style and register style. We cannot, therefore, simply set aside genre considerations until diachronic factors have been ruled out. That approach is too simplistic. All potential factors need to be considered equally and at the same time.

Aside from critiquing the traditional view, Rezetko and Young develop their own methodologies (based on current linguistic theory) and arrive at different conclusions. Rezetko and Young rely heavily on historical and social linguistic theories, such as cross-textual variable analysis and corpus linguistics. I will be utilizing both cross-textual variable analysis and corpus linguistics throughout this project and will discuss them at length in Chapter III. A. below.

Linguistic research on the Hebrew language has been strongly focused on how it changed over time, as the above summary shows. And while it is true that the DSS, particularly the 'biblical' scrolls, can add significantly to the diachrony discussion, more work needs to be done on understanding the linguistic nature of these witnesses before scholars rely too heavily upon the evidence they provide. Though several scholars have described in part different aspects of the language of the DSS, no one has yet produced a comprehensive analysis. This project fills part of that gap by presenting a thorough analysis of the language found in the 'biblical' DSS. It is hoped that along with previous scholarship this work will function as foundational for future projects engaging the language of these scrolls.

My research begins with the question: 'Do the "biblical" Dead Sea Scrolls contain any distinctive linguistic characteristics, beyond orthography and morphology, when compared with other witnesses to the "biblical" text?' As I show in my review of the pertinent scholarly literature below, there are various answers to this question, both positive and negative. Some argue that there are distinctive linguistic characteristics found in the scrolls, while others take the opposite stance. For the purposes of this project, I will proceed with the following hypothesis: The 'biblical' DSS do not contain any distinctive linguistic characteristics beyond orthography and morphology. Defaulting to the negative hypothesis is common in scientific studies, since assuming no statistically significant patterns will be found helps to avoid bias and the influence of presuppositions. Yet most scientific studies aim to disprove their starting hypothesis. For example, researchers who develop a new drug hope that drug will prove more effective than previous treatments. If the new drug ends up being less effective, then it is often considered to be a failure. But this is not the case for the project at hand. Though patterns of variation may be interesting, it would be just as informative to find a lack of consistent change.

Therefore, I begin with the hypothesis that there are no statistically significant patterns of difference between the 'biblical' scrolls and other witnesses. In Chapter II, I review scholarly discussion regarding the linguistic nature of the 'biblical' scrolls, with special attention paid to their place within the history of the Hebrew language. In the next chapter, I present the methodology that I use to test my hypothesis. As mentioned above, this methodology is firmly grounded in statistical theory, but it is also influenced heavily by modern linguistic methodology. In Chapter IV, I test my hypothesis by undertaking a global review of all the variations between the 'biblical' DSS and the Masoretic Text (MT), as well as other major witnesses. In Chapter V, I test the conclusions of Chapter IV by reviewing the linguistic character of five individual manuscripts. In Chapter VI, I connect my results to the sociolinguistic setting in which the 'biblical' DSS were produced. The final chapter presents a summary of my conclusions. Here, I begin by discussing my aims and objectives, terminology, corpora issues and linguistic issues.

A. Aims and Objectives

The recent publication of the Isaiah Scrolls in the *Discoveries in the Judaean Desert* series marks the culmination of over seventy years of work. This milestone is accompanied by the digital publication of all of the scrolls through Accordance Bible Software[21] and The Dead Sea Scrolls Electronic Library,[22] giving scholars access to powerful search- and data-gathering features. Those resources mark a watershed in DSS research since scholars have never before had access to all of the DSS. And scholars have never been able to leverage the power of computers to enhance their research potential as they can today. Because of these resources, the time is ripe to undertake new research and to update past work.

The topic of this project, the linguistic character of the 'biblical' DSS, is not new. Indeed, from the early days of scrolls research, scholars have focused on

---

21 M.G. Abegg, Jr. and C. Toewes, *Qumran Biblical Texts*, Version 1.0 (Altamonte Springs, FL 2007). Also, M.G. Abegg, Jr., *Qumran Non-biblical Manuscripts*, Version 2.5 (Altamonte Springs, FL 1999).

22 E. Tov and N.B. Reynolds (eds), *The Dead Sea Scrolls Electronic Library* (Leiden 2006).

this work. Yet my objective, methodological approach, as well as my conclusions, are new. In this chapter, I will develop my main objectives and in subsequent chapters develop in detail my methodology and conclusions.

My main objective is to provide a comprehensive review of the linguistic character of all of the 'biblical' DSS. I will use every 'biblical' scroll (as defined below) and every variation between the 'biblical' scrolls and the MT. However, I do not intend to provide a detailed account of each individual linguistic aspect of the 'biblical' scrolls, such as E.Y. Kutscher undertook for 1QIsa^a.[23] Instead, I will focus on patterns of variations that set the linguistic character of the 'biblical' DSS apart from their parallel representations in other manuscript traditions such as the MT. This project will focus on the linguistic nature of the 'biblical' scrolls, an approach that stands in contrast to the focus of many scholars primarily interested in Qumran Hebrew (QH); for some that includes the 'biblical' scrolls and for others it does not. By starting with QH and then analysing the 'biblical' scrolls, scholars tend to read too much into rare features. However, by starting with the 'biblical' scrolls, the rare features take their appropriate place and the more common linguistic patterns start to become clear. This approach also helps to simplify the goals of the project. Instead of connecting the linguistic features found in the 'biblical' scrolls to a group of people who may or may not have produced those scrolls, I will first focus on the scrolls themselves and then progress to tentative connections to the sociological environment from which they came.

Thus the broad objective of this project is to analyse comprehensively the linguistic character of the 'biblical' DSS. A secondary, yet clearly related, objective is to identify and explain previously unknown linguistic characteristics of the 'biblical' scrolls. Scholars have long noted the distinctive orthographic and morphological features found in some of the scrolls, but little attention has been given to other grammatical features. Some scholars, like Kutscher who analysed one scroll, or T. Muraoka,[24] who focused on a small set of features within a select corpus of manuscripts, have moved beyond orthography and morphology. However, as I will discuss in Chapter II, their work needs updating and reassessment based on the newly available resources.

---

23   E.Y. Kutscher, *The Language and Linguistic Background of the Isaiah Scroll (1QIsa^a)* (STDJ 6, Leiden 1974).
24   T. Muraoka, 'An Approach to the Morphosyntax and Syntax of Qumran Hebrew', in T. Muraoka and J.F. Elwolde (eds), *Diggers at the Well: Proceedings of a Third International Symposium on the Hebrew of the Dead Sea Scrolls and Ben Sira* (STDJ 36, Leiden 2000), 193–214.

I also test claims scholars have made, such as Muraoka's assumption that 'one should be able to learn about the nature of Qumran Hebrew ... by analysing cases where Qumran biblical texts differ and deviate from the standard biblical text, namely the MT'.[25] Muraoka does not test this assumption, nor does he discuss the problems that it raises. M.G. Abegg, Jr. follows Muraoka by theorizing that through a comprehensive analysis of the linguistic character of the 'biblical' DSS, '[w]e will likely conclude that subsets of syntactic features will help define particular scribal associations influenced by the language that the scribes spoke'.[26] This is a broader and more open-ended suggestion than Muraoka's, yet Abegg's work (as he notes) is still preliminary. Over against Kutscher, Muraoka, Abegg and others, some scholars claim that the 'biblical' scrolls do not contain useful data for characterizing Second Temple Hebrew. The following quotations, both coming from linguistic profiles of QH published in an encyclopaedia/handbook, reveal the contrast between scholars who rely on the 'biblical' scrolls for data reflecting QH and those who avoid the 'biblical' scrolls. S. E. Fassberg states: 'In the following description of the language the examples are cited from the Great Isaiah Scroll (1QIs^a) wherever possible, in order to highlight the differences between the Hebrew found in the scrolls and that of Tiberian Hebrew as reflected in the Masoretic text'.[27] In contrast, J. Joosten says: 'Fragments of the books that ended up in the canon of the Hebrew Bible will be disregarded in the present survey to the extent that they represent writings that are very much older than the sectarian scrolls'.[28] Thus, one scholar looks to the 'biblical' scrolls whenever possible, while the other sets them aside. Through a comprehensive analysis of the linguistic nature of the 'biblical' DSS, I assess those two contrasting approaches.

In summary, my aims and objectives focus on comprehensively analysing the linguistic nature of the 'biblical' DSS, identifying distinctive linguistic features that are not orthographic or morphological, and testing previous claims about the connection between those scrolls and QH.

---

25 Ibid., 194.
26 M.G. Abegg, Jr., 'The Biblical Dead Sea Scrolls and Second Temple Hebrew Syntax', in P.W. Flint, J. Duhaime and K.S. Baek (eds), *Celebrating the Dead Sea Scrolls: A Canadian Collection* (SBLEJL 30, Atlanta 2011), 163–72.
27 S.E. Fassberg, 'Dead Sea Scrolls: Linguistic Features', *EHLL* 1 (2013), 673–84.
28 J. Joosten, 'Hebrew, Aramaic and Greek in the Qumran Scrolls', in J.J. Collins and T.H. Lim (eds), *The Oxford Handbook of the Dead Sea Scrolls* (Oxford 2010), 354.

B. Terminology

Several terms become problematic in discussions of the linguistic character of the 'biblical' DSS, which I will focus on here: Qumran, biblical, plus and minus.

1. Qumran

Many scholars use the term 'Qumran Hebrew' when referring to the distinctive linguistic features found in the DSS. Yet this term is problematic. To begin with, not all of the scrolls found at Qumran were produced there.[29] A more appropriate term for this style of Hebrew may be DSS Hebrew. However, that term has its own problems. Most notable is the linguistic diversity found in the scrolls.[30] While some scrolls such as 11Q13 (a Jubilees manuscript) and 11Q19 (a Temple Scroll manuscript) share distinctive traits, others such as 3Q15 (Copper Scroll) are closer to previously known forms of Hebrew. This linguistic variety has led some scholars to develop categories within QH, such as S. Morag's General QH, Copper Scroll Hebrew and Qumran Mishnaic.[31] Labelling the form of Hebrew found in the scrolls 'DSS Hebrew' does not avoid the issue of diversity, but since we lack a better alternative, I have used QH as a label for the style of Hebrew found in the scrolls from the Judaean Wilderness, while recognizing its problems.

2. 'Biblical'

In this study, I will be working primarily with texts that have been labelled 'biblical'. Throughout, I will place the term 'biblical' in quotation marks whenever it is used as a label for manuscripts that contain almost exclusively passages now to be found in Rabbinic Bibles.[32] There are two reasons for this.

---

29 'Not all the scrolls found at Qumran were copied on site. Some were certainly copied before the site was reoccupied in the early first century BCE'. J.J. Collins, 'Sectarian Communities in the Dead Sea Scrolls', in *The Oxford Handbook of the Dead Sea Scrolls*, 160.
30 Joosten, 'Hebrew, Aramaic and Greek', 354.
31 S. Morag, 'Qumran Hebrew: Some Typological Observations', *VT* 38 (1988), 148.
32 As the following explanation will show, my approach to this subject closely follows that of E.D. Reymond who states: 'Another common way of dividing the texts is between biblical manuscripts and non-biblical manuscripts (in other words, manuscripts that contain texts that would later become part of the Bible and those that did not). Here, too, categorizing texts is not always as unambiguous as one might initially think. First, the very concept is anachronistic since what the ancients felt to be scripture and what moderns think of as scripture are not coterminous. Second, some scrolls are made up of only portions of what we identify as scripture; the other material does not belong to any modern canon. For the sake of simplicity, 'biblical' in relation to the scrolls will refer to those nonpesher, nonreworked scrolls that contain texts that are currently

First, the term 'biblical' is anachronistic when applied to ancient texts. Modern readers of the Qumran texts may naturally separate the manuscripts into two groups: 'biblical' and non-biblical. But the people who used those manuscripts would not have viewed their collection in this way. Discussing the term 'rewritten Bible', S. White Crawford explains, 'A bible, in the sense of a fixed collection of sacred books regarded as authoritative by a particular religious tradition, did not exist during the time in which the Qumran corpus was copied (roughly 250 BCE to 68 CE)'.[33]

Second, I use quotation marks around the term 'biblical' when applied to Qumran texts because it is not always possible to determine what is 'Bible' and what is a text that uses quotations from the biblical books. On the one hand, this is due to the small size of many fragments, and on the other hand to the nature of texts in the Second Temple period. A small fragment that has ten words from Exodus on it may have originally been part of a Torah scroll, but it could also have been part of a text such as the Temple Scroll. Further, how 'pure' does a text need to be in order to be considered 'biblical'? Should 1QIsa[a] be considered 'biblical' even though it has numerous differences when compared with the Leningrad Codex?[34] Or should phylacteries be placed in this group even though they only contain excerpts from books that are now considered part of the Bible?[35] One possible response to those questions is to avoid the term 'biblical' all together. However, finding an alternative that does not have similar problems is difficult. Thus, for this study I have chosen to continue with the term 'biblical' for the sake of convenience. I place this term in quotation marks

---

part of the Jewish canon, though portions of them may have no parallel in the contemporary Tanakh. The phylactery texts, although of a different character than the biblical texts, will here be labelled 'biblical' based on the similar labeling in the DSS Concordance and in Accordance software. 'Nonbiblical' will refer to everything else'. E.D. Reymond, *Qumran Hebrew: An Overview of Orthography, Phonology, and Morphology* (SBLRBS 76, Atlanta 2014), 5–6.

33 S. White Crawford, 'The "Rewritten" Bible at Qumran: A Look at Three Texts', in J.H. Charlesworth (ed.), *The Bible and the Dead Sea Scrolls, Volume One: Scripture and the Scrolls: The Second Princeton Symposium on Judaism and Christian Origins* (Waco, TX 2006), 131–48.

34 S. Talmon argues that some early Qumran scholars characterized 1QIsa[a] as sectarian due to its 'vulgar' language and many discrepancies with the MT. See F.M. Cross, 'The History of the Biblical Text in the Light of Discoveries in the Judaean Desert', in F.M. Cross and S. Talmon (eds), *Qumran and the History of the Biblical Text* (Cambridge 1975), 177–8.

35 G. Geiger includes the phylacteries and *mezuzot* because 'sie sind per definitionem eine Zusammenstellung biblischer Texten'. G. Geiger, *Das hebräische Partizip in den Texten aus der judäischen Wüste* (STDJ 101, Leiden 2012), 10. Cross and Talmon deal with similar questions in their contributions to F.M. Cross and S. Talmon (eds), *Qumran and the History of the Biblical Text* (Cambridge 1975), as well as White Crawford, 'The "Rewritten" Bible'.

not to alleviate its inherent shortcomings but to draw attention to them.

3. Plus and Minus

The last problematic terms are 'plus' and 'minus' (e.g. 1QIsa^a has a plus of the definite article in 1:2). I use 'plus' and 'minus' when speaking of variations between two manuscripts to move away from the loaded terms 'addition' and 'omission', which imply a chronological relationship among the witnesses. 'Addition' and 'omission' imply that the scribe of the scroll either added something that was not in his *Vorlage*, or omitted something that was. Yet we cannot always determine if that is actually the case. If 1QIsa^a has ארץ preceded by a definite article where the MT does not, it is possible that the scribe of the Leningrad Codex removed the article. It is also possible that the article was not in 1QIsa^a's *Vorlage;* there are other possibilities as well. So, to say 1QIsa^a has an addition of the definite article assumes more than can be demonstrated. I have moved to 'plus' and 'minus', which are softer terms, though they are still not entirely neutral. Just as I articulated above, I am forced to settle for certain terms even though they do not convey the desired specific meaning. That is to say, 'plus' and 'minus' may seem to carry more meaning than is intended. All I mean by either of those terms is that the manuscript with the plus has a word or phrase that another manuscript does not.

C. Linguistic Issues

A number of linguistic issues are involved in discussions of the linguistic character of the 'biblical' DSS. Here I will discuss three: register, genre and style.

Research on ancient Hebrew often lacks clarity regarding the nature of register and dialects, as well as in regard to modern linguistic theory. To alleviate that lack of clarity, I offer definitions of these terms as I analyse current research and suggest a few refinements.

The first, and maybe the most significant, linguistic concept for ancient Hebrew studies is register. There is considerable disagreement even in current linguistic literature on the subject,[36] but the lack of clarity on this issue in Hebrew studies is particularly pronounced.[37] The concept of register in ancient Hebrew

---

36 D. Biber and S. Conrad, *Register, Genre, and Style* (Cambridge 2009), 15.
37 G.A. Rendsburg even uses register and dialect interchangeably. At one point he calls Mishnaic Hebrew a colloquial dialect and in the next sentence he calls it a register. G.A. Rendsburg, 'Northern Hebrew Through Time: From the Song of Deborah to the Mishnah', in *Diachrony*, 356. While

studies focuses almost entirely on 'high/low'[38] and 'spoken/literary'[39] varieties. Three points need to be made regarding this focus of register studies in Hebrew. First, the terms 'high/low' and 'spoken/literary' are misleading. High and low are often connected to a view of the low variety as vulgar[40] and/or corrupt. This is clearly a misunderstanding of language varieties. Some readers of the ancient Hebrew texts may see the infiltration of a spoken version of Hebrew into the 'original' compositions as a corruption of the pure language. Yet in historical linguistics all forms of language are studied for their own value; one is not 'better' or a purer representation of the language.

Second, a common example of the dichotomy between high and low registers is the interchange between שׁ and אשׁר. This stems from what I believe to be a misunderstanding of the differences between register and dialect studies. D. Biber argues that '[w]hen dialects are studied, analysts usually focus on linguistic features that are not associated with meaning differences… Linguistic variables in dialect studies almost always consist of a choice between two linguistic variants'. In contrast 'the linguistic variables used in register studies are exactly the opposite from those used in dialect studies: register variables are functional… Linguistic variables in register studies are the rate of occurrence for a linguistic feature, and a higher rate of occurrence is interpreted as reflecting a greater need for the functions associated with that feature'.[41] One of the main functions associated with the switch between שׁ and אשׁר is the scribe's desire to distinguish between a high and low variety. Yet שׁ and אשׁר retain essentially the same meaning and thus essentially the same function within the context of the clause in which either choice is used. Therefore, the choice between those two linguistic variants should be characterized as a difference in dialect — probably a social dialect.[42] The use of the interchange between שׁ and אשׁר to differentiate

  a dialect can be chosen by an individual for use in a specific situation, thus making it a register, Rendsburg does not highlight this nuance, making his discussion of these varieties vague.
38 See Kutscher, *Language*, 62–71.
39 See J. M. Grintz, 'Hebrew as the Spoken and Written Language in the Last Days of the Second Temple', *JBL* 79 (1960), 32–47. Also, A. Hurvitz, 'Was QH a "Spoken" Language? On Some Recent Views and Positions: Comments', in *Diggers*, 110–14.
40 For a helpful summary of this position and its critiques, see S. Talmon, 'The Old Testament Text', in P.R. Ackroyd and C.F. Evans (eds), *The Cambridge History of the Bible* (Cambridge 1970), 1, 159–99.
41 Biber and Conrad, *Register, Genre, and Style*, 11–12.
42 Biber defines social dialects as 'varieties associated with speakers belonging to a given demographic group (e.g., women versus men or different social classes)'. Biber, *Dimensions of Register Variation: A Cross-Linguistic Comparison*, 1. Thus, the difference in use between שׁ and אשׁר could be attributed to the scribe's place in society.

between registers highlights the lack of clarity surrounding register and dialect studies within Hebrew linguistics.

The third issue surrounding recent studies of Hebrew registers is the focus on the dichotomy between spoken and literary language. The labels 'spoken' and 'literary' suggest that some forms were only used in written Hebrew and the others were characteristic of the 'natural' language. The problem with this dichotomy resides in the fact that we have no direct evidence of spoken forms of ancient Hebrew. Because register studies focus on functional variations, direct evidence is necessary for proper analysis. The lack of direct evidence can be overcome sometimes, as D.-H. Kim discusses,[43] but the results are not always satisfactory.[44]

One way to alleviate some of the difficulties surrounding the concept of register is to define the terms clearly. Biber and S. Conrad argue that the terms 'register', 'genre', 'style' and 'dialect' should be regarded 'as different approaches or perspectives for analysing text varieties, *not* as different kinds of texts or different varieties. In fact, the same texts can be analysed from register, genre and style perspectives'.[45] For the purpose of this project, I will adopt Biber and Conrad's general approach. They argue that register analysis focuses upon linguistic characteristics that are functional and can be connected to the social situation in which the text was created. The situational context of the text is also included in genre analysis, but it focuses on 'conventional structures used to construct a complete text',[46] such as introductory formulae for letters and the use of the Hebrew phrase ויהי to begin a narrative. In contrast with both register and genre, style is not connected to situational context: 'rather, style features reflect aesthetic preferences, associated with particular authors or historical periods'.[47] Identifying the key characteristics of register, genre and style analysis is essential to clarify disagreements within historical linguistic research concerning them.

To avoid confusing definitions of register, genre, style and dialect, I will characterize the linguistic nature of the 'biblical' DSS simply as a 'variety'. This

---

43 Kim, *Early Biblical Hebrew*, 79–84.
44 R. Rezetko, 'Evaluating a New Approach to the Linguistic Dating of Biblical Texts', review of *Early Biblical Hebrew, Late Biblical Hebrew, and Linguistic Variability: A Sociolinguistic Evaluation of the Linguistic Dating of Biblical Texts*, by D.-H. Kim (JHS 13, 2013), http://jhsonline.org/reviews/reviews_new/review678.htm.
45 Biber and Conrad, *Register, Genre, and Style*, 15 (italics original).
46 Ibid., 2.
47 Ibid.

term does not intend to imply any connection between the distinctive features found in the scrolls and a specific group of people, time period, social setting or locale, but does intend to provide an unbiased analysis of the manuscripts at hand. However, in my final chapter, I will argue that one possible cause of the distinctive linguistic features found in the scrolls is register choices made by the scribes who produced them and who may have chosen specific linguistic features based on the context in which they were copying their manuscripts.

D. Nature of the Corpus and Justification of Its Use

In section I. B. 2. above, I discussed the term 'biblical' and its application to a portion of the DSS. There I concluded that for the purposes of this study, the 'biblical' DSS corpus consists of all manuscripts that contain portions of what today is known as the Hebrew Bible. The 'biblical' DSS may contain small amounts of text that are not found in the current canon, but generally speaking they reflect the same text that has been transmitted to the modern reader. This omits *pesher* and some rewritten works, but includes phylacteries (even though they are excerpted texts). This approach follows that of Abegg et al. in their various publications of the 'biblical' scrolls.[48] This corpus totals 257 manuscripts,[49] and contains roughly 94,500 words. In this section, I will provide a rationale for working with the 'biblical' texts as opposed to the non-biblical texts.

As noted above on the aims and objectives of this project, I am primarily concerned with the linguistic nature of the 'biblical' DSS. I have chosen to focus upon this sub-corpus of the DSS collection for six reasons.

First, scholars disagree about the usefulness of the 'biblical' scrolls for linguistic analysis. I will develop this theme in Chapter II where I present the history of research on the 'biblical' DSS. There I discuss the contrasting approaches to the 'biblical' scrolls, wherein one scholar focuses primarily on the 'biblical' scrolls due to the contrast that they provide with the MT, while another

---

[48] M.G. Abegg, Jr., et al., *The Dead Sea Scrolls Concordance*, 3 vols. (Leiden 2003). Also, Abegg and Toewes, *DSSB-C*. And, E.C. Ulrich, *The Biblical Qumran Scrolls: Transcriptions and Textual Variants* (Leiden 2009). However, Ulrich does not include the phylacteries.

[49] See the appendices for a list of manuscripts included in this study. Note that the naming of the phylacteries is difficult at times due to J.T. Milik's multiplying of titles for each item, see J.T. Milik (ed.), *Qumran Grotte 4, Volume 6: II. Teffillin, Mezuzot et Targums (4Q128–4Q157)* (DJD 12, Oxford 1977), 34–7. Since, for this project I am primarily utilizing the Accordance Bible Software modules to collect and reference data I will follow the identification of phylacteries found in Abegg, *Qumran Non-biblical Manuscripts*.

scholar excludes the scrolls because of that same connection. The history of research on the 'biblical' scrolls leaves us with the question, 'What can be learned from studying the linguistic character of the "biblical" DSS?' I will consider this question throughout the following chapters.

Second, there is a known scribal practice (*plene* versus defective) that differentiates the 'biblical' DSS corpus from parallel corpora. Further, this scribal practice separates the 'biblical' DSS corpus into two sub-corpora, which can act as a helpful control for testing the validity of other possible linguistic patterns of change. In Chapters II and III, I develop this concept in detail.

Third, working with the 'biblical' scrolls avoids issues of genre that can cloud comparative linguistic studies focused on the non-biblical scrolls. Comparing the linguistic character of the non-biblical texts to other Hebrew texts may seem to be the most straightforward way to better understand QH, yet this approach entails significant challenges, primary among them are issues of genre. Differences in the linguistic character between the two corpora are just as likely to be due to differences in genre as to diachronic changes or register differences. By comparing parallel texts, this challenge is avoided since each copy of a scroll retains its genre. That is to say, if we compare three copies of Genesis (DSS, MT and SP) we are comparing three manuscripts that contain the same genre. Thus, differences in genre need not be considered and variations can be more easily attributed to register differences and possibly diachronic development.

Fourth, this corpus works well with modern comparative linguistic methodology. As I discuss at length in my methodology chapter, a major branch of modern historical linguistics is characterized by comparing parallel texts. This methodology is highly developed and tested, providing a scientifically based approach to a field that has been lacking one.

Fifth, the linguistic development of witnesses to the 'biblical' text is integrally connected to the diachronic development of Hebrew. As the ancient Hebrew texts were copied from generation to generation, the Hebrew language was continually developing. This development likely had an impact upon the copying of the texts over time. Thus, as we see variation among parallel copies of the same text, we are likely viewing different stages of the Hebrew language. However, lining up the parallel witnesses in a diachronic fashion is not straightforward. To claim that the MT version is earlier than the DSS version is overly simplistic. As I discussed above, since this project is not focusing specifically upon the diachronic development of Hebrew, I will not be engaging this difficulty in an in-depth way. However, I will return to possible diachronic explanations for the variations found between the 'biblical' DSS and other witnesses throughout the following chapters.

Finally, the 'biblical' DSS provide a variety of possible controls, all of which aid in removing 'background noise'.[50] My primary control and point of interest will be comparing *plene* and defective scrolls,[51] but I will also analyse groups of texts according to other possible controls such as text type. This array of controls will help narrow the possible explanations for the variations that are identified.

The benefits of working with the 'biblical' scrolls outweigh the disadvantages, but the challenges should be recognized. I have already mentioned the challenge of diachronically organizing witnesses to the 'biblical' text. Another challenge is the relatively small size of the 'biblical' DSS corpus, which contains just over 94,500 words, compared with the more than 160,300 words found in the non-biblical corpus and the more than 425,000 words contained in the MT corpus. Nevertheless, as I will discuss at length below, the size of the 'biblical' corpus is large enough to produce statistically valid results, even though we could wish for a more complete set of texts. A final challenge in working with the 'biblical' scrolls is the lack of sociological information available about the people who produced and used them. But this difficulty is well-known to those who study most ancient texts, including the non-biblical manuscripts from Qumran. I will return to the advantages and challenges of working with the 'biblical' texts in the following chapter.

---

50 I discuss background noise in Chapter III. B. 2. a. 2.
51 In Chapter II. E., I discuss Tov's 'Qumran Scribal Practice' in detail. All I will note here is that I do not utilize Tov's construction as a way to separate the 'biblical' scrolls into sub-corpora. Instead I group manuscripts based on orthographic style, that is *plene* versus defective. I return to this topic in Chapter III. B. 2. a. 1.

Chapter II

History of Linguistic Studies on the 'Biblical' Scrolls

Linguistic analysis of the non-biblical scrolls has progressed steadily since the early days of DSS research. Scholars have undertaken comprehensive studies on the nature of QH as well as analyses of the language of individual scrolls. Researchers have discussed all parts of the grammar of QH, including orthography, phonology, morphology and syntax. However, a limited amount of attention has been given to the language of the approximately 257 'biblical' scrolls. In this section, I will review research on the linguistic character of the 'biblical' DSS. This review will highlight five main shortcomings of past scholarship. First, the majority of past scholarship on the 'biblical' DSS has, what I am calling, an unprincipled corpus upon which the work is based. By this I mean that scholars used sets of texts that were not appropriate for the questions they were asking. The two main reasons for this were lack of access (scrolls were not published) and over utilization of small texts that might skew results. Second, most research has not been grounded well in a sound linguistic methodology. Modern historical, social and corpus linguistics have come a long way in the past few decades, yet the study of ancient Hebrew varieties has not kept up with developments in linguistic theory. Third, many scholars were working with deficient datasets, either due to poor data collection or incomplete corpora (as noted above). Some scholars have been able to develop sound data, yet fail to analyse this data with robust statistical techniques. Fourth, the MT has been assumed to contain the oldest form of Hebrew, while considering most linguistic variations from it to be modernizations. Even when this assumption is successfully set aside, many scholars still struggle with proposing a methodology that does not place the MT at the centre. Lastly, orthography, phonology and morphology have been the focus of most linguistic studies on the 'biblical' scrolls leaving the area of syntax neglected. Scholars working on the 'biblical' scrolls have produced outstanding work, but none, in my view, have been able to avoid all five of these limitations, as I will show in the following sections that discuss the primary scholars who have worked with the language of the 'biblical' DSS.

A. Burrows

M. Burrows, well-known for publishing an edition of 1QIsa[a] just two years after its discovery, was director of the American Schools for Oriental Research from 1947–8. Burrows also published a brief, yet comprehensive analysis of the linguistic 'peculiarities'[1] of 1QIsa[a]. He stated that he was unable '[t]o appraise and expound the significance of these phenomena for the historical grammar of the Hebrew language'[2] due to lack of time. Burrows foreshadowed Kutscher's analysis of 1QIsa[a] by stating that those who were more interested in the topic would complete his work. Thus Burrows's 1949 article simply presented a concise description of the distinctive linguistic features of 1QIsa[a].

Burrows skilfully presented the orthography and morphology of 1QIsa[a], but of more significance for the present study is his review of the syntactic nature of this manuscript. The importance of his work on 1QIsa[a]'s linguistic features is not mainly in his conclusions, but merely in the fact that he covers syntax at all.

In his review of the syntax of 1QIsa[a], Burrows highlighted four features that distinguish this scroll from its MT counterpart. Yet in his analysis of all four of those features, Burrows fails to rigorously analyse his data. The first feature Burrows works with is the scribe's 'tendency to avoid the ו-consecutive, though not consistently carried through and perhaps hardly conscious'.[3] While there is some evidence to support this view, a comprehensive analysis of the data does not reveal a strong case. As I will discuss in the following chapter, it is common for researchers to notice and emphasize rare linguistic characteristics. This seems to be the case in Burrows's analysis of the preterite. A full analysis of the data does not show any pattern of avoiding this form. I will return to the use of the preterite in the 'biblical' DSS in Chapter IV. B. 4., but this is a significant point to raise at this stage because Burrows was the first of many to argue that the scribe of 1QIsa[a] avoided the preterite.

The second syntactical feature that Burrows discussed is a 'preference for the use of the preposition ל with the [infinitive construct] …'[4] Of the 209 occurrences of the preposition *lamed* plus infinitive construct found in 1QIsa[a], 8 are not found in the MT. Again, the scribes' preference for this form must

---

1 M. Burrows, 'Orthography, Morphology, and Syntax of the St. Mark's Isaiah Manuscript', *JBL* 68 (1949), 195.
2 Ibid.
3 Ibid., 209.
4 Ibid., 210.

be questioned due to the lack of data.[5] Is an increase of four percent enough to reveal a significant scribal pattern? I will discuss answers to this question in Chapter III. B. 4.

The final two features that Burrows presents are the pluses and minuses of the definite article and conjunction *vav*. Burrows simply lists the occurrences of those features and does not discuss them except to say that they are 'of no apparent importance'.[6] Scholars such as P. Pulikottil and Abegg, have challenged Burrows's conclusion. Pulikottil has found exegetical significance in the additions and omissions of the conjunction *vav*. He claims that the scribe(s) of 1QIsa^a was punctuating his text by marking or unmarking clause boundaries with this conjunction.[7] Abegg, on the other hand, highlights the increased use of the conjunction *vav* plus simple imperfect to account for some of the variations involving *vav*.[8] The theories presented by Pulikottil and Abegg are only two of the ways in which scholars have sought to explain the use of the definite article and conjunction *vav* within the scrolls. Due to the lack of rigorous analysis, Burrows's conclusions can be called into question, as I will show in more detail in the following chapters.

Burrows's work on the linguistic character of 1QIsa^a sets the stage for further research in this area. Those scholars that followed usually accepted his conclusions without a comprehensive analysis of the data, perpetuating questionable conclusions. In general, Burrows provides a useful analysis of the linguistic character of 1QIsa^a. But rigorously analysing the data and referring to other witnesses instead of focusing mainly on the MT could have strengthened his work.

---

5   Abegg also questions whether the scribe actually had a preference for the *vav* consecutive and *lamed* plus infinitive (2011, 167–8). He further points out that Kutscher, Muraoka and Fassberg have argued the same point as Burrows without a significant amount of data to support their conclusions. These conclusions may come about by imprinting characteristics of MH upon the evidence found in the scrolls. One could hypothesize that since MH does not utilize the *vav* consecutive and increases the use of *lamed* plus infinitives construct, these characteristics are unduly highlighted within the scrolls to support the claim that QH is a bridge between LBH and MH.
6   Ibid., 211.
7   P. Pulikottil, *Transmission of Biblical Texts in Qumran: The Case of the Large Isaiah Scroll 1QIsa^a* (JSPSup 34, Sheffield 2001), 82–6.
8   Abegg, 'The Biblical Dead Sea Scrolls', 168–9.

B. Mansoor

Nearly a decade after the work of Burrows, M. Mansoor produced a linguistic analysis of the (published) DSS. In contrast to Burrows who analysed the language of 1QIsaᵃ by itself, Mansoor evaluated seven scrolls from Cave 1: 1QIsaᵃ, 1QpHab, 1QHᵃ, 1QM, 1QS, 1QpPs and CD. Mansoor's study stands out due to its comparative nature. Mansoor was able to compile a broad set of data, yet he did not take full advantage of this larger corpus. As an example, of the seventy-six passages from the scrolls that Mansoor uses, fifty are from 1QIsaᵃ.

While Mansoor focuses mainly on orthography, phonology and morphology, he does discuss six syntactical characteristics of the DSS: 1) the retention of אשר 2) the use of a preposition where את is expected, 3) the use of the conjunction *vav*, 4) preference for active over passive, 5) the minus of the definite article between the preposition *lamed* and an infinitive construct and 6) the increased use of the preposition *lamed* before infinitives construct. All but one of the features discussed by Mansoor prove to be rare in the 'biblical' scrolls, the exception being variations involving the conjunction *vav*. Mansoor follows Burrows by concluding:

> Hebrew grammarians who may venture to conduct an investigation into the use of the prefix ‑ו in the Qumran writings will be simply baffled...The scribes inserted or omitted *waw* with utter defiance of grammatical rules. There is also a general, though inconsistent, tendency to avoid the *Waw* Consecutive.[9]

As was noted above, a comprehensive analysis of the conjunction *vav* reveals some scribal patterns not noticed by Burrows or Mansoor, while demonstrating that the scribes did not avoid the preterite in any significant way.

Mansoor's work was one of the first to be comparative in nature. He brought together a larger collection of texts (although he works mostly with 1QIsaᵃ), while also referring to a broad range of Semitic language traditions. Yet he falls short by focusing on rare features instead of on characteristics that are supported by significant data. This was also a shortfall of Burrows's work, which was likely the result of both scholars writing a short article with space restrictions. Kutscher's lengthy analysis of 1QIsaᵃ, which followed quickly after Mansoor's work, was not constrained by such limitations.

---

9 M. Mansoor, 'Some Linguistic Aspects of the Qumran Texts', *JSS* 3 (1958), 42.

C. Kutscher

The research of Burrows and Mansoor was swiftly overshadowed when Kutscher published his monograph on the Great Isaiah Scroll. We cannot overstate Kutscher's impact on the study of the Hebrew and Aramaic languages and the same holds true for his influence on QH research. H.B. Rosen, in his obituary of Kutscher, captures the essence of his influence:

> Kutscher introduced linguistics into the study of Hebrew and Aramaic and their history, and carried out that immense self-imposed task almost single-handedly through many years. Departing from interpretation-oriented atomistic and itemistic ways of looking at written texts, he achieved his goal of an overall view, grammatical as well as lexical, of two of the culturally most significant language-forms in Judaism: Rabbinical Hebrew and Jewish Palestinian Aramaic, and it was he who created Hebrew and Aramaic historical linguistics.[10]

Maybe Kutscher's greatest contribution to the study of the linguistic character of the scrolls was his use of current (at the time) linguistic methodology. Kutscher's historical linguistics seems to have been influenced by the work of the Danish philologist, O. Jespersen and the American linguist, L. Bloomfield, who were major contributors to the development of historical linguistics. We can see their influence in Kutscher's application of comparative philology to the study of Hebrew and Aramaic and, specifically, to the Great Isaiah Scroll.

Kutscher's work is notable for two further contributions to the study of QH. First, Kutscher completed what Burrows began nearly ten years earlier. Kutscher's monograph titled *The Language and Linguistic Background of the Isaiah Scroll* provided a systematic and comprehensive description of the language of 1QIsa^a. Second, as a complement to that synchronic approach, Kutscher takes up Mansoor's discussion of the relationship between the language found in the scrolls and the languages current at the time of the production of the scrolls. To do this, Kutscher provided a diachronic analysis of the grammar of 1QIsa^a, comparing it to other stages of Hebrew as well as to Aramaic.

Kutscher's analysis of the language of the Great Isaiah Scroll has become an essential resource for any student of QH. It remains, even today, the most comprehensive work on any single scroll found near the Dead Sea. Kutscher meticulously details the distinctive features of 1QIsa^a, while comparing those features to various forms of Hebrew and other Semitic languages. In Part One of *The*

---

10 H.B. Rosen, Obituary of Prof. E.Y. Kutscher, published in: Kutscher, *Language*, ix–xi.

Linguistic Background, Kutscher introduces the language of this scroll as well as more detailed analysis of proper nouns and orthography. Part Two is comparative, with sections on the influence of Aramaic, the different stages of BH, as well as a synchronic analysis of the phonetic and phonological traits of this scroll.

Finding fault in Kutscher's analysis of 1QIsa^a is difficult. Even without the assistance of technology, he was able to collect and analyse almost every variant between the Isaiah Scroll and other relevant witnesses. Kutscher's breadth and depth of knowledge of Semitic languages imbues his research with copious amounts of evidence to support his arguments. Yet there are a few places where his description of this scroll can be refined and updated.

Kutscher follows previous scholars in overstating the influence of certain sets of data. As an example, Kutscher perpetuates Burrows's claim that the scribe of 1QIsa^a had an aversion to the preterite. As evidence, Kutscher notes that 1QIsa^a has twelve non-preterite forms where the MT has the preterite. He then states: '… here and there one may find examples of the opposite nature'.[11] As noted above, there are four places where 1QIsa^a has the preterite and the MT does not. Thus there is a decrease of only eight preterite forms in the scroll (twelve shifts away from the preterite and four shifts towards). Kutscher claims that the shift away from the preterite is 'clearly reflected' in 1QIsa^a[12] but a decrease of 8 out of 244 total occurrences of this form may not be enough to support this claim.[13] While Kutscher's review of the data is generally accurate, his perception of the relationship between QH and LBH/MH may have overly influenced his analysis.

Also, we can note that Kutscher's historical linguistic methodology needs updating. During the past sixty years the field of historical linguistics has matured greatly and complementary fields of linguistics have been developed, all of which need to be taken into account in future work on the linguistic nature of the 'biblical' scrolls.

Aside from a few places where Kutscher may have overstated the evidence, his description and analysis of specific features of the language of 1QIsa^a has been the focus of little scholarly criticism. M. Goshen-Gottstein is one of the few that has challenged Kutscher's work. At almost the same time that Kutscher was focusing on 1QIsa^a, Goshen-Gottstein argued that 1QIsa^a had mistakenly become the representative of QH. He states that once all the Qumran documents are compared, '[t]he first manuscript, which had been taken to represent a cer-

---

11 Ibid., 352.
12 Ibid.
13 Abegg, 'The Biblical Dead Sea Scrolls', 167–8. Abegg develops a similar argument in this article.

tain "tradition", may turn out to be the exception with that alleged "tradition" rather than the rule'.[14] Goshen-Gottstein questions whether the distinctive features found in 1QIsa[a] can be considered features of QH as a whole or whether they should be 'discarded as mistakes perpetrated by its scribe, characteristic of nothing but his own carelessness'.[15]

The remainder of Goshen-Gottstein's article presents a comparative analysis of 1QIsa[a] with the other Qumran documents published up to that point in time.[16] The aim of his article was to 'show in a pilot study what picture would emerge if each of the major linguistic features said to be characteristic of [the Qumran Scrolls] and each of the major documents were analysed'.[17] Goshen-Gottstein then worked his way through the orthography, morphology and syntax of QH, as described by previous research based on 1QIsa[a], to see if the other scrolls shared the same features. He concluded as follows: 'The foregoing investigation of each of the phenomena which may be said to be common to QS, at least to some degree, have impressed upon us the difference between the picture emerging from QS as a whole and that provided by IsA'.[18] Goshen-Gottstein's analysis reveals 1QIsa[a] to represent one extreme, while 1QIsa[b] represents the other extreme as a conservative document. The other manuscripts, according to Goshen-Gottstein, fall on a spectrum between 1QIsa[b] and 1QIsa[a], but are still closer to the former than the latter. Goshen-Gottstein's conclusion caused 1QIsa[a] to be marginalized in the discussion, as will be seen below. Recently this scroll has returned to the spotlight in a revised version of the official publication in Discoveries in the Judaean Desert series.[19]

Kutscher seems to respond to Goshen-Gottstein's critique in two ways. First, he repositions 1QIsa[a] as the representative of QH even if only by default. In a survey of the language of the DSS, Kutscher writes, '*Isaiah* is the only DSS text which has been extensively dealt with from the linguistic point of view. The following survey, therefore, will be based mainly on the language of this scroll'.[20] Thus Kutscher seems to consider 1QIsa[a] a good starting point for understanding QH.

---

14 M. Goshen-Gottstein, 'Linguistic Structure and Tradition in the Qumran Documents', *ScrHier* 4 (1958), 101.
15 Ibid.
16 1QIsa[b], 1QS, 1QpH, 1QM, 1QT, 1QG, CD, 1QS[a].
17 Ibid., 102.
18 Ibid., 130.
19 E. Ulrich and P.W. Flint (eds), *Qumran Cave 1. II: The Isaiah Scrolls, Part 2: Introductions, Commentary, and Textual Variants*, DJD 32 (Oxford 2010).
20 E.Y. Kutscher, 'Hebrew Language: The Dead Sea Scrolls', *EncJud* 8:636 (italics original).

E. Qimron, a student of Kutscher's, produced a dissertation that presented a comprehensive synchronic analysis of the language of every published DSS. This, in an indirect way, appears to be Kutscher's second response to Goshen-Gottstein's critique.

D. Qimron

Kutscher provided a comprehensive analysis of 1QIsa^a that was consistent with previous work on this scroll and which became the basis for the general understanding of QH at the time. Goshen-Gottstein pointed out the flaw in allowing 1QIsa^a to be the representative of this type of Hebrew. His work, although preliminary, showed that there was a need for a full description of the language found in all of the DSS. Qimron provided this (at least for the non-biblical scrolls published before 1986).

Under the supervision of Kutscher and Hurvitz, Qimron produced a dissertation that contained a full grammar of the DSS in 1976. In 1986, Qimron condensed and published his research in a monograph.[21] If Kutscher erred on the side of favouring one 'biblical' manuscript, then Qimron erred on the opposite end of the spectrum. Qimron's analysis of QH focused mainly on the non-biblical scrolls, while referencing 'biblical' manuscripts in rare cases and only as secondary examples. This work is one of the most comprehensive analyses of the orthography and morphology of the non-biblical manuscripts. Qimron completed what Goshen-Gottstein began years earlier. Yet his brief analysis of the syntax of DSS documents as well as his lack of interaction with the 'biblical' manuscripts left room for more research to be done. E. Tov, especially in the area of analysing the 'biblical' manuscripts, fills this gap.

E. Tov

Tov provides an exemplar of a holistic approach to the DSS. Through an analysis of thousands of different details, Tov groups the DSS manuscripts into two collections: manuscripts that contain a distinct orthography, morphology and scribal practice and those that do not. While Tov based his conclusions on many different types of data, a large portion of his work focused on linguistic evidence. Tov notes that 'One hundred and sixty-seven Qumran texts ... are characterized

21 E. Qimron, *The Hebrew of the Dead Sea Scrolls* (HSM 29, Atlanta 1986), 17–24.

Chapter II History of Linguistic Studies on the 'Biblical' Scrolls

by a distinctive orthography and morphology which has no equal among the documents known from other places'.[22] Tov not only attempts to show that this set of manuscripts is different than those manuscripts found elsewhere, but that they are also different from other manuscripts found at the Dead Sea. Further, Tov claimed that there is a close connection between a small set of 'biblical' scrolls and the sectarian scrolls.

Yet, as important as Tov's research is, it is not without its critics. E.J.C. Tigchelaar presents a summary of Tov's work (especially as found in Tov's 2004 monograph), a review of past critiques, and his own analysis. I will focus here on the specific challenges set against Tov's conclusions.

F.M. Cross challenged Tov's analysis of the orthographic and morphological features of the Qumran manuscripts. Tigchelaar points out that Cross[23] argued that most of the orthographic and morphological features found in the Qumran scrolls are not distinctive. Cross reasoned that since those features are found in the MT and Samaritan traditions they cannot be used to identify sectarian works written at Qumran.

A second critique focuses on the lack of consistency in the Qumran manuscripts. Tov identifies eighteen categories of orthographic, morphological and scribal features that set some manuscripts apart from others. Yet the DSS do not use Tov's features consistently and none except 1QIsa^a has all eighteen.

A third objection highlights the fact that not all of the Sectarian texts employ the Qumran Scribal Practice. Because of this, Tov's sceptics argue that his features cannot be used to identify manuscripts that were produced at Qumran.

As Tigchelaar points out, Tov has addressed most of the challenges levied against his theories throughout his extensive publications on this topic. Yet Tigchelaar's analysis of Tov's data and conclusions reaffirms some of the above criticisms. Tigchelaar's main critique focuses on the dichotomy between Qumran Scribal Practice manuscripts and non-Qumran Scribal Practice manuscripts. Tigchelaar argues for a spectrum approach. Qumran Scribal Practice manuscripts make up a cluster upon this spectrum, but those manuscripts are not distinct enough to be set completely apart.

A further detail of Tov's work that needs consideration is his corpus design.

---

22 E. Tov, *Scribal Practices and Approaches Reflected in the Texts Found in the Judean Desert* (STDJ 54, Leiden 2004), 252.
23 For this discussion and references to further reviews of Tov's work, see E.J.C. Tigchelaar, 'Assessing Emanuel Tov's "Qumran Scribal Practice"', in S. Metso, H. Najman and E. Schuller (eds), *The Dead Sea Scrolls: Transmission of Traditions and Production of Texts* (STDJ 92, Leiden 2010), 178–9.

Tov, in a couple of cases, notes that a fragment or manuscript is too small for analysis or does not contain enough data to determine its alignment.[24] Unfortunately Tov does not explicitly state how big a manuscript must be in order for it to be analysed. In Chapter III. B. 2. b., I will develop my approach to considering this issue.

Finally, since Tov focuses mainly on orthography and morphology there is room for adding syntactic elements to his discussion of 'scribal schools'. This will become central in the following chapters.

F. Muraoka

Goshen-Gottstein's critique of 1QIsa[a] as representative of QH and Qimron's grammar of QH based on the non-biblical scrolls has led most scholars to give little attention to the 'biblical' manuscripts. One notable exception, beyond Tov, is Muraoka's analysis of the syntax of QH. Muraoka states that '[t]he basic point of departure of my presentation is that one should be able to learn about the nature of Qumran Hebrew ... by analysing cases where Qumran biblical texts differ and deviate from the standard biblical text, namely the MT'.[25] An analysis of Muraoka's research on the 'biblical' scrolls is fitting at this point for he himself hoped that the '[r]esults of such an analysis [would] be able to complement a picture obtained by studying non-biblical DSS texts as found, for instrance [sic], in Qimron 1986...'[26] Muraoka also saw himself following in the footsteps of Kutscher by linguistically analysing parallel witnesses.[27]

Through this analysis, Muraoka identified twelve distinctive syntactical features that he argued set the language of the 'biblical' scrolls apart from the language found in the MT. Muraoka concludes by stating, 'Our study has also indicated that the description of QH by Kutscher with reference to 1QIsa[a] on the one hand and by Qimron with reference to non-biblical DSS on the other is at places in need of revision or supplementation'.[28] This conclusion is relevant due to the continued publication of the DSS. Muraoka analysed every scroll available to him; since then however, more scrolls have been published and his work can also be updated. Abegg develops just this point.[29]

---

24 Tov, *Scribal Practices*, 228.
25 Muraoka, 'An Approach', 193.
26 Ibid.
27 Ibid.
28 Ibid., 214.
29 Abegg, 'The Biblical Dead Sea Scrolls', 163–72.

G. Abegg

Abegg begins his article by stating: 'If such a noted grammarian as Muraoka has been down this path, what new insights might I hope to offer? The answer comes in one word: completeness'.[30] Abegg was able to obtain a higher level of comprehensiveness for two reasons. First, as was mentioned above, Abegg had access to the most complete corpus of 'biblical' DSS manuscripts to date. Second, Abegg used computer software in order to gather a complete set of data. In contrast, Kutscher, Qimron, Muraoka and others were gathering data by hand. The completeness of Abegg's corpus and his access to powerful technologies provided a way forward in linguistic analyses of the 'biblical' DSS.

Abegg's study also sheds light on a path of inquiry that may prove to be fruitful. Abegg stated: 'an initial study that I undertook using the 20 syntactic categories in Qimron's *Hebrew of the Dead Sea Scrolls* revealed no discernible influence among the biblical scrolls'.[31] Abegg noted that he was surprised by this result. Indeed, one would have expected the distinctive syntactical features found in the non-biblical scrolls to have influenced the production of the 'biblical' scrolls, yet apparently this is not the case. After considering Qimron's syntactical features, Abegg pressed on to those characteristics that are distinctive of LBH in general. This proved to be a more worthwhile undertaking. Abegg summarizes his results as follows:

> For some of these features, the focus on a few examples discovered early on has brought too much emphasis in the secondary literature. For others, the data have verified earlier expectations. In addition, in a few instances there are some surprises in corners where it seems no one has thought to look until now.[32]

The details of Abegg's study will be dealt with in the following chapters. However, his methodology is the important factor at this point because Abegg demonstrates the usefulness of comparing the 'biblical' scrolls with the MT in order to learn about the language that influenced their production. Not all scholars have agreed with this approach. As an example, Joosten disregards the 'biblical' manuscripts because 'they represent writings that are very much older than the sectarian scrolls'.[33] Joosten goes on to note that scribes modernized the

---

30 Ibid., 165.
31 Ibid.
32 Ibid.
33 Joosten, 'Hebrew, Aramaic and Greek', 354.

language of some of the 'biblical' scrolls, yet he still does not use this evidence in his analysis. As Abegg demonstrates, this is a missed opportunity.

However, Abegg's research can be strengthened in two main areas. First, by adding in comparisons to other witnesses, such as the SP and the LXX, we can gain a more balanced view of the linguistic nature of the 'biblical' scrolls. Second, while Abegg focuses upon patterns within the data and his methodology of analysis is sound, he lacks robust statistical models to test his conclusions. Specifically, as will be discussed in Chapter II. B. 4., statistical significance tests can be used to see if observed patterns are relevant or the result of random chance.

H. Fassberg

While some scholars, such as Joosten, have set aside the 'biblical' scrolls in their research, others have focused on those manuscripts in detail. Fassberg published an analysis of the syntax of some of the 'biblical' scrolls in the same collection as Muraoka's work discussed above. Fassberg's approach to studying the syntax of the 'biblical' scrolls was distinct from those that came before him. He removed the MT as the base text and instead compared 'biblical' manuscripts from Qumran that shared parallel passages. In Fassberg's words, 'I propose to focus on biblical texts of which multiple copies exist at Qumran in order to see if, in addition to the obvious orthographic differences that exist between the manuscripts, there are also syntactic ones, and if so, what kind'.[34] This methodology provided a distinctive take on the syntax of the 'biblical' scrolls, yet Fassberg's results were consistent with the results of those who came before him. Fassberg concludes his article by stating:

> The picture that emerges from a comparison of syntactic features in multiple copies of biblical books is clear: in the case of many variants, one syntagm or form is well attested in Classical Hebrew whereas the second is well-known from post-classical Biblical Hebrew, namely Late Biblical Hebrew, Tannaitic Hebrew, or Samaritan Hebrew.[35]

Fassberg is careful to note, however, that the variations between the manuscripts do not align with text type (e.g. proto-Masoretic or LXX).[36]

---

34 S.E. Fassberg, 'The Syntax of the Biblical Documents From the Judean Desert as Reflected in a Comparison of Multiple Copies of Biblical Texts', in *Diggers*, 95.
35 Ibid., 106.
36 Ibid., 106–7.

Fassberg's conclusions suggest that the MT should not play the central role in research on the syntax of the 'biblical' DSS. A balanced approach, with a comparison of all manuscripts, provides a clearer picture of scribal activity and the influence that their language may have had upon the production of their manuscripts.

In another publication of Fassberg's, he continues his reliance upon the 'biblical' scrolls to aid in describing QH. Fassberg writes: 'In the following description of the language the examples are cited from the Great Isaiah Scroll (1QIsa) wherever possible, in order to highlight the differences between the Hebrew found in the scrolls and that of Tiberian Hebrew as reflected in the Masoretic text'.[37] This approach is the opposite of that taken by Joosten (discussed briefly above) and highlights the importance that Fassberg places on 1QIsa^a for understanding the nature of QH. A similar, although much broader, approach is taken by E.D. Reymond in his analysis of QH.

I. Reymond

Very recently Reymond published a grammar of QH that focuses on orthography, phonology and morphology. In his introduction, Reymond details his reasons for publishing another grammar of QH in light of the significant work already done by Kutscher and Qimron. Reymond lists five problems that he sees with past research, specifically Qimron's QH grammar. I will reference two of the five because they relate specifically to the present project and the weaknesses I have already discussed. Reymond states: '[Qimron] proposes dramatic differences between the language of the DSS and the Hebrew as evidenced in the MT, though the evidence for these differences is sometimes tenuous (based on a single example) and often ambiguous'.[38] I have made this same point above. Due to lack of data or weak analysis of data, scholars have emphasized phenomena that are not supported by a careful review of the material. Reymond goes on to state that '[Qimron's] book, although it has recently been reprinted in 2008, contains no references to recently published texts…'[39] Again, I have mentioned this criticism above. The corpora upon which much of past research has been based is either incomplete or unprincipled. Reymond's work has overcome (at least in part) those two problems. He uses computer software to gather data, al-

---

37 Fassberg, 'Dead Sea Scrolls', 1.
38 Reymond, *Qumran Hebrew*, 1–2.
39 Ibid., 2.

lowing him to see and analyse a more complete picture and he works with every published DSS. Yet his work falls short in at least three other areas.

Probably the most significant shortcoming of Reymond's grammar is his lack of work on syntax. Both Kutscher and Qimron deal with syntax in some detail, yet Reymond's updated grammar entirely ignores this important and neglected part of language.

Reymond's work could also be strengthened through the use of statistical analysis. He appeals to data throughout his text, yet a more robust descriptive statistical methodology would clarify his arguments in places. As an example of this, we can look at Reymond's discussion of מאדה. Reymond claims that the *he* is often affixed to adverbs in the MT as well as in the DSS, but that they are far more common in the scrolls. However, he does not support this conclusion with any data. At the least, the raw numbers would be helpful for the reader to assess his conclusions. Some basic comparative graphs would be more helpful. As it stands, Reymond's conclusions are difficult to confirm due to the lack of supporting data.

Finally, Reymond's work is comparative in nature, as the above example shows. Yet he does not explicitly use any modern linguistic methodology to inform his work. Some sub-disciplines of historical linguistics would serve to guide and clarify Reymond's work throughout. In my analysis of Rezetko and Young's work below, I focus on the specific historical linguistic methodologies that would be helpful in improving Reymond's research since Rezetko and Young have successfully used linguistic theory in their own analyses of ancient Hebrew.

J. Hornkohl

A.D. Hornkohl is undertaking 'a large-scale project involving the diachronic comparison of Hebrew as it is found in the MT and the "biblical" DSS'. Hornkohl presented some 'preliminary and tentative'[40] conclusions at the Seventh International Symposium on the Hebrew of the Dead Sea Scrolls and Ben Sira. The main focus of Hornkohl's analysis is upon how a comparison between the 'biblical' DSS and the MT can impact our understanding of the diachronic development of Ancient Hebrew. While Hornkohl's focus is different than that of this project, his work still deals with many of the same issues.

---

40 A.D. Hornkohl, 'Diachronic Exceptions in the Comparison of Tiberian and Qumran Hebrew: The Preservation of Early Linguistic Features in the Biblical Dead Sea Scrolls' (Paper presented at The Seventh International Symposium on the Hebrew of the Dead Sea Scrolls and Ben Sira, Strasbourg, Germany 22–25, June 2014).

Hornkohl analyses two features that he argues reveal the 'discernibly later character of DSS BH relative to MT BH'.[41] The first of these is the long form of the 3rd masculine plural suffix יהם-. Hornkohl shows that the DSS contain the long form of this suffix in 10 out of 72 cases where the MT has the short form. He also states the MT has the long form 1 time out of 23 cases where the DSS have the short form. From this data, Hornkohl concludes 'Neither proportion is overwhelming, but, clearly, in cases where the two corpora differ with respect to the suffixal forms under discussion the DSS are more than three times as likely to opt for the typically post-classical one'.[42]

The second feature that Hornkohl analyses is the infinitive construct as verbal complement with and without a preceding preposition -ל. Hornkohl summarizes this analysis by stating:

> [I]n at least twelve cases the difference between the MT and parallel material in the DSS centers on the presence or absence of -ל preceding an infinitive construct in service as a verbal complement. In all twelve the DSS have the -ל and the MT the bare infinitive.[43]

Hornkohl argues that this comparison between the 'biblical' DSS and the MT shows a 'trend in the direction of replacement'.[44]

The two examples given by Hornkohl are, if taken at face value, rather convincing. While a full critique of Hornkohl's work is not justified due to the pre-publication and preliminary nature of his analysis, one major issue needs to be addressed. Both of Hornkohl's examples are based on very small datasets, just 10 tokens related to the use of the long form of the 3mp suffix on feminine plural construct nouns and 12 tokens related to the preposition ל and certain types of infinitives construct. As I will argue below, these very small datasets may not be statistically reliable. Further, Hornkohl does not use any inferential statistical tools to assess the validity of his data. With the very small datasets and lack of inferential statistical analysis, Hornkohl's conclusions regarding these two features should be considered anecdotal at best.

---

41 Hornkohl, 'Diachronic Exceptions in the Comparison of Tiberian and Qumran Hebrew: The Preservation of Early Linguistic Features in the Biblical Dead Sea Scrolls Hebrew', in J. Joosten, D. Machiela and J.-S. Rey (eds), STDJ Series, Prepublication draft, 8.
42 Hornkohl, 'Diachronic Exceptions', 9.
43 Hornkohl, 'Diachronic Exceptions', 13.
44 Hornkohl, 'Diachronic Exceptions', 14.

K. Rezetko and Young

Rezetko and Young have published several valuable articles and monographs related to Hebrew linguistics.[45] While a number of their publications are relevant here, I will focus on their most recent monograph as it synthesizes and updates their previous work. In their new text, Rezetko and Young focus upon 'constructing a more philologically robust approach to the history of ancient Hebrew...'[46] To accomplish their goal, Rezetko and Young use, among other texts, the 'biblical' scrolls from Qumran.

Rezetko and Young's end goal in this book is different than that of my project. They are working towards developing a better approach to ancient Hebrew studies, while I am narrowly focused upon possible correlations between *plene* orthography/long morphology and other grammatical phenomena. Our end goals are different, but some of the steps to our goals are similar. The linguistic nature of the 'biblical' manuscripts needs to be analysed in order to reach both of our goals. Rezetko and Young focus on the linguistic nature of the Qumran Samuel manuscripts in order to consider their questions and some of their conclusions are relevant here.

In contrast to Muraoka and others who believe we can learn about QH through linguistically analysing the differences between the 'biblical' DSS and the MT, Rezetko and Young conclude differently. The following passage summarizes their views well:

> Based largely on Kutscher's monograph on 1QIsa^a, Hebraists have come to assume that usually the MT will have early or 'original' language whereas the Qumran, both the non-biblical and biblical scrolls, will have diachronically later linguistic items.... This widespread belief, however, is at best problematic and at worst false.[47]

To support that conclusion Rezetko and Young cite the mixed linguistic character of 4QSam^a, which contains both 'early' and 'late' forms, as well as the differences between Samuel manuscripts where one will consistently have early features while the other has the corresponding late feature. Thus they conclude that there is 'inconsistent "direction of (early/late) movement" between the MT and Qumran Samuel'.[48] In the following chapters, I will review their conclu-

---

45 See for example Young, Rezetko and Ehrensvärd, *Linguistic Dating of Biblical Texts*.
46 Rezetko and Young, *Historical Linguistics*, 269.
47 Ibid., 141.
48 Ibid., 142.

sions. For now, it is enough to say that Rezetko and Young find little evidence of systematic linguistic changes in the Qumran Samuel manuscripts.

I will now turn to the methodology that led Rezetko and Young to their conclusions. That methodology has helped them to successfully overcome a number of the shortcomings found in previous research on the 'biblical' scrolls. I will discuss their methodology in more detail by focusing on the five inadequacies of previous research that I listed at the beginning of this chapter. This will serve a dual purpose. First, a review of the five shortcomings will highlight the contributions as well as the weaknesses of Rezetko and Young's work. And second, it will provide a helpful summary of the main points developed throughout this chapter.

1. Unprincipled Corpus

Nearly all previous researchers on the 'biblical' scrolls based their work on unprincipled corpora. The use of such corpora was mainly due to the fact that not all the DSS had been published when most research upon the scrolls was being undertaken. The lack of full access to the scrolls necessarily led to conclusions that were tentative pending the complete publication of all the scrolls. The exceptions to this are those researchers that focused upon the linguistic character of a single scroll such as Kutscher.

Other scholars fell short of a principled corpus by including all available manuscripts. This is problematic due to the fragmentary nature of some manuscripts, causing them to be too small for analysis. Tov, to his credit, removed manuscripts that were too small for analysis, but unfortunately he did not explicitly state his methodology for doing so.

Rezetko and Young clearly present a methodology by which they evaluate the usefulness of manuscripts. The linguistic framework that they use is called corpus linguistics and the principle of sufficient tokens is used. Their approach allowed them to build a principled corpus that contains only manuscripts of sufficient size for analysis. However, they appear to apply their principles inconsistently.[49] I will return to corpus linguistics and sufficient number of tokens in Chapter III. B. 3.

---

49 As an example of this inconsistency, in their analysis of some pronominal endings they exclude all manuscripts that do not contain at least ten tokens of each form, but in their work on the directive *he* they appear to analyse all available manuscripts.

2. Lack of Linguistic Theoretical Foundation

Unlike the majority of previous scholarship on the 'biblical' scrolls, Rezetko and Young use a wide range of modern linguistic theories. The two main theories that they focus on are cross-textual variable analysis and variationist analysis. Both of those methodologies draw from other linguistic disciplines, such as historical linguistics, social linguistics, corpus linguistics, among others, aspects of which will be discussed in detail in the following chapters. However, I will mention one main issue here. Probably the most important methodological concept discussed by Rezetko and Young is a focus on identifying patterns. This is a hallmark of modern historical and corpus linguistics. They quote A. Marantz to emphasize this need: 'It's very difficult to argue anything from idiosyncrasies — one argues from systematic differences'.[50] Thus they avoid basing their conclusions on rare variations or small amounts of data, but instead focus on patterns that are supported by the bulk of the data and that stand out as distinctive.

3. Deficient Data or Rigorous Analytical Analysis of the Data

Rezetko and Young handle the collection and analysis of their data well: they gather their data comprehensively; they analyse the data for individual books/manuscripts as well as for collections of books; and they use descriptive statistical tools to describe their data. Yet they fall short in one main aspect of data examination — inferential statistical analysis, which is a corner-stone of corpus linguistics. This involves not just describing the data but also testing it. Rezetko and Young briefly consider the possibility of using statistics to mine data for patterns. Yet they state,

> [T]here are several potential caveats in this kind of research… First, there are the problems of low-density and non-categorical distributions of many data in the surviving sources, so that it may be challenging to find ample variables that are attested sufficiently and have adequately distributed variants in order to give meaningful and conclusive results. Second, there is the problem of the complete nonexistence of dated and localized (authentic) manuscripts for biblical writings, which means that any 'associative patterns' that are identified will inevitably be open to more than one interpretation.[51]

---

50 A. Marantz, 'No Escape From Syntax: Don't Try Morphological Analysis in the Privacy of Your Own Lexicon', in A. Dimitriadis et al. (eds), *University of Pennsylvania Working Papers in Linguistics: Proceedings of the 21st Annual Penn Linguistics Colloquium* (Philadelphia 1997), 4:2, 215.

51 Rezetko and Young, *Historical Linguistics*, 273.

Here, Rezetko and Young, are concerned about the lack of data and the possibility of multiple interpretations of the data, which are important points to consider when utilizing statistics to help analyse data. However, such concerns can be overcome, in part, with the proper tools. Moving beyond descriptive statistics to inferential[52] statistics is a necessary step, even if these tools fail us at times. In Chapter III. B., I will discuss how inferential statistics can be used to improve upon past research.

4. MT Centred Comparisons

One of the main critiques of past research developed by Rezetko and Young is the centrality of the MT. They argue that many scholars assumed the MT reflects the original linguistic character of the text and any linguistic variation from the MT reflects modernizations on the part of subsequent scribes.[53] In contrast to this, Rezetko and Young state:

> This assumption, however, is out of line with the consensus view of specialists on the history of the text of the Hebrew Bible, who consider that the details of the biblical writings were so fluid in their textual transmission that we have no way of knowing with any degree of certainty what the original of any biblical composition looked like.[54]

Rezetko and Young's challenge to the place of the MT in linguistic studies needs to be seriously engaged. A balanced and unbiased view of all text forms and types is necessary if one wishes to arrive at solid conclusions. In Chapter III. B. 2., I will discuss my approach to the MT and its impact upon my conclusions.

5. Neglected Syntactic Variations

As I have also noted above, compared with the other areas of linguistic study, syntax has received relatively little scholarly attention. Rezetko and Young take note of this fact and respond by focusing upon syntactical issues throughout their work.[55] This focus upon syntax helps to round out previous research upon the linguistic character of the 'biblical' DSS and it will be continued in this project as I will discuss in the following chapter.

---

52 Inferential statistics is also referred to as analytical statistics.
53 See especially 4.4.2.1 of Ibid.
54 Ibid., 38.
55 See especially pages 94–5 of Ibid. Geiger is another scholar who focuses on the syntax of QH, specifically the use of the participle, both in the 'biblical' and non-biblical manuscripts. See especially pages 202–370 of Geiger, *Das hebräische Partizip in den Texten aus der judäischen Wüste*.

This review of Rezetko and Young's most recent contribution to Hebrew linguistics has provided a catalyst for reviewing the merits and shortfalls of previous research, while also providing a helpful segue into my own methodological considerations. In the following chapter, I will present my answers to the problems present in this literature review.

Chapter III

Methodology

In the previous chapter, I discussed the five main shortcomings of past research on the linguistic nature of the 'biblical' DSS. In this chapter, I will develop my methodology for analysing the linguistic nature of the 'biblical' scrolls and will show how this methodology accounts for the problems in previous work. First, in a short section on cross-textual variable analysis, I will develop the basic approach taken in this study. Second, I will discuss at length corpus linguistics and its application to Hebrew and the linguistic character of the 'biblical' scrolls.

A. Grammatical Variable Analysis

Grammatical variable analysis seeks to describe and explain variables in the grammar of a language. In this approach, a variable is 'a set of at least two grammatical, that is, morphological[1] or syntactic variants, which may be used alternatively'.[2] A. Auer and A. Voeste use 'dived' and 'dove' as examples of an English grammatical variable.[3] The phrases 'he dived' and 'he dove' mean the same thing, but use different grammatical elements. Such variables are at the heart of grammatical variable analysis.

Grammatical variable analysis can be applied in three ways: intra-textually, inter-textually and cross-textually. Intra-textual variable analysis works with grammatical variation within one text or corpus. Inter-textual variable analysis deals with variant grammatical elements in two or more texts or corpora. And cross-textual variable analysis compares different versions of the same text. For the purposes of the present project, I will mainly be working with cross-textual variable analysis, but will also use inter-textual variable analysis, and thus will briefly provide a description of both below. I will not be utilizing intra-textual variable analysis as it focuses upon only one text or corpus without detailed remarks about the parallel versions of the texts.

---
1   As has been noted in previous chapters, I will not be analysing morphological variants due to the extensive attention they have already received in previous scholarship.
2   A. Auer and A. Voeste, 'Grammatical Variables', in J.M. Hernández Campoy and J.C. Conde Silvestre (eds), *The Handbook of Historical Sociolinguistics* (Malden, MA 2012), 253.
3   Ibid., 254.

1. Cross-Textual Variable Analysis and the 'Biblical' DSS

I will begin with cross-textual variable analysis as it is the foundation of my methodological approach. Auer and Voeste define this approach as follows: '[C]ross-textual variable analysis compares the variants in different versions of the same text. The main purpose of this method is to focus on the alterations from one version to another in order to detect a pattern of deliberate changes'.[4] This method fits linguistic studies of the 'biblical' texts well. By comparing different versions, we are able to highlight the differences in linguistic style that exist between them.

Anytime two or more versions of the same texts are linguistically analysed, cross-textual variable analysis is being used. Thus scholars have used this approach in biblical Hebrew studies for decades, though few have recognized it as such. By intentionally engaging this sub-discipline of historical linguistics, we are able to obtain the greatest benefit from this approach. Two aspects of cross-textual variable analysis have historically been under-utilized: the technical definition of 'variable' and a focus on patterns of change.

As was noted above, a variable is a set of two or more grammatical variants that can be used interchangeably, which are usually small, such as single words or short phrases. Because of this I will not focus in detail upon large pluses or minuses, although I will discuss them on occasion. I will also attempt to distinguish between variants where meaning is changed and those where the meaning stays the same. However, this is a difficult distinction to make. Does the addition of a *vav* between two clauses change the meaning of those clauses? We cannot always answer this type of question. But by focusing on variant types instead of individual variants when making this determination, I will be able to establish a set of data for analysis without having to make a subjective decision for every single variation.

The second aspect of cross-textual variable analysis that provides a corrective to past research is the focus on patterns of change. I will discuss this in more detail below, so it is sufficient to state here that rare variations should not be the primary focus of linguistic analysis. Further, a pattern can be established even when there are some contrary examples. I will return to this topic in a following section in order to define what should be considered rare and how to determine if a pattern is significant.

The application of cross-textual variable analysis in this study is straight-

---

4   Ibid., 260.

forward. I start with a comparison between the MT and the 'biblical' DSS. This provides the raw data that is useful in analysing the linguistic differences between those two versions of the text. Next, I identify readings that are only found in the 'biblical' DSS and not other witnesses such as the Samaritan Pentateuch (SP) and the Septuagint (LXX), allowing for a more holistic approach by moving the MT out of the centre.[5]

Generally speaking cross-textual variable analysis is used to connect patterns of change to the sociological influences that brought about that change, whether linguistic or non-linguistic.[6] Yet the primary focus of this project is the linguistic character of the 'biblical' manuscripts. Due to insufficient background details regarding our witnesses (dates, authors, provenance) and the internal literary development of many texts, identifying sociological influences is particularly challenging. In Chapter VI, I will return to the challenges involved in sociolinguistic analysis and will propose a tenuous connection between the sociological context of the scrolls and their linguistic character.

2. Inter-Textual Variable Analysis and the 'Biblical' DSS

I will primarily be utilizing cross-textual variable analysis in this project to analyse the linguistic character of the 'biblical' DSS. However, inter-textual variable analysis will also be used. As I briefly noted above, inter-textual variable analysis compares the use of grammatical variables in two or more texts or corpora. This is done to highlight the different uses of the grammatical variables within each group. The 'biblical' DSS are often treated as one corpus, but these manuscripts can also be grouped into different corpora and each manuscript can be analysed individually. One of the main divisions within the 'biblical' DSS that will be explored here is the *plene* and defective manuscripts, which will allow us to see if there are any grammatical (non-orthographic or morphological) differences between the two. Further, comparing the *plene* and defective scrolls will help to control for the potential influence of register choices based on genre and style of manuscript. I will discuss the different sub-corpora of the 'biblical' DSS in more detail below. I will also use inter-textual variable analysis to compare the linguistic character of the 'biblical' DSS to other corpora, such as the non-biblical scrolls and the Mishnah.

---

5   Due to the inherent problems with comparing Hebrew and Greek manuscripts, I followed the decisions made in the DJD series when collecting this data. This approach allows for my data to be easily reproduced by others.

6   Ibid., 253.

B. Corpus Linguistics

As I noted above, many scholars have (some unknowingly) used grammatical variable analysis in their work with ancient Hebrew texts. Even the basic step of intentionally engaging this methodology adds some clarity and precision to this project. Yet the main shortcomings of past research will be addressed in this project by utilizing another modern linguistic methodology, corpus linguistics. Biber summarizes the essential characteristics of corpus linguistics with the following four points:

> [1] it is empirical, analyzing the actual patterns of use in natural texts; [2] it utilizes a large and principled collection of natural texts, known as a 'corpus', as the basis for analysis; [3] it makes extensive use of computers for analysis, using both automatic and interactive techniques; [4] it depends on both quantitative and qualitative analytical techniques.[7]

The application of any one of Biber's four principles would, and has, enhanced the study of ancient Hebrew. The application of all four to the current study of the linguistic character of the 'biblical' DSS will provide reliable conclusions based upon reproducible results. In this section, I will breakdown Biber's four principles of corpus linguistics and discuss their application to the current study. To do this, I focus on each of Biber's four characteristics in turn.

1. Empirical Analysis

Empirical analysis is the starting place of any study based on corpus linguistics. Biber clearly states the need for this type of analysis when comparing different registers:

> An analyst cannot legitimately claim that a feature is more frequent in one register than another unless he has counted the occurrences of the feature in each register. Since most people notice unusual characteristics more than common ones, simply relying on what you notice in a register is not a reliable way to identify register features.[8]

Biber makes two points in this statement that can be applied to different types of linguistic analysis. First, one must gather data. This is a labour intensive and tedious work, but it is necessary. And this data must be comprehensive and reliable. Early studies on the DSS were necessarily incomplete as the entire corpus

---

7 D. Biber, S. Conrad and R. Reppen, *Corpus Linguistics: Investigating Language Structure and Use* (Cambridge 1998), 4.
8 Biber and Conrad, *Register, Genre, and Style*, 56.

was not available. Their data was also understandably prone to errors since early scholars did not have the benefit of modern technology. As an example of this issue, Abegg updates Muraoka's work when he writes, 'Muraoka documents 28 [added] direct object markers. I have now accounted for 67'.[9] Muraoka himself draws attention to the need for data in the same article that Abegg spoke about. Muraoka writes, '[Kutscher] goes on to say: "the את becomes less common in Rab. Hebr.," without any substantiating statistics or examples'.[10] So, Kutscher's work is found lacking by Muraoka and Muraoka's work is improved upon by Abegg. All three scholars focus heavily on data, but the analysis of all three can also be improved upon. Scholarship in general sees the need for empirical data and when research falls short of this mark, scholars are often called out for it.

Biber's second point, made in the above quote, is '...most people notice unusual characteristics more than common ones...'[11] As an example of Biber's point we find scholars claiming things like the preterite is avoided in the 'biblical' DSS and that the scribes often add the preposition *lamed* to the infinitive construct. Yet a thorough analysis of the data suggests that both claims are based on relatively little data.[12] Through comprehensive data collection that does not simply focus on what seems to be relevant, but upon a wide selection of variations, more common trends can be identified and analysed. Thus empirical analysis moves beyond the intuition of the scholar (granted the intuition of many Hebraists has produced some outstanding research) towards verifiable and replicable results.

2. Corpus Design

The second characteristic of corpus linguistics that Biber discusses is the development of a large and principled corpus upon which research is based.[13] I will review this characteristic in two parts: the guiding principles behind the corpus and the size of the corpus.

a. A Principled Corpus

The selection of texts for a corpus must be principled. That is to say, specific texts should be chosen in order to answer specific questions. There are three

---

9   Abegg, 'The Biblical Dead Sea Scrolls', 165.
10 Muraoka, 'An Approach', 204.
11 Biber and Conrad, *Register, Genre, and Style*, 56.
12 See, Abegg, 'The Biblical Dead Sea Scrolls', 167–8, 170. As well as the section below, 'Global Analysis of the Verbal System', IV. B.
13 See note 1 above.

aspects to developing principled corpora that are essential for this study: 1) types of texts, 2) background 'noise' and 3) relative text size.

1) Types of Texts

This study focuses on the linguistic character of the 'biblical' DSS, which naturally leads to the corpus for this study being those scrolls. Yet not all the 'biblical' scrolls are useful for analysis, as will be seen in the next section. So, care needs to be taken to make sure there are samples that address the questions at hand. The broad question of this study will focus on the linguistic character of all the scrolls as a group. But, further refinement will take place by comparing the character of subgroups and individual manuscripts. One of the main comparisons for this study will be between those scrolls that were written mostly in a *plene* orthographic style and those that were not.[14] This comparison will help to identify any scribal patterns that correlate with this known, although debated, scribal practice. Thus there must be representatives of the *plene* and defective manuscripts included in the corpus. This will play a major roll in the selection of manuscripts for this study.

2) Background 'Noise'

Another issue that is addressed by selecting a principled corpus is background 'noise'. P. Cantos Gómez presents the issue of noise as follows:

> [I]t is important to note that in order to carry out comparisons we should use similar corpora whenever possible, that is, corpora that are alike or comparable in size, content, and design, in order to avoid too much 'noise' and prevent or reduce the interaction of too many variables.[15]

As has been noted above, previous historical linguistic scholarship on Hebrew has been plagued by problems of background 'noise'. This has mostly stemmed from the lack of proper corpus design. As an example, Holmstedt's recent contribution to *Diachrony in Biblical Hebrew* ignores the genre of the manuscripts being compared.[16] Without controlling for genre his conclusion that the diachronic development of Hebrew caused the shift from אשר to ש may not be as sound as he presents. One could argue that genres such as narrative and prophetic litera-

---

14 The advantages and shortcomings of dichotomizing the 'biblical' scrolls in this way have been discussed in Chapter I. D.
15 P. Cantos Gómez, 'The Use of Linguistic Corpora for the Study of Linguistic Variation and Change: Types and Computational Applications', in *The Handbook of Historical Sociolinguistics*, 104.
16 Holmstedt, 'Historical Linguistics', 97–124.

ture that are prevalent in EBH texts favoured אשר, while ש was preferred by the more legally focused genre of 4QMMT or the book of Ben Sira. There may be a diachronic explanation for this shift, but the background noise of genre makes it difficult to determine this for certain. Thus we must control for variables such as genre in order to isolate the target variable (time in Holmstedt's study) by only comparing manuscripts of the same genre. If the target variable is genre, then we would want to compare texts from different genres while controlling for time by selecting texts from the same period.

By working with parallel copies of manuscripts ('biblical' DSS, MT, SP, etc.) I am able to control more easily for variables. Indeed, the issue of genre need not be considered at all since each copy contains essentially the same text. With the variable of genre set aside, other variables such as time, register and scribal practice can be focused on with less background noise. I am able to analyse synchronic registers particularly effectively by comparing different types of manuscripts. If the linguistic character of *tefillin* can be shown to be different than Torah scrolls, as an example, then one possible explanation could be a difference in register.

3) Relative Text Size

Relative text size is another aspect of selecting a principled corpus that is related to background noise. Ideally all of our manuscripts would be the same size. This would aid in analysis by allowing us to compare the raw data of each sample. Of course the 'biblical' DSS manuscripts are not all the same size, so we must control for this variable. In order to do this, I will use ratios throughout this study. Instead of simply saying that the first half of 1QIsa[a] has less variations than the second half because there are 693 variants in the first 27 columns and 1,001 in the remaining columns, we need to convert such numbers into ratios in order to understand their significance. The first half of 1QIsa[a] contains 10,945 words and the second half has 11,751, resulting in ratios of 6.3% and 8.5% respectively. By controlling for sample size we can now clearly see the difference between the two parts of 1QIsa[a]. Whenever possible, this study uses controls as specific as possible (i.e. number of variations involving verbs to the number of verbs, number of variations involving nouns to the number of nouns, number of variations involving *vav*s to the number of *vav*s, etc.)

b. Corpus Size

More is always better, or at least that is prevailing modern wisdom. Yet this saying seems to be actually true in historical linguistic studies — large corpora are desirable.[17] The push for large corpora is seen in the size of modern corpora such as the Brown University Standard Corpus or the London-Lund Corpus, each containing about one million words. Even with such large collections available some have argued that they are not big enough.[18] On the other hand, Biber has argued against the trend toward large corpora. As a test, Biber built a corpus of just ten texts from eleven different categories, each just a thousand words long.[19] His test showed that in many cases ten texts were enough to obtain representativeness for a specific category. Further, the experience of some sociolinguists has shown that fifteen is the minimum number of samples needed to reach statistical relevancy, with thirty or more being ideal.[20] These results provide a range of corpus size between ten and thirty texts. This large range is reflective of the present state of the historical linguistics discipline, which has yet to decide upon how many words is enough.[21] But, in general, all agree that researchers should include as many samples as possible. I will discuss the implications of these criteria for the 'biblical' DSS corpus in the following three sections: 1) the 'biblical' DSS and corpus size, 2) analysis of sample manuscripts for representativeness and 3) making the best of bad data.

1) The 'Biblical' DSS and Corpus Size

The 'biblical' DSS corpus is restricted to the number of manuscripts that were found that are classified as 'biblical'. As I have discussed in section I. B. 2. above, the present study will define 'biblical' as those manuscripts that contain only portions of the canonical Hebrew Bible as we have received it today. This definition leaves out parabiblical material, commentaries, quotations of biblical

---

17 For a general discussion of sample size and the idea that more is better, see C. Feagin, 'Entering the Community: Fieldwork', in J.K. Chambers, P. Trudgill and N. Schilling-Estes (eds), *The Handbook of Language Variation and Change* (Malden, MA 2001), 29.

18 See A. Renouf, 'Lexical Resolution', in W. Meijs (ed.), *Corpus Linguistics and Beyond: Proceedings of the Seventh International Conference on English Language Research on Computerized Corpora* (Costerus 59, Amsterdam 1987), 121–32.

19 D. Biber, 'Representativeness in Corpus Design', *LLC* 8 (1993).

20 J.M. Hernández-Campoy and N. Schilling, 'The Application of the Quantitative Paradigm to Historical Sociolinguistics: Problems With the Generalizability Principle', in *The Handbook of Historical Sociolinguistics*, 67.

21 S. Romaine, *Socio-Historical Linguistics: Its Status and Methodology* (Cambridge Studies in Linguistics 34, Cambridge 1982), 105–10.

passages in nonbiblical texts, etc.[22] This approach has been taken for two main reasons. First, it creates a homogenous corpus in that all the manuscripts that have been included are of the same type with respect to their relationship to their *Vorlagen* (they are all copies). The second reason is more practical. The editors of the Qumran manuscripts for the Accordance Bible Software program have used this definition for creating their two modules — 'biblical' and nonbiblical texts from Qumran. As a result, the total Qumran 'biblical' manuscript corpus, for the purposes of this study, contains 257 total manuscripts. Yet not all of these manuscripts are useful for some aspects of the current study. This is due to issues of representativeness.

Biber states that '[r]epresentativeness refers to the extent to which a sample includes the full range of variability in a population'.[23] Due to the fact that all of the 'biblical' DSS are fragmentary to one extent or another, all of the potential samples for this corpus are simply samples of the whole. Because of this, we must decide if the sample that we have of each text is representative of the whole. There is large disagreement within the historical linguistic community over how large a sample must be before it can be considered representative. E. Schneider states: '[t]here is no figure specifying any precise minimum number of words required — but usable texts must provide reasonably large token frequencies of individual variants'.[24] Thus Schneider argues that the number of words is less critical than the number of tokens (occurrences) of a given variant.[25]

---

22 These are of course categories with a lot of grey areas making it difficult to ascertain the exact nature of some of the manuscripts.
23 Biber, 'Representativeness', 1.
24 E. Schneider, 'Investigating Variation and Change in Written Documents', in *The Handbook of Language Variation and Change*, 71.
25 A token is an occurrence of a target variable. As was noted in the section on grammatical variable analysis above (III. A.), a variable is any two grammatical variants that can be used interchangeably. When focused on the interchange between the prepositions אל and על, any occurrence of either is considered one token. When focused on the overall variation rate within a manuscript (as we are when selecting texts for our corpus), every word is a token since each word is a potential textual variant. Thus the principle of sufficient tokens applies to this study on a number of levels. The first level of investigation is the variation rates for each manuscript. As has been mentioned above, a minimum of fifteen and ideally thirty tokens is necessary for sound statistical results. Since every word is a potential textual variant, manuscripts with at least thirty words are necessary for statistical validity according to the principle of sufficient tokens. This principle does not raise any issues at the level of variation rates, but when the focus is upon specific variation types, such as the interchange between the prepositions אל and על, issues arise. Many manuscripts contain at least thirty tokens of this interchange (at least thirty occurrences of either אל and על) but many others do not. I will not work further with the principle of sufficient tokens in this section since it does not play a major role in selecting manuscripts based on varia-

While Schneider does not focus on the number of words in a text, Biber settles on 1,000-word samples for some research questions and argues that much larger sample sizes are needed in some cases.[26] This highlights the need to evaluate the type of questions being asked and the manuscripts being used to address them.

The minimum benchmarks outlined above (ten plus texts of at least one thousand words or more) have significant implications for the study of the linguistic nature of the 'biblical' DSS. Of the 257 'biblical' scrolls only 16 contain at least 1,000 words. For many aspects of this study, it will be essential to divide the scrolls into two groups such as those written with a *plene* orthography and those that are not. Of the sixteen scrolls that contain at least one thousand words only, six are written *plene*. Clearly this is not ideal, as it does not reach Biber's minimum of ten texts for each group within the corpus. This state of affairs reflects the fact that historical linguistics is necessarily tasked with making the best of bad data. While the DSS have changed our understanding of the biblical text in major ways and at first we could hardly have wished for better, we must now recognize the limitations inherent in the texts found near the Dead Sea. The following quote from W. Labov helps to put this situation into perspective:

> Texts are produced by a series of historical accidents; amateurs may complain about this predicament, but the sophisticated historian is grateful that anything has survived at all. The great art of the historical linguist is to make the best of this bad data, 'bad' in the sense that it may be fragmentary, corrupted, or many times removed from the actual productions of native speakers.[27]

So, with the encouragement of Labov, this study will attempt to make the best of this data, while continually keeping in mind the limitations inherent in the study of the DSS. In order to make the best of this data, we are left with two options: decrease the minimum number of words required for a text or decrease the minimum number of texts required for each category. A thorough analysis of the 'biblical' DSS in relationship to the current research project shows that decreasing the minimum number of words is the better of these two 'bad' options.

As Biber has argued,[28] the selection of texts and their size must be directly related to the questions being asked. Since the primary questions being asked in this study revolve around variation between our witnesses to the Hebrew Bible, I will focus primarily on the variations found within the 'biblical' DSS in order

tion rates. But, as my focus shifts to individual variation types, I will return to token sufficiency in order to gauge the validity of the data at hand.
26 Biber, Conrad and Reppen, *Corpus Linguistics*, 249.
27 W. Labov, 'Some Principles of Linguistic Methodology', *LS* 1 (1972), 98.
28 Biber, 'Representativeness', 248–52.

to decide which texts can be considered representative of the whole of which most are only a small fraction.

Simply selecting any text that has at least one thousand words is not desirable as this approach might exclude relevant manuscripts. As an example of this, using the criteria of 1,000 words or more we would include 1QIsa^b since it contains 4,603 words, but would exclude 4QDan^a because it only has 803 words. But is 1QIsa^b more likely to be representative of the entire manuscript from which it is a sample because it has more words? Just the opposite, it seems likely that 4QDan^a would prove to be the better representative of its whole as it preserves roughly ninety percent of the text of Daniel while 1QIsa^b only preserves about twenty percent of the book of Isaiah. This example helps to show that the sample size should be linked to the size of the whole. This is supported by research within the social sciences field. W. L. Neuman argues the following:

> For small populations (under one thousand), a researcher needs a large sampling ratio (about thirty percent). For example, a sample size of about 300 is required for a high degree of accuracy. For moderate populations (10,000), a smaller sampling ratio (about ten percent) is needed to be equally accurate, or a sample size of around 1,000. For large populations (over 150,000), smaller sampling ratios (one percent) are possible, and samples of about 1,500 can be very accurate.[29]

If we take Neuman's methodology and apply it to the 'biblical' DSS we would include in our corpus only those manuscripts that preserve ten percent (for all of the 'biblical' books) and thirty percent for *tefillin*. This would leave us with 30 of the 257 'biblical' manuscripts. Of these thirty manuscripts, fifteen are written with a *plene* orthography while the others are not. This meets Biber's criteria of at least ten texts for each group within the corpus. However, a sample size of ten percent for books with less than ten thousand would not fulfil Biber's criteria of one thousand word samples. In fact, if Neuman's benchmark of ten percent is used, nineteen of the twenty-nine texts have less than one thousand words. The application of either of these criteria to the 'biblical' scrolls proves to be problematic, as the following analysis shows.

Simply assuming that ten percent of a text is representative of the whole does not go far enough. Using statistical analysis, we can ascertain what proportion of a text is representative within a given margin of error. The control I propose using for this analysis is the rate of variation across the extant text since the

---

29 W.L. Neuman, *Social Research Methods: Qualitative and Quantitative Approaches* (Boston 1997), 222.

variation between our witnesses is the primary area of interest for this study. I will analyse five sample texts from the 'biblical' DSS corpus to explore further this issue of representativeness.

2) Analysis of Sample Manuscripts for Representativeness

In this analysis, I will chart the rate of variation across five sample texts: 1QIsa^a I, 1QIsa^a II,[30] 1QIsa^b, 11QPs^a, 4QpaleoExod^m. If the rates of variation are consistent throughout these texts, then a small sample would prove to be representative of the whole. But if the rates of variation differ significantly from one section of the text to the next, a larger portion of that text would need to be sampled in order to gain representativeness.

i) 1QIsa^a I[31]

The first manuscript that I will analyse is 1QIsa^a I. This manuscript contains a total of 695 variations and preserves 10,945 words.[32] Thus 1QIsa^a I preserves roughly 98% of the first half of the book of Isaiah and has about 1 variant for every 16 intact words (or 6.4%). If the variation rate for 1QIsa^a I was perfectly consistent throughout the manuscript, then a sample size of just sixteen words could be considered representative of the whole. Yet obviously this sort of consistency is not expected. In fact, 1QIsa^a I shows a large range of variation rates. Figure 1 provides a visual representation of the variation rates of 1QIsa^a by column.

---

30 1QIsa^a will be analysed as two separate texts. 1QIsa^a I contains columns 1–27 and 1QIsa^a II contains columns 28–54. In general, this division is required due to the likelihood that this scroll was copied from two different *Vorlagen*.

31 E. Tov, 'Scribal Features of Two Qumran Scrolls', in S.E. Fassberg and M. Bar-Asher (eds), *Hebrew in the Second Temple Period: The Hebrew of the Dead Sea Scrolls and of other Contemporary Sources* (Leiden 2013), 241–58.

32 Accordance search: DSSB-M, ignore words inside brackets (excludes reconstructed words), range 1QIsa^a 1–27, total words ([range 1qisa^a 1-27] <and> *) = 10,945.

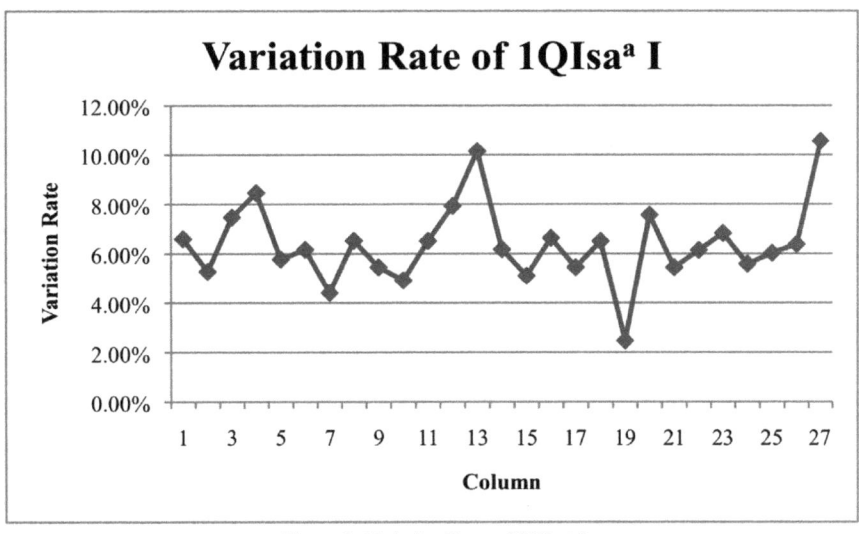

Figure 1. Variation Rate of 1QIsa[a] I

The highest rate of variation is found in column 27 at 10.6% (32 variations in 303 words) and column 19 has the lowest with 2.5% (just 9 variations in 365 words). This gives us the rather large range of 2.5% to 10.6%. Thus if we sampled only three hundred words from this manuscript at random we could end up with a completely non-representative sample of the whole. Because of this it is clear that a larger sample of the whole is needed in order to obtain representativeness. To determine how large a sample is needed, I will compare the data to a Gaussian Curve,[33] determine the standard deviation for the dataset, and calculate the number of words needed in a sample size to bring the sample size's variation rate within one standard deviation[34] of the mean of the whole. By increasing the size of the sample until it is within one standard deviation of the whole, we guarantee that the variation rate of the sample will not fall to the extremes of the data.[35]

The standard deviation for 1QIsa[a] I is 1.6%. Nineteen of the twenty-seven columns of 1QIsa[a] I fall within one standard deviation of the mean. That is to say, these 19 columns have a mean of between 4.75% and 8.01%. This tells us that if we selected a column at random from 1QIsa[a] I, we would have about a seventy percent chance of selecting one that falls within one standard deviation. But, we would also have a thirty percent chance of selecting one that falls out-

---

33 This is also known as a Normal Curve or Bell Curve.
34 The standard deviation is the square root of the variance, which is the average of the squared differences (between variation rates) from the mean. See section III. B. 4. below for further development of this concept.
35 In section III. B. 4., I will develop the theory behind and application of the relevant statistical methodologies that I will be utilizing.

side of this range. By increasing the sample size, we can increase the likelihood that our selected sample will have a mean between 4.75% and 8.01%. If the sample size is increased to three columns,[36] the chance of randomly selecting a non-representative sample is just 4%.[37] This falls below the five percent threshold commonly considered valid by statisticians.[38] Further, columns 11–13 (the only contiguous three column set that does not fall within the target range) have a mean variation rate of 8.19%, which is very close to being within the target range. Those results show that by selecting any set of three columns from 1QIsa^a I, we can obtain a representative sample. The only exception to this is columns eleven through thirteen that fall just outside of the representative range.

By using a sample size of three columns, we are nearly able to guarantee representativeness. For 1QIsa^a I, the largest three-column set contains 1,473 words, which is about 13 percent of the total word count for the book of Isaiah. Therefore, we can consider all samples from 1QIsa^a I that contain thirteen percent or more of the first half of Isaiah to be representative. This shows that neither Neuman's benchmark of ten percent nor Biber's criteria of a thousand words is sufficient for selecting a representative sample of 1QIsa^a I.

ii) 1QIsa^a II

I will analyse the second half of the Great Isaiah Scroll next. 1QIsa^a II contains a total of 989 variations and preserves a total of 11,751 words. Even though some of this scroll has been lost to decay, it preserves more total words than the corresponding half in the MT. This is due to the expanding tendencies of the scribe, which will be discussed below. The variation rate found in 1QIsa^a II is roughly 8.5% or about 1 in every 11 words. This is compared with the 6.4% variation rate found in 1QIsa^a I. Just as in the first half of this scroll, the second half reveals a wide range of variation rates from column to column as can be seen in Figure 2.

---

36 I am assuming contiguous columns. While some of the 'biblical' manuscripts are not contiguous, the chances of randomly selecting three sections of a text that contain rates of variation that differ greatly from the mean is not statistically relevant.

37 This is because of the twenty-five contiguous three column possibilities, only one falls outside of the one standard deviation range being used for this analysis.

38 I will discuss the five percent threshold in section III. B. 4. b. below.

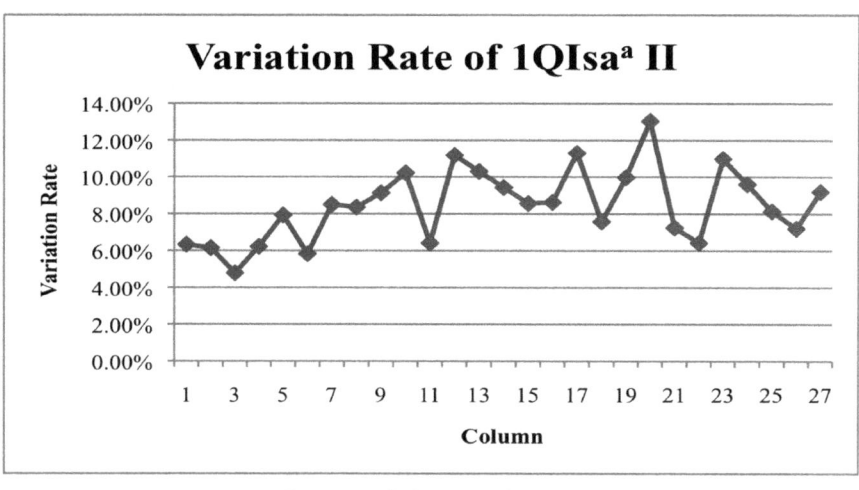

Figure 2. Variation Rate of 1QIsa^a II

The highest rate of variation in this manuscript is found in column 47 with 13% and the lowest is in column 30, which has only 4.7%. The standard deviation for 1QIsa^a II is 2.0%, resulting in a representativeness range of 6.5% to 10.5%. Of the twenty-seven columns in this half of the Great Isaiah Scroll, seventeen fall within this range. But due to the low variation rate found at the beginning of this scroll, we have to increase our sample size to a minimum of five columns. If sample sizes of three columns were used (as with the first half of this scroll) there would be three places where the sample would fall outside of the representativeness range (these ranges are found from columns twenty-eight to thirty-three). This would leave us with a twelve percent chance of selecting a non-representative sample, which is above the five percent threshold discussed earlier. The same is true for four column sample sizes. By increasing our sample size to five columns we have a ninety-six percent chance of selecting a representative sample. However, these five columns account for 2,806 words, which is about 24% of the total words found in Isaiah. While a sample size of thirteen percent will produce representative results for 1QIsa^a I, sample sizes of at least twenty-four percent are needed to get the same results for 1QIsa^a II. While Neuman states that a sample size of ten percent will produce representative results and Biber argues that one thousand-word sample sizes work for most studies, the above results for 1QIsa^a II show that a much larger sample size is needed for this manuscript.

iii) 1QIsa^b

In contrast to the relatively high sample sizes needed for the two sections of 1QIsa^a, the following three manuscripts require significantly smaller samples. 1QIsa^b contains a total of 4,627 words (roughly 20% of Isaiah) and 157 variations. This scroll has a much lower variation rate than 1QIsa^a with just 1 in every 37 words or 2.7%. Yet due to the very fragmentary nature of the first fifteen columns of this scroll, I will focus only on columns sixteen through twenty-eight. These columns have a variation rate of 1 in 27 words or 3.6%. Figure 3 presents the individual variation rates for each of these columns.

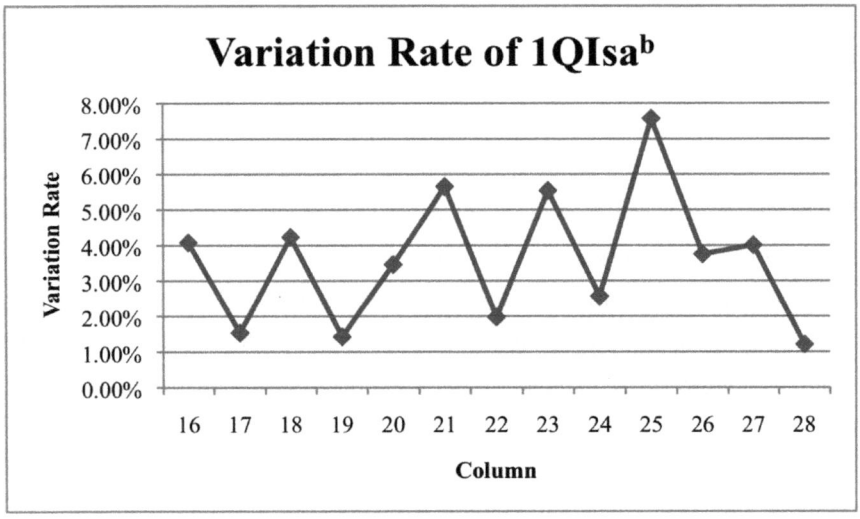

Figure 3. Variation Rate of 1QIsa^b

Column 25 has the highest rate of variation with 7.5% and column 28 has the lowest with 1.2%. The standard deviation for these columns is 1.9%, resulting in a range of 2.7% to 5.4%. Of the thirteen columns being analysed, six fall within this range. To obtain representativeness, the sample size for 1QIsa^b needs to be increased to 3 columns or a total of 1,224 words. This sample size accounts for about 5.4% of the total word count for Isaiah. This falls below Neuman's ten percent mark, but the sample size needed based on the variation rates for 1QIsa^b is over the one-thousand-word mark set by Biber.

iv) 11QPs^a

11QPs^a contains 303 variations and a total of 3,298 total words (about 13% of the book of Psalms). This manuscript has a relatively high variation rate of 8.8% or about 1 in every 11 words. The range of variation found in this scroll is presented in Figure 4.

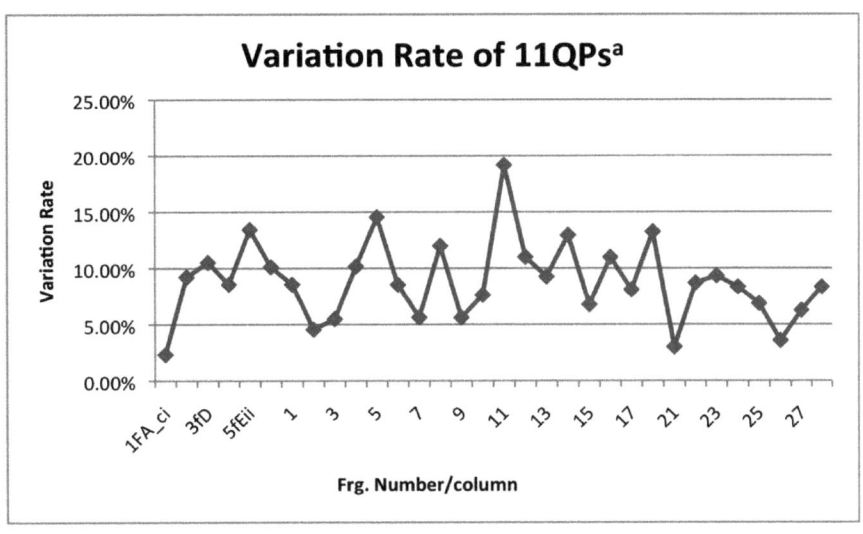

Figure 4. Variation Rate of 11QPs[a]

The highest rate of variation is found in column 11 with 19% and the lowest rate is in column 1 with 2.3%. This range of variation is significantly larger than those found in the previous three manuscripts. The standard deviation for this manuscript is 3.6%, creating a representativeness range of 5.3% to 12.4%. Of the thirty-two columns in 11QPs[a], twenty-three fall into this range. The sample range for this manuscript needs to be raised to 5 columns, or a total of at least 683 words, to result in a high probability of selecting a representative portion of the text. Six hundred and eighty-three words accounts for about 2.7% of the total word count for the Psalms. Unlike the first three manuscripts analysed thus far, this sample size fits both Neuman's and Biber's criteria.

v) 4QpaleoExod[m]

The final scroll that I will analyse to assess representativeness within the 'biblical' DSS is 4QpaleoExod[m]. This scroll contains 2,622 preserved words accounting for about 11% of the book of Exodus. 4QpaleoExod[m] has 84 variations when compared with the MT, resulting in a variation rate of 3.1% or 1 in every 33 words. Figure 5 presents the range of variation found in this scroll.

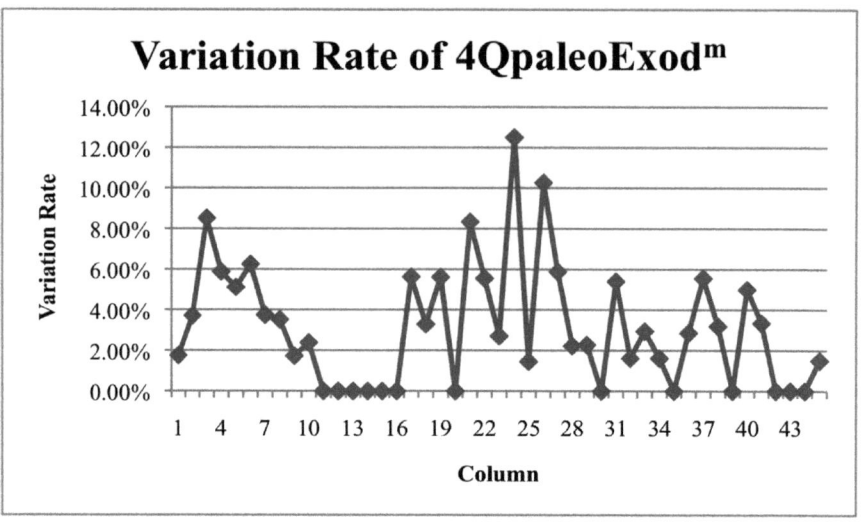

Figure 5. Variation Rate of 4QpaleoExod[m]

4QpaleoExod[m] has a range of variation from 0% in a number of relatively fragmentary columns to 12.5% in column 24. The standard deviation for this scroll is nearly identical to the mean, standing at three percent. This is due to the low variation rate and the significant number of columns that preserve very little of the original manuscript. This results in a representativeness range of 0.1% to 6.2%. The variation rates for twenty-six of the total forty-five columns are within this range. Increasing the sample size to 6 columns or more than 282 words results in a high probability of obtaining representativeness. Two hundred and eighty-two words is just 1.2% of the total word count for the book of Psalms. This analysis of 4QpaleoExod[m] shows that Neuman's and Biber's criteria are far too restrictive for some manuscripts.

3) Making the Best of Bad Data

This review of variation rates in five manuscripts from the 'biblical' Qumran corpus results in the following representativeness sample sizes: 1QIsa[a] I – 13% (1,473 words), 1QIsa[a] II – 24% (2,806 words), 1QIsa[b] – 5.4% (1,224 words), 11QPs[a] – 2.7% (683 words), 4QPaleoExod[m] – 1.2% (282 words). While Neuman's mark of ten percent and Biber's criteria of one thousand words fit some of these results, others show that using either of these methods would at times be too restrictive and at other times unnecessarily inclusive. In an ideal situation, we would simply take the most restrictive path, that found in 1QIsa[a] II of 24% (2,806 words). By selecting only those manuscripts that preserve at least twenty-four percent of the book that it represents, our corpus would have a very high chance of containing only representative samples. Yet this approach would only include twenty manuscripts, fourteen of which are *tefillin*. While this corpus would have representative samples, it would not have a sufficient number of diverse manuscripts. We are then left with the conclusion that the 'biblical' DSS corpus does not simply contain 'bad data',[39] but in fact it contains 'very bad data'.[40] The corpus appears to have enough manuscripts and enough of these manuscripts appear to be large enough for analysis, but when these criteria are taken together (number and size) the corpus falls short.

On the one hand, scholars could abandon this corpus as too fragmentary for linguistic analysis. On the other hand, we can attempt to make the best of the data that is available while recognizing its limitations.[41] In order to make the best of what time has left us, we need to focus on building a corpus that contains as many texts as possible from as many different groups as possible.[42] I will use Biber's criteria of ten texts per group as the guiding principle for this corpus. The main groups that I will focus on are the following: scrolls written with a *plene* orthography and those written in a defective orthographic style; and content of scroll (Torah, Prophets, Writings).

Since it is not possible to produce a corpus containing only representative samples, we need to focus on the overall statistical relevancy of the whole. A statistically relevant whole will help counteract the impact of individual manuscripts that might not be representative. In order to gauge the statistical relevance of the 'biblical' Qumran corpus, we can use histograms. A histogram graphically represents the distribution of a set of data.[43] This data is plotted on a graph according to a given set of frequencies. The resulting shape of the data can be compared with a Gaussian Curve to test for statistical relevancy. Data that aligns closely with a Gaussian Curve is more likely to produce relevant results than data that is heavily skewed to the right or left.

In order to build a histogram, the data must be organized into categories. For

---

39 Labov, 'Some Principles of Linguistic Methodology', 97–120.
40 Rezetko and Young, *Historical Linguistics*, 105.
41 A. Rubinstein, 'Singularities in Consecutive-Tense Constructions in the Isaiah Scroll', *VT* 5 (1955), 26.
42 Biber argues that diversity is more important than sample size. Biber, Conrad and Reppen, *Corpus Linguistics*, 249.
43 'A graphical representation of a set of observations in which class frequencies are represented by the areas of rectangles centred on the class interval'. B. Everitt, *The Cambridge Dictionary of Statistics* (Cambridge 1998), 193.

our purposes, I continue to use the percent of variation found in each manuscript. My categories are variation rates of 0% to 1%, 1.1% to 2%, etc. The resulting plot on the graph will represent the number of manuscripts for each category. First, I place all of the 'biblical' scrolls into these categories and then plot the results onto a graph to ascertain if the entire corpus follows a Gaussian Curve. Figure 6 is the resulting histogram:

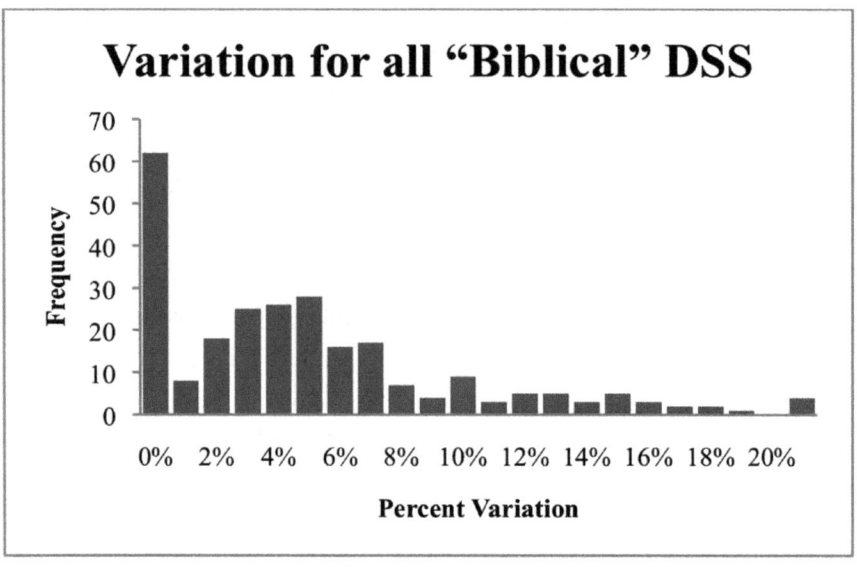

Figure 6. Histogram of Variation Rates for All 'Biblical' DSS

This histogram reveals two key characteristics of the 'biblical' DSS corpus. First, this corpus contains more manuscripts with low variation rates than high variation rates. These low variation scrolls skew the data heavily to the left. Second, aside from the low variation scrolls, this corpus does contain a bell shaped curve. Yet because this data is skewed, any statistical analysis will be overly influenced by those manuscripts containing low variation rates. One would normally allow each manuscript to play its role in the statistical analysis, even if more of those manuscripts have low variation rates. But, closer analysis reveals a correlation between low variation rates and number of words in a manuscript. The following histograms demonstrate this connection.

When the 'biblical' DSS corpus is restricted to those manuscripts that contain at least one hundred words, the following histogram is produced.

Chapter III Methodology

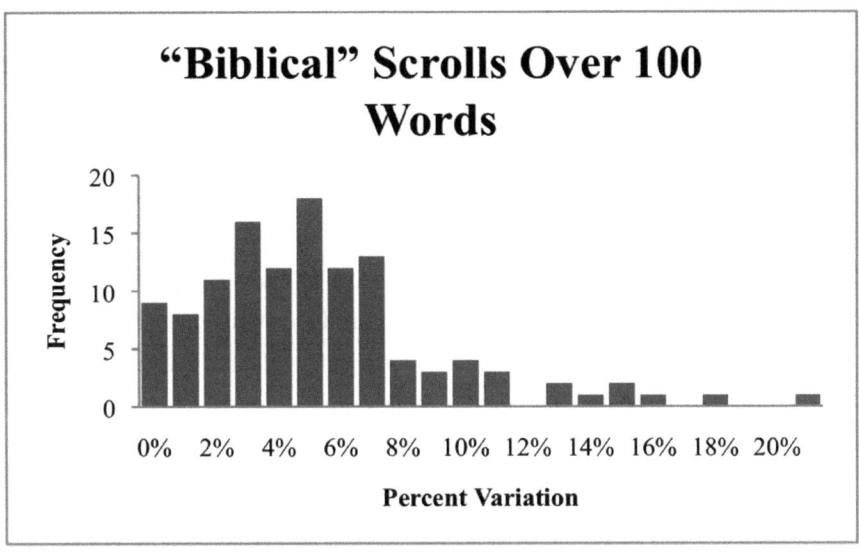

Figure 7. Histogram of 'Biblical' Scrolls Over 100 Words

The most significant aspect of this histogram is the first bar, which represents the category zero percent to one percent. This category contains significantly fewer manuscripts compared with this category in the histogram for the entire corpus. Fewer manuscripts end up grouping to the left of the histogram when manuscripts with less than one hundred words are excluded. Yet the histogram for the remaining scrolls is still tilted in that direction. By restricting our corpus to those manuscripts with at least two hundred words we get a set of data that much more closely aligns with a Gaussian Curve.

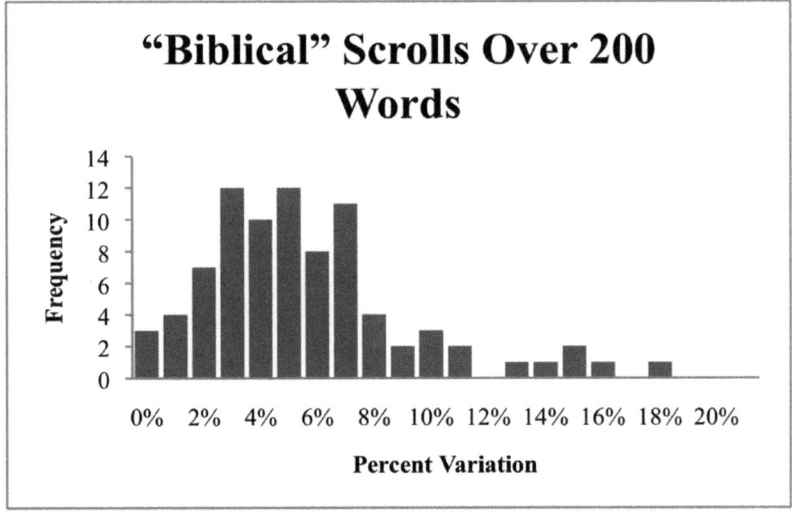

Figure 8. Histogram of 'Biblical' Scrolls Over 200 Words

The histogram for scrolls containing at least two hundred words presents a good bell shaped curve, although it should be noted that it is still slightly skewed to the left. However, excluding manuscripts with less than two hundred words has reduced this problem significantly. This brief analysis of three histograms shows the impact smaller manuscripts have upon the whole. Because these smaller manuscripts skew the data they need to be removed from the corpus before statistical analysis is undertaken. The resulting corpus fits much closer to a Gaussian Curve and thus is much more likely to produce statistically relevant data. Because the whole is likely to produce statistically relevant results, the impact of individual manuscripts that are not representative will be negated or at least reduced greatly.

The manuscripts in Table 1 contain at least two hundred words and thus will make up the corpus upon which this study will be based.[44]

---

44 Two manuscripts, 4QGen^f and 11QPs^c, that have at least two hundred words have been excluded from this corpus because they do not have an intact reading of לא. Because the main comparison for this project is between *plene* and defective scrolls, specifically between those scrolls reading לא and those reading לוא, these two scrolls that do not contain this negation cannot be utilized for this work.

Scroll Name	Scroll Number	Scroll Name	Scroll Number	Scroll Name	Scroll Number
1QDeut^a	1Q4	4QJosh^a	4Q47	4QDan^b	4Q113
1QDeut^b	1Q5	4QSam^a	4Q51	4QDan^c	4Q114
1QIsa^b	1Q8	4QSam^b	4Q52	4QPhyl A	4Q128
1QPhyl	1Q13	4QSam^c	4Q53	4QPhyl B	4Q129
1QIsa^a	1QIsa^a	4QIsa^a	4Q55	4QPhyl C	4Q13
2QJer	2Q13	4QIsa^b	4Q56	4QPhyl G	4Q134
2QRuth^a	2Q16	4QIsa^c	4Q57	4QPhyl H	4Q135
4QGen-Exod^a	4Q1	4QIsa^d	4Q58	4QPhyl J	4Q137
4QGen^b	4Q2	4QIsa^e	4Q59	4QPhyl K	4Q138
4QGen^c	4Q5	4QIsa^f	4Q6	4QPhyl M	4Q14
4QGen^j	4Q9	4QJer^a	4Q7	6QpapKgs	6Q4
4QpaleoGen-Exod1	4Q11	4QJer^c	4Q72	8QPhyl	8Q3
4QExod^b	4Q13	4QEzek^a	4Q73	8QMez	8Q4
4QExod^c	4Q14	4QXII^a	4Q76	11QpaleoLev^a	11Q1
4QExod-Lev^f	4Q17	4QXII^c	4Q78	11QPs^a	11Q5
4QpaleoExod^m	4Q22	4QXII^e	4Q8	5/6Hev1^b	5/6Hev1^b
4QLev-Num^a	4Q23	4QXII^g	4Q82	Mas1b	Mas1b
4QLev^b	4Q24	4QPs^a	4Q83	Mas1d	Mas1d
4QNum^b	4Q27	4QPs^b	4Q84	Mas1e	Mas1e
4QDeut^b	4Q29	4QPs^c	4Q85	Mur Gen 1	Mur1
4QDeut^c	4Q3	4QPs^e	4Q87	MurEx	Mur4
4QDeut^d	4Q31	4QPs^f	4Q88	MurXII	Mur88
4QDeut^f	4Q33	4QJob^a	4Q99	XHev/Se5	XHev/Se5
4QDeut^h	4Q35	4QCant^b	4Q17	XQPhyl 1	XQ1
4QDeut^j	4Q37	4QLam	4Q111	XQPhyl 2	XQ2
4QDeutⁿ	4Q41	4QDan^a	4Q112	XQPhyl 3	XQ3
4QpaleoDeut^r	4Q45				

Table 1. 'Biblical' DSS Corpus for Statistical Analysis

'This corpus contains seventy-nine manuscripts (twenty-seven[45] *plene* and fifty-two defective). These scrolls contain eighty-five percent of the total variations found in the 'biblical' DSS. Further, it is diverse in nature, while also providing enough texts in each group to allow for statistically relevant analysis. This corpus has been shown to align closely with a Gaussian Curve, meaning it will not produce heavily skewed results. It is not perfect, but it appears to be the best possible corpus given the manuscripts that are available. I will primarily focus on this corpus when utilizing inter-textual variable analysis, since this approach focuses on comparing variation rates between corpora and relies heavily upon statistical testing. However, I will discuss features of manuscripts not included in this corpus

---

45 I will be treating 1QIsa^a as two manuscripts throughout this project, which is accounted for in this number. See note 30, above.

throughout the following chapters in order to provide the most holistic description of the language of the 'biblical' DSS as possible. Including all the 'biblical' manuscripts will be particularly relevant when utilizing cross-textual variable analysis. Since cross-textual variable analysis focuses mainly on comparing the use of grammatical variables in two or more versions of the same text, it does not heavily rely on comparing variation rates nor does it use significance tests. Now I will turn to the methodology that I will use to analyse this corpus.

3. Data Collection

The third characteristic of corpus linguistics that Biber discussed is the use of computers to aid in data collection.[46] As I mentioned above, the need for good data has been recognized in the field of Hebrew linguistics for a long time. But up until the last two decades data collection had to take place by hand. This process was necessarily prone to error. But, with the development of powerful personal computers and the digitization of 'biblical' manuscripts, scholars are able to obtain large amounts of data with relative ease. Computer programs such as Accordance Bible Software allow researchers to search the 'biblical' corpus for a wide range of linguistic features, from orthographic and morphological characteristics to more complex syntactic phenomena. Accordance Bible Software even allows the user to compare parallel passages in different witnesses, allowing scholars to analyse variations. In order to make this analysis less labour intensive, I (along with Abegg) developed a module for Accordance Bible Software that contains every true variation between the 'biblical' DSS and the MT.[47] This is a searchable tool which allows the user to gather a significant amount of data quickly. For this study, I have categorized this data into groups such as variations involving verbs or nouns and more specific types of variations such as those that include a plus of a conjunction *vav*. I further annotated this database so that I am able to identify readings that are only found in the 'biblical' DSS manuscripts (readings not found in the MT, SP or LXX).[48] This allows my analysis to move beyond a simple comparison between the DSS and the MT. This collection of data enables me to empirically analyse the variations between

---

46 Biber, Conrad and Reppen, *Corpus Linguistics*, 4.
47 To this database I have added notes for my personal research that document every true variant reading found in the 'biblical' DSS, but not in other major witnesses.
48 For the DSS and MT readings, I compiled my own set of variants. For the SP and the LXX I followed DJD. Since comparing versions, especially Hebrew texts to Greek texts, is problematic at times, I chose to follow the decisions found in the DJD series to allow for my data to be easily referenced by others.

our witnesses while supplying supporting examples and comprehensive counts for all my conclusions. For complete documentation of all relevant data for this study including references and counts, see the attached appendices. While no dataset can be perfect, with the assistance of computer software and by checking the data against reference works,[49] a high level of confidence can be achieved.[50]

Another significant benefit of basing linguistic analysis upon publicly available computer software is that it allows for the replication and verification of all data and conclusions.[51] These are two hallmarks of scientific study. Before computer software, scholars were left with two options. One, they could trust the data that was presented to them and the conclusions upon which that data was based. Or two, they could manually reproduce the data, which likely took the original researcher years to gather. In order to avoid these two problematic choices, I will provide complete search details for data that is easily collected via Accordance Bible Software.[52] For data that is not easily replicated I will include complete documentation in the attached appendices.

4. Quantitative Analysis

The fourth and final characteristic of corpus linguistics discussed by Biber is quantitative and qualitative analysis. The strength of past research on the Hebrew language has been qualitative analysis, but quantitative techniques have not been used to their full potential. This study will make use of both types of analyses, starting with a quantitative approach and basing all qualitative conclusions upon empirically valid statistical analysis. Because quantitative statistical methodologies are not common in Hebrew linguistics, I will briefly describe the techniques that I will be using throughout this study.

a. Hypothesis Testing

In the corpus linguistics approach to language study, a typical research question takes the form: 'is variable x used differently in corpus A compared with corpus

---

49 Ulrich, *The Biblical Qumran Scrolls*, as well as the DJD series.
50 Yet it is important to note that minor errors in data collection due to human or software errors should not impact the results of this type of study in significant ways. These small errors can be overcome through rigorous statistical analysis and by working with large datasets.
51 Cantos Gómez, 'The Use of Linguistic Corpora', 100.
52 All Accordance searches for this study were done in version 10, with the most up-to-date modules available at the time. However, it is important to note that even small updates in the Accordance software can change the results of searches. Further, modules are continually updated, so small differences in search results from module to module are to be expected.

B?'[53] In order to be answered this question needs to be stated in the form of a hypothesis that can be tested. Typically, this hypothesis states that any difference between the use of variable x in corpus A and corpus B is due to random chance. This is called the null hypothesis and is represented by 'H_0'. Once the null hypothesis is formulated, the alternative hypothesis needs to be stated. Normally this takes a form similar to: variable x is used differently in corpus A compared with corpus B and this difference is not due to random chance. The alternative hypothesis is represented by 'H_1'. Once these hypotheses are developed, a statistical test is selected to analyse the truth of H_0. If H_0 is found to be false, then H_1 is assumed to be true.

Before discussing the different statistical tests that can be used to analyse hypotheses, a couple of notes are needed. First, I will briefly consider the concept of random chance in linguistic analysis. In linguistic studies, randomness is not equated with accident. Clearly authors do not accidentally choose one linguistic form over another. There are reasons and motivations behind these choices. Even scribal errors do not happen 'randomly'. A scribe produces an error for specific reasons (e.g. some words get omitted from a manuscript do to *homoeoteleuton*, thus there was a cause for the omission). Let us return to our null hypothesis to investigate the idea of random chance further. And let us suppose that we are comparing a corpus of EBH books to LBH books. Further, the variable that we want to analyse is the use of verbs in these corpora. Our H_0 could be: There is no difference that cannot be attributed to random chance, between the use of verbs in EBH and LBH. And our H_1 could be: There is a difference between the use of verbs in EBH and LBH and it is not due to random chance. In this example, let us assume that the mean ratio of verbs to total number of words in EBH is one to twenty and in LBH it is one to ten.[54] With these assumptions in place, there appears to be a clear difference in the use of verbs between these two corpora. Now let us imagine that we apply a statistical test to these corpora and it states that our H_0 is true. This means that statistically speaking the difference between the use of verbs in EBH compared with the use of verbs in LBH is simply due to random chance. This is possible because many of the statistical tests that are used to analyse linguistic hypotheses focus on the internal variation within each corpus. That is to say, the likelihood of a difference occurring between two corpora is based on the internal differences observable within each individual corpus. Table 2 helps to make this clear.

---

53 Ibid., 103.
54 In order to keep this example as simple as possible, I will fabricate numbers that will clearly demonstrate the necessary points.

Corpus	EBH	LBH
Sample 1	5.0%	10.0%
Sample 2	0.5%	1.0%
Sample 3	2.0%	5.0%
Sample 4	10.0%	15.0%
Sample 5	19.0%	3.0%
Sample 6	0.6%	20.0%
Sample 7	2.0%	12.0%
Sample 8	0.5%	14.0%
Mean	5.0%	10.0%

Table 2. Hypothetical Comparison Between EBH and LBH

As Table 2 shows, our fabricated data produces a mean of five percent for EBH and ten percent for LBH. Further, a brief look at each sample ratio gives the impression that EBH contains far less verbs per word on average than LBH. But a two-tailed t-test (described below) confirms that there is no statistical difference between these two sets of data. This is due to the internal variation of each corpus. For EBH, there is a range from 0.5% to 19% and for LBH the range is from 1% to 20%. Because of the internal variation the t-test concludes that the difference in mean between the two corpora is due to random chance. There is a high probability that, had more data for each corpus been available, the difference in the usage of verbs would be wiped away.

An intuitive example of this comes from flipping a coin. If we flip a coin ten times and it comes up heads eight times, is that enough evidence to claim that the coin is unfair? The answer is no, because flipping a coin and having it land on heads eight of ten times occurs roughly once every twenty attempts. The variability of possible coin flips tells us that eight of ten is not that rare. The same is true for our sample Hebrew study. The variability within each corpus tells us that a mean of five percent or ten percent is not that rare and given more data the means for each corpus could be significantly different.

These examples lead to another topic that needs some brief discussion — significance level. When a null hypothesis is analysed, the results are normally presented in the form of a significance level. The Cambridge Dictionary of Statistics defines 'significance level' as '[t]he level of probability at which it is agreed that the null hypothesis will be rejected'.[55] Significance tests report a percentage, the P-value,[56] which tells '[t]he probability of the observed data (or data showing a more extreme departure from the null hypothesis) when the

---
55 Everitt, *The Cambridge Dictionary of Statistics*, 345.
56 Ibid., 304.

null hypothesis is true'.[57] This score ranges from one hundred percent to zero percent, with higher P-values telling us that the observed data is highly likely if the H_0 is true and lower values telling us that the observed data is very unlikely if the H_0 is true. The significance level is set by consensus at a specific point, so that if the P-value falls below this level we reject the null hypothesis as false. The significance level is arbitrarily set at five percent in many fields of study. Yet W.S. Browner argues that there is 'nothing magical about the value 0.05. Why should a result that has a P value of 0.049 be important, while one with a P value of 0.051, or 0.07, is meaningless?... Almost every investigator understands that it is silly to look askance at results that have P values that are barely nonsignificant'.[58] Because of this, the 'best course of action depends on whether results with a P value that is "right around 0.05" make sense'.[59] Since the significance level is subjectively set by researchers within a particular field, it needs to function as a guideline, not a hard and fast rule. This study will adopt the five percent significance level, but will follow Browner's lead in treating it carefully. If a P-value falls near five percent the null hypothesis will not be accepted/rejected without further consideration of the plausibility of the result.[60]

Up to this point, I have discussed the development of hypotheses, random chance and significance levels. Now I will present the different significance tests that will be used in this study as well as some other useful statistical tools.

b. Significance Tests

At their most basic, significance tests are used to test the validity of a null hypothesis. But more precisely a significance test is applied to a set of observations and produces a P-value related to a null hypothesis. The P-value states the probability of the data if the null hypothesis is true. I will return to the flipping of a coin to demonstrate the application of a significance test. First we develop our hypotheses:

H_0 The coin is fair

H_1 The coin is not fair (it has been tampered with)

Then we gather data. For this example, let us assume we ran one hundred tests of ten flips. We can then use a significance test, in this case a one-sample t-test,

---

57 Ibid., 304.
58 W.S. Browner, *Publishing and Presenting Clinical Research* (Philadelphia 2006), 63.
59 Browner, *Publishing and Presenting*, 63.
60 The plausibility of all results need to be questioned and will be in this study. But this is particularly true in cases where the P-value falls near the significance level.

Chapter III Methodology

to produce a P-value. Let us assume our P-value came out as 98.7%. This tells us that if the H_0 is true then the observed data has a 98.7% chance of occurring. Since this P-value is far above the five percent significance level, we can accept the H_0 and reject the H_1. Now, let us imagine that we ran the same scenario with a different coin producing a different set of data. We then applied the one sample t-test to the data and got a P-value of 3.5%. This tells us that if the H_0 is true then this new set of data only has a 3.5% chance of occurring. Because this P-value falls below the five percent threshold, we should reject the H_0 as untrue. We would therefore accept the H_1 and conclude that the coin is not fair and has probably been altered in some way. Thus, the significance test helps us to sift through a large amount of data in order to test hypotheses.

Choosing the appropriate significance test is vital for obtaining reliable results. It is therefore important to understand the assumptions made by the tests being used, the purpose for which the tests were developed, and the possible applications for which they are useful. I will thoroughly examine the main test that I will use in this study, the Student's t-test developed by W.S. Gosset in 1908. The Student's t-test, or simply t-test, is used to assess a hypothesis based on population means. The t-test assumes normalized data, equal variance, and independent sampling. When a set of data is normalized, its dispersion follows a Gaussian Curve. The t-test has been shown to produce reliable results even when the assumption of normalcy is not met[61] as long as the dataset contains a large number of samples (less than one hundred can prove to be enough at times).[62] Normalcy tests will be used to see if each sample meets the first assumption of the t-test. To meet the assumption of equal variance both datasets being compared must have equal internal variation within a margin of error. For this study, the f-test[63] will be used to test for equal variance.[64] The assumption of independent sampling states that all samples found in one dataset cannot be included in a second.[65] This is true of all corpora in this study; no single manuscript is included in two corpora that are being compared. As an example, I

---

61 Everitt, *The Cambridge Dictionary of Statistics*, 366.
62 T.P. Lumley et al., 'The Importance of the Normality Assumption in Large Public Health Data Sets', *ARPH* 23 (2002), 151–70.
63 'A test for the equality of the variances of two populations having normal distributions, based on the ratio of the variances of a sample of observations taken from each. Most often encountered in the analysis of variance, where testing whether particular variances are the same also tests for the equality of a set of means'. Everitt, *The Cambridge Dictionary of Statistics*, 153.
64 For datasets that do not have equal variances, I will use the heteroscedastic t-test (which assumes unequal variances), as opposed to homoscedastic t-test (which requires equal variances).
65 Romaine, *Socio-Historical Linguistics*, 107.

would not compare all *tefillin* to all *plene* manuscripts as some of the *tefillin* are written with *plene* orthography. This sort of comparison would cause errors in the statistical calculation due to having some of the same witnesses in each corpus. The t-test is a good fit for this study because all of the data upon which my conclusions are based meet the three assumptions of the test. The corpus is normally distributed (roughly) and contains enough samples to overcome the slight skewness observed in some datasets. The t-test assumes equal variance, but there is an alternative version that allows for unequal variance — the heteroscedastic t-test. This version of the t-test is used throughout because all of the datasets used in this study have unequal variance. And, as I have just discussed above, all of the data has been independently sampled.

While I will use the t-test throughout, there are three forms of this test that will be applied in different contexts. Those three forms are the one sample t-test, the one-tailed t-test and the two-tailed t-test. Each of these has different applications. I have already used the one sample t-test above, but a further example and some explanation are needed.

The one sample t-test is used to compare the mean of a single group of observations with a specific value.[66] The coin flip example that has already been used a few times provides a basic way of looking at this t-test. If we flipped a coin one hundred times, recorded the results, and then wanted to know if those results are statistically different than what is expected we could use the one sample t-test. This test would compare the results of the one hundred flips to the expected value of fifty/fifty (or stated in the form of a mean, fifty percent heads). If the test produced a P-value of five percent or lower, then we would conclude that our test results are abnormal and would question the fairness of the coin that we flipped. Thus the one sample t-test assess the possibility of obtaining the observed results given the expected mean.

The one sample t-test will be used in a number of contexts in this study. As an example, if one particular corpus, say all Torah manuscripts, displays a particularly high variation rate of a given type this test will be applied in order to calculate the probability of that variation rate occurring given the overall variation rate for all manuscripts.

The other two forms of the t-test are related. Both of these tests analyse the means of two independent samples (e.g. the control group and the test group in a medical trial). These tests compute the similarity of each group given the

---

66   D.G. Altman, *Practical Statistics for Medical Research* (New York 1991), 183.

internal variation of each and determines whether they are statistically the same. The Gaussian Curve is used by both tests. The mean of each group is calculated in relationship to the normal distribution of the data. If the mean of one group falls to the extremes of one of the 'tails' of the curve, then that data is considered extreme. The use of the Gaussian Curve and the tails of this curve as a reference point gives rise to the names of each form of this test. The one-tailed t-test only calculates the probably of obtaining a statistically relevant result on one half of the curve (one tail). This test is commonly used in medical testing since researchers are often only trying to find out if a new drug produces better results in the test group compared with the control group. As an example, let us say a research group wants to test a new blood pressure medication. They know that the medication is likely to lower blood pressure, but they want to know if it lowers it more than the standard drug on the market. In this case, the one-tailed t-test can be used because the researchers know upon which tail they should focus – the reduction of blood pressure. Any significant result for this research project will fall to one tail of the Gaussian Curve.

In contrast, the two-tailed t-test needs to be used when we do not know in which direction to look for significant results. As an example of this let us return to the medical field. Imagine a group of researchers want to study the impact of coffee upon the well-being of people. They set up two groups. One group will drink coffee everyday, the other will not. These researchers are interested in knowing if coffee improves the test groups' overall feeling of well-being or if it negatively influences it. After running their experiment and gathering the data, the researchers would use a two-tailed t-test because significant results could be found at either tail of the Gaussian Curve. A non-significant result would show at the peak of the curve, while the researchers would be particularly interested in any result that fell to either tail.

The various versions of the t-test will be used throughout this study to determine if there are statistically relevant differences between two sets of manuscripts. The results of these tests help to guide data analysis by testing hypotheses, but they do not replace the need for qualitative analysis. I will therefore apply these tests to the extent that they are useful, but all my conclusions will be based upon further analysis and comparison with the conclusions of past research.

c. Standard Deviation

An analysis of the standard deviation will be used to test for statistical relevancy for the basic analysis of means (that are not grouped into two corpora). As I noted above, the standard deviation of a set of data is the square root of the variance, which is the average of the squared differences (between variation rates) from the mean. The standard deviation of a dataset is useful information since it can clearly show what data points are statistically 'normal' and which are outliers. By simply overlaying a Gaussian Curve onto a plot of data and determining the standard deviation for the dataset, we can identify statistically relevant outliers. As has already been discussed above, the ninety-five percent mark is the common threshold for statistical relevancy. Ninety-five percent of data that follows a Gaussian curve falls within two standard deviations of the mean. Any data point that falls outside of the ninety-five percent is considered statistically abnormal. Figure 9 presents a visual presentation of this concept:

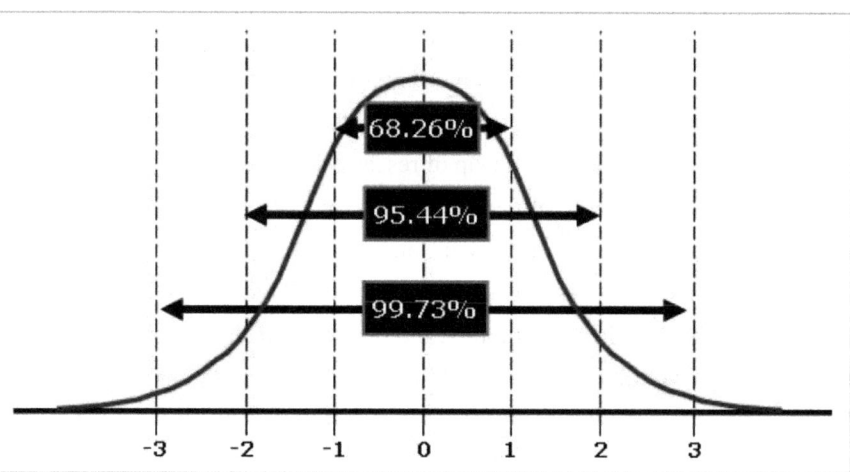

Figure 9.[67] Gaussian Curve and Standard Deviations

This graph shows that, for normally distributed data, 68.26% of data points will fall within 1 standard deviation, 95.44% within 2 and 99.73% within 3. Any data point that falls to the left of negative two or to the right of positive two is considered abnormal. The place where a specific data point falls is normally reported as a z-score. Thus a data point that is 2.25 standard deviations to the left of the mean has a z-score of -2.25. A basic example of how this can be used is the average heights of people. While the mean adult height of a male born

---

67 'Normal Distribution', Six-Sigma-Material.com, http://www.six-sigma-material.com/Noral-Distribution.html.

in Austria in 1950 is about 164.0 cm, most in that population are not that tall. But, most Austrian males born in 1950 (in fact 95% of all Austrian males born in that year) are between 150 cm and 178 cm.[68] In other words, ninety-five percent of Austrian males fall within two standard deviations of the mean height. Those outside this range can be considered abnormal (although we would likely find a different word for this section of the population). This type of analysis is particularly useful for the study of the 'biblical' DSS when comparing different types of variation rates within the entire corpus. An example question that can be answered by using standard deviations is the following: Do 'biblical' DSS manuscripts contain significantly more shifts away from the preterite form when compared with other shifts in the verbal system? If the variation rate for preterites falls outside of two standard deviations (the ninety-five percent) then it can be considered statistically relevant. This question will be considered in the section on the verbal system of the 'biblical' DSS below and by using the standard deviation of variants involving verbs we can arrive at solid answers.

C. Conclusion

In the above sections, I have reviewed cross-textual variable analysis and the four characteristics of corpus linguistics: empirical analysis; principled corpora; data collection; and quantitative analysis. Cross-textual variable analysis as well as the first and third characteristics of corpus linguistics needed little discussion as the field of Hebrew linguistics has incorporated their application in some productive ways. The second and fourth characteristics of corpus linguistics were covered at length since their application to Hebrew studies has been limited. Thus this review primarily focused on presenting the corpus of 'biblical' DSS upon which this study will be based. Secondarily, this section presented the main statistical tools that will be applied to this corpus. This review also showed how my methodological approach addresses the five main shortcomings found in past research. Through the application of cross-textual variable analysis and corpus linguistics, I have based my work on robust modern linguistic theories. Corpus linguistic theories as well as statistical analysis has helped to make the best of 'bad data' by developing a corpus that is diverse and statistically valid. I have decentralized the MT by also comparing the 'biblical' DSS to the LXX and

---

68 J. García and C. Quintana-Domeque, 'The Evolution of Adult Height in Europe: A Brief Note', *EHB* 5 (2007), 340–9.

SP.⁶⁹ And I have focused primarily upon syntactical variations to begin to fill the gap that has been left by previous scholarship.

While the methodology that has been developed above makes some significant steps forward, it also has some limitations that need to be recognized. The first and most substantial of these is the limited data found in the 'biblical' DSS corpus. As has been discussed in detail above, we are working with 'bad data'. The limitations of this data will be discussed throughout the following chapters.

As I have discussed above, variants that are most useful for cross-textual variable analysis are those that are interchangeable and do not influence the meaning of the text in any way. This is problematic since it is very difficult to know if there are subtle meaning differences between variables.⁷⁰ The prepositions על and אל are good examples of this difficulty. It is often suggested that in EBH, there are clear differences, but over time these distinctions may have been lost.⁷¹ I use variations such as these on the assumption (good or bad) that they are interchangeable. I will return to this issue throughout my analysis.

Another constraint of this methodology is its narrow focus. The following analyses are focused on the linguistic character of the 'biblical' DSS. This work does have implication for understanding QH and Second Temple Hebrew in general, which I will discuss in my concluding chapter, but the core of this study does not make claims about the relationship between the linguistic character of the 'biblical' scrolls and nonbiblical forms of Hebrew.

Finally, this methodology is limited in its ability to connect the linguistic differences between the corpora being analysed and the influences that may have caused those differences. This is mostly due to the lack of background data regarding the scrolls and to the complex textual nature of our witnesses. I will begin to consider this issue in my closing chapter, but much more work needs to be accomplished in the areas of Hebrew social and historical linguistics before further progress can be made.

---

69 In order to control the scope of this project, only the SP and LXX were chosen as additional witnesses. While adding more witnesses would help to further balance this analysis, in order to keep the linguistic character of the 'biblical' scrolls as the central focus, I chose to limit the number of witnesses. I also selected the SP and LXX, as opposed to other possible witnesses, due to their common prioritization in current scholarly works (see for example Reymond's grammar on QH where he references the SP over ten times and the LXX over twenty, but calls upon the Targums and Syriac versions only a few times each). This may not be the ideal approach, but it seems to be standard and thus, because it was possible only to include a few witnesses, I have defaulted to the SP and LXX.
70 Auer and Voeste, 'Grammatical Variables', 256.
71 Reymond, *Qumran Hebrew*, 76.

Now that I have introduced my thesis, analysed the shortcomings of past research, and presented my methodology, I will move into analysing the corpus of 'biblical' DSS manuscripts. I will do this in two parts. First I will present a global analysis of the entire corpus as defined above. And second, I will analyse five representative manuscripts to test the conclusions of that global analysis.

Chapter IV

Global Analysis of the Linguistic Character of the 'Biblical' Dead Sea Scrolls

In Chapter III, I outlined the methodological approach that I will be taking in my analysis of the linguistic character of the 'biblical' DSS. That methodology starts with a comparison of the 'biblical' scrolls with the MT as well as with other major witnesses. Through a comparison of these manuscripts, I identified 4,993 variations between the MT and the 'biblical' DSS.[1] As I mentioned in the previous chapter, not all of these variations are useful for analysing the linguistic character of the 'biblical' DSS. For the purposes of this study, I will be focusing on select grammatical variables from the particle system, verbal system and nominal system.

I will start with a cross-textual variable analysis that will provide a comprehensive picture of the linguistic differences between witnesses. Next, I will use inter-textual variable analysis to compare sub-corpora within the 'biblical' DSS. The main sub-corpora that I will compare are *plene* and defective manuscripts, although I will also discuss the characteristics of other sub-corpora at times. I will use descriptive statistics to present the data as clearly as possible. Through general observation of this data as well as by applying statistical tests, I will identify, describe and attempt to explain any patterns of linguistic differences that are found. Finally, I will compare these results to past research in order to place the current project within the larger context of scholarly inquiry.

A. Global Analysis of the Particle System

I will begin my analysis by working with grammatical variables that involve particles. In order to narrow the focus of this analysis, I have selected nine particles for consideration: the directive *he* with comments on מאדה, the definite article, the direct object marker, the prepositions ב, כ and ל, the interchange between אל and על and the conjunction *vav*. I have selected these particles for two reasons. First, they have the highest rates of occurrence in the Hebrew Bi-

---

[1] J. Jacobs and M.G. Abegg, *Dead Sea Scrolls and Masoretic Text Variants*, Version 1.0 (Altamonte Springs, FL 2013). Search: 'vr' in Signs/Abbreviations.

ble, and second, scholars have claimed that variations involving these particles reveal scribal patterns of intervention. In order to provide a broad picture from which to start, I will compare the variation rates for these nine particles. As a control, I will include the overall variation rate for all variant types throughout all the manuscripts. This comparison will help identify any variation type that is unusually widespread or infrequent. The following table presents the raw data for variations involving particles.

Global Variation Rate	Direct Object Marker	Definite Article	*Vav*	Directive *he*	Prepositions
Pluses	66	125	483	40	77
Minuses	22	84	314	27	32
Total occurrences	1914	4043	9312	207	7120
Percent increase	3.45%	3.09%	5.19%	19.33%	1.08%
Percent decrease	1.15%	2.08%	3.37%	13.04%	0.45%
Total variation	4.60%	5.17%	8.56%	32.37%	1.53%

Table 3. Variations Involving Particles

The pluses column shows the number of places where the 'biblical' scrolls contain each particle where the MT does not, while the minuses column shows the opposite. These numbers are normalized against the total number of occurrences of these particles (found in the fourth column) which results in the variation rates shown in the columns labelled percent increase and percent decrease. Finally, the total variation rate for each particle is listed in the last column.

Two items stand out in this data. First, and this is an overall trend with most variation types, there are more pluses than minuses of all nine of these particles. I will return to this phenomenon throughout this chapter. Second, the directive *he* has a much higher variation rate than any of the other particles. The mean variation rate for particles is 10.44%, which is clearly being inflated by the high variation rate for the directive *he*. This mean variation rate is also nearly double the global variation rate[2] for all of the scrolls, which is 5.44%. When this data is plotted on a graph, the difference between the rates of variation for the directive *he* and the other particles becomes clear.

---

2   Global variation rate (5.44%) = All variations (4,993) divided by total words in the 'biblical' DSS corpus (91,716).

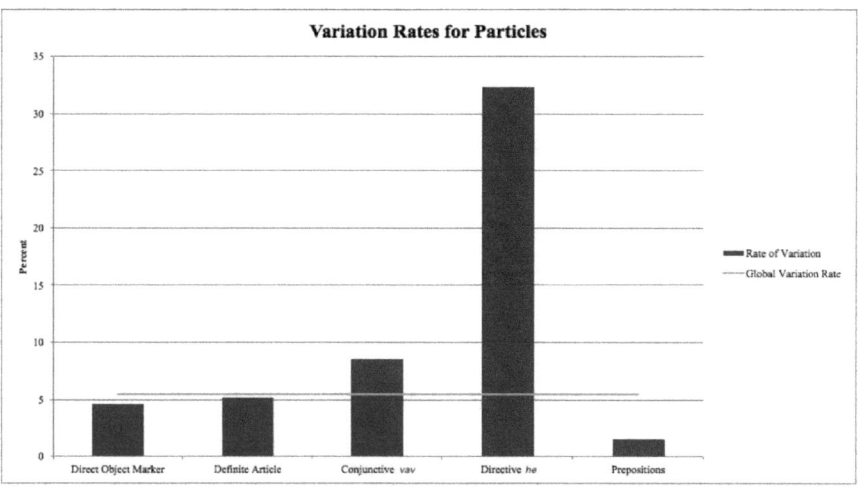

Figure 10. Variation Rates for Particles

Figure 10 compares the variation rates of particles to the global variation rate. While the rates of variation for the direct object marker, the definite article, *vav* and prepositions are relatively close to the global variation rate, the variation rate for the directive *he* is far higher. In order to determine if this difference is statistically valid or just slightly higher than expected, I will calculate the standard deviation[3] for this dataset. As was discussed in Chapter III. B. 4., any data point that falls more than two standard deviations away from the mean can be considered statistically relevant. The standard deviation for this set of data is 11.37% and the mean is 9.61%. Thus two standard deviations from the mean is 32.35%. The variation rate for the directive *he* is 32.37%, which is more than two standard deviations from the mean. Therefore, we conclude that the high variation rate for the directive *he* is statistically relevant and in need of further analysis. However, the fact that the other particles are within two standard deviations of the mean does not mean that they are of no interest; it simply helps guide us towards those variations that are more likely to reveal significant patterns of difference between the 'biblical' DSS and the other witnesses. Because of this, I will begin an in-depth analysis of these particles with the directive *he*. I will then consider the remaining particles in turn, proceeding in three parts. First, I will compare the use of each particle across manuscripts. This will show which manuscripts (if any) contain statistically more variations of a given type. If this analysis reveals statistically relevant patterns, I will consider possible

---

3   See section III. B. 4. c. for a description and uses of standard deviations

explanations. This step will focus especially, but not exclusively, on any patterns of variation that align with *plene* manuscripts.

Second, I will place the comparison between the 'biblical' DSS and the MT into the broader context of other witnesses. While a comparison between the scrolls and the MT provides a useful starting place, this approach is not without its problems – as is discussed in the methodology section above. Therefore, as a balance to this initial comparison I will consider those variations that are found in the 'biblical' DSS, but not in any of the other major witnesses (MT, SP and LXX).

Third and finally, I will conclude each analysis of individual particles with a review of past scholarship. If previous scholars have argued that variations involving a specific particle reveal a pattern of difference, I will test their claims and compare them to my results.

1. Directive he

The directive *he* will be analysed first due to its comparatively high rate of variation. As noted above, the variation rate for the directive *he* is 32.37% compared with the overall mean for particles of 10.44%. This high rate of variation, statistically speaking, marks these variations as significant and in need of further analysis and explanation.

Num. 13:22 and Deut. 10:22 are good examples of this relatively common variation.

Num. 13:22

4Q27

ויבוא עד חברון ושמה אחימן

MT

ויבא עד־חברון ושם אחימן

Deut. 10:22

4Q128

ירדו אבו[תיכה מצרים

MT

ירדו אבתיך מצרימה

Table 4 contains a summary of the data[4] for the distribution of these variations across the 'biblical' DSS corpus.

---

4 The full set of data can be found in Appendix A, chart 1.

Orth. Style	Number of Manuscripts	Number of Directive *hes*	Number of Pluses	Mean Percent Change (Pluses)	Number of Minuses	Mean Percent Change (Minuses)
Defective	52	82	4	2.05%	11	3.83%
Plene	27	102	36	14.30%	12	7.46%
N.E.D.[5]	179	28	5		0	

Table 4. Directive *hes*

In the 'biblical' DSS there are forty-five places that have the directive *he* where the MT does not. On the other hand, there are twenty-three places where the 'biblical' scrolls do not have the directive *he* where the MT does. These variations are spread over twenty-nine manuscripts, five of which have both pluses and minuses.

Statistical analysis of these variations reveals some significant insights. Those manuscripts that contain only the defective spelling of לא contain only four of the additional directive *hes*, an overall increase of just 4.88%. Those manuscripts that contain at least one *plene* spelling of לוא contain 36 additional directive *hes*, an increase of 35.29%. These numbers suggest a clear distinction between defective and *plene* manuscripts. Statistical testing confirms that this distinction is relevant and not just due to random chance.

In order to test the relevance of the difference between the use of the directive *he* within the *plene* and defective manuscripts, I will use a one-tailed t-test to compare the corpora. First I will propose a null hypothesis and the corresponding alternative hypothesis.

H_0 The difference in the use of the directive *he* between the two corpora is due to chance.

H_1 The difference in the use of the directive *he* between the two corpora is statistically significant.

By applying a one-tailed t-test to the data a P-value will be obtained that will either confirm or reject the null hypothesis. Table 5 presents the results of the t-test:

A one-tailed t-test applied to these two corpora results in a P-value of 1.02%, well below the 5% threshold of statistical relevance. Therefore, we reject the null hypothesis and accept the alternative: The difference between the use of the directive *he* in these corpora is statistically significant. The one-tailed t-test thus

---

[5] N.E.D. stands for 'Not Enough Data' and includes all manuscripts under two hundred words as well as those that do not contain any intact occurrence of the negation לא. This row is included in order to be comprehensive, but this data is not utilized for statistical testing. Because of this, and because of the lack of data for these manuscripts, mean percentages of change are not given as this data would simply be misleading.

Comparing Means [t-test assuming unequal variances (*heteroscedastic*)]			
Descriptive Statistics			
Corpus	Sample Size	Mean	Variance
Defective	52	0.02051	0.0055
Plene	27	0.14304	0.06678
One-Tailed Distribution			
P-value	0.01016	*t Critical Value (5%)*	1.69913

Table 5. T-Test Applied to the Directive *he* (Pluses) Data

strongly confirms that the *plene* scrolls contain significantly more pluses of the directive *he* than the defective scrolls.

A comparison of the 'biblical' scrolls to the other major witnesses (besides just the MT) lends credence to this correlation between *plene* orthography and the pluses of the directive *he*. Thirty-eight of the forty-five pluses found in the 'biblical' DSS are not found in any other major witnesses. This suggests that these variations were not inherited by the 'biblical' scrolls from their *Vorlagen*, but are more likely to have developed alongside the full orthographic nature of these scrolls.

An analysis of the minuses of the directive *he* also supports the conclusion that the *plene* scrolls contain significantly more pluses of this particle. When a one-tailed t-test is applied to the data for the minuses with the same hypotheses as above, the following results are found:

Comparing Means [t-test assuming unequal variances (*heteroscedastic*)]			
Descriptive Statistics			
Corpus	Sample Size	Mean	Variance
Defective	52	0.0383	0.01131
Plene	27	0.07463	0.0255
One-Tailed Distribution			
P-value	0.14295	*t Critical Value (5%)*	1.68385

Table 6. T-Test Applied to the Directive *he* (Minuses) Data

With a P-value of 14.30% and means that are relatively close (especially when compared with those found for the pluses), we can conclude that there is no statistically significant difference between the *plene* and defective scrolls when the minuses of the directive *he* are analysed. This stands in clear contrast to the results found for the pluses of this particle. Further analysis of the variations involving the directive *he* reveal a more refined picture.

Twenty-one of the forty-five pluses of the directive *he* and seven of the twenty-three minuses are found on שם. All but one of the pluses are found in manuscripts that contain *plene* readings of לוא. The only exception is the one found in 11Q7, which does not contain לא in any form. In contrast, all but one of the minuses of the directive *he* are found in manuscripts that do not contain any *plene* readings of לא. This data is summarized in Table 7:

	Pluses to שם	Minuses from שמה
Defective	0	6
Plene	21	1
N.E.D.	1	0

Table 7. Directive *he* and שם

The data in Table 7 shows that the manuscripts that use the *plene* לוא also contain the long שמה, which shows a clear correlation between *plene* readings and the long form of this particle. Muraoka developed a similar point. However, he claimed that only 1QIsaª showed a 'preference' for the long form of שמה, while the other manuscripts contained both additions and omissions.[6] Yet his work did not take into account the corresponding *plene* reading of לוא, which has proven to be a helpful control feature in this case, showing that the distribution of שמה is not random amongst the 'biblical' DSS. On the contrary, it reveals a correlation between *plene* orthography and the long form of שמה.

Aside from this significant pattern of preference for שמה, there are two other smaller trends of note. The first is seen when we focus on the context in which nine of the twenty-three minuses of the directive *he* are found. These particular variations result in the minus of the directive *he* from a place-name (there is only one occurrence of a plus of this particle to a place-name). This seems likely to have been caused by the loss of the locative force of this suffix, and thus it must have appeared to the scribes as out of place.[7]

The second trend may be explained by what Muraoka calls 'fossilized lexemes'.[8] He argues that MH lost the directive *he* all together, except in a few phrases such as למעלה. In the 'biblical' DSS, we find three places where the MT has מ/למעל and the scroll has a plus of the directive *he*. These few pluses may have developed under the influence of the spoken language or later written register of the scribes, since they may have been more familiar with the long form. This is supported by the fact that the Mishnah only contains the long form. Yet

---

6 Muraoka, 'An Approach', 207.
7 Ibid.
8 Ibid.

the limited amount of data makes any conclusions tentative at best.

The loss of the locative force of the directive *he* over time may account for some of the above variation types. Yet the correlation between the long form of שמה and the *plene* scrolls seems to be the key to understanding these variations on a large scale. In general, the *plene* scrolls use far more long orthographic and morphological forms than the defective scrolls. Because the *plene* scrolls also favour the long form of שמה, it seems possible that this form should simply be considered a long morphological form akin to the long suffixes such as המה instead of הם.

2. מאדה

Some scholars have connected the long form of מאדה to the development of the directive *he*. Qimron seems to be the first to make this connection when he mentions מאדה and איכה in the context of his discussion on the directive *he* in the Qumran documents. Yet he does not develop any connection between the directive *he* and these two words; he simply states: 'Cf. the adverbs מאדה "very" M 19: 5 et al., איכה H 10: 7 et al...'[9] Muraoka follows Qimron's lead by loosely connecting the directive *he* and מאדה. Muraoka writes, 'the long form [of שמה] has mostly lost its directional force, and the ending is that of locative adverbial, cf. the ubiquitous and typical Qumranic מאודה/מואדה for the MT מאד'.[10] Rezetko puts the finest point on this issue with the following statement: 'In QH the [directive *he*] occurs predominantly in the fixed adverbial expressions שמה, למעלה, מואדה (unknown in BH)...'[11] Yet, these three statements do little to explain why the *he* on מאדה should be considered a locative particle. Perhaps Qimron's discussion of חוצה can shed some light on their thinking. Qimron writes: 'The final *he* here, as well as in some other adverbs, should be considered as an adverbial termination. Originally, this *he* expressed the direction, but in postexilic Hebrew, it became meaningless and prepositions were added to the adverb'.[12] If מאדה can be considered one of the adverbs to which Qimron is alluding, then his conclusion proves helpful. Since this *he* no longer functioned as a locative in later forms of Hebrew but more simply as an adverbial termination, then its use with מאד seems more plausible. While this explanation is helpful in understanding how מאדה developed, its actual use does not seem to be dictated by a need to mark מאד as an adjective. The correlation

---

9   Qimron, *Hebrew*, 69.
10 Muraoka, 'An Approach', 206.
11 R. Rezetko, 'The Qumran Scrolls of the Book of Judges: Literary Formation, Textual Criticism, and Historical Linguistics', *JHS* 13 (2013), 50.
12 Qimron, *Hebrew*, 90–1.

between the use of מאדה and *plene* orthography suggest that the scribes who utilized מאדה had a preference for the long form. This correlation will now be explored in more detail.

The 'biblical' DSS contain מאדה where the MT has מאד twenty-six times with two more additional readings of מאדה found where the MT does not contain מאד at all. Table 8 summarizes this data.[13]

	מאדה	מאד
Defective	3	16
Plene	25	5
N.E.D.		5

Table 8. מאד and מאדה Data

The following are good examples of this type of variation:

Isa. 52:13

1QIsa[a]

וגבה מואדה

MT

וגבה מאד

Ps. 139:14

11Q5

ונפשי ידעת מואדה

MT

ונפשי ידעת מאד

These variations are spread over thirteen manuscripts with 11QPs[a] containing the most (ten) and 1QIsa[a] having six (one in 1QIsa[a] I and the remaining five in 1QIsa[a] II). Of the thirteen scrolls that contain this variation, there are three that have both מאדה and מאד - 1QIsa[a] (I and II): two מאד; 4Q22: four מאד (one מאדה); and 4Q78: one of each. With the exceptions of 4Q13, 4Q22 and 4Q23, all of the scrolls that contain מאדה also only have *plene* spellings of לוא. Further, there is just one manuscript which uses only *plene* spellings of לוא that has the short מאד - 4Q83. Thus with only a few exceptions, *plene* scrolls read מאדה while defective scrolls read מאד. This reveals a correlation between the long form מאדה and the full לוא.

---

13 For the complete set of data, see Appendix.

מאדה is also used twenty-eight times in the nonbiblical texts of Qumran. Many of these are found in the 'sectarian' texts as is seen in the following examples:

1QS 10:16

בהפלא מודה ובגבורתו אשוחח

Upon his very wonderful deeds and his mighty acts I will meditate

1QHª 19:6

וביצר חמר הגברתה מודה

and you have worked so very powerfully with vessels of clay

1QM 19:5

ציון שמחי מואדה

O Zion, rejoice greatly

While the long מאדה is found relatively often in the Qumran texts it is not found at all in the MT, the SP or the Mishnah. Thus מאדה appears to be a distinctive feature of a select group of manuscripts from Qumran. Y. Yadin, in his work on the excavation of Masada, appears to be the first to note this. In reference to the occurrence of מאדה found in MasapocrJosh,[14] Yadin states: 'The spelling מואדה for מאוד is interesting; it resembles that in the "War of the Sons of Light" ציון שמחי מואדה (19.5)'.[15] Further investigation[16] into this form by Tov confirms that this 'Qumran feature' is 'not known beyond the corpus'[17] and that with one possible exception,[18] המאד occurs only in manuscripts that use 'Qumran Orthography'.[19] Most of the texts that have מאדה only have this form and only use the full לוא, but there are exceptions. These exceptions demand some caution regarding any conclusions, but in general מאדה has been shown to be correlated with *plene* manuscripts.

This correlation, just as with the directive *he* as discussed above, may help us to better understand this form. Instead of considering the added *he* on מאד to be some form of the directive *he*, it may be possible to simply regard מאדה as a long morphological alternative to מאד.

---

14 Tov argues that the occurrence of מאדה in this Masada manuscript supports his claim that this manuscript along with others were produced at Qumran and later brought to Masada. Tov, *Scribal Practices*, 301.

15 Y. Yadin, 'The Excavation of Masada—1963/64: Preliminary Report', *IEJ* 15 (1965), 105.

16 Qimron also notes the distinctive nature of מאדה within his discussion of the directive *he*. Qimron, *Hebrew*, 51.

17 Tov, *Scribal Practices*, 301.

18 Tov does not note what this exception is and up to this point I have been unable to find it.

19 Ibid., 301, n. 374.

3. The Definite Article

Table 9 presents a summary of the pluses and minuses of the definite article found in the 'biblical' DSS.

Corpus	Number of Manuscripts	Number of Definite Articles	Definite Article Plus	Mean Percent Change (Pluses)	Definite Article Minus	Mean Percent Change (Minus)
Defective	52	1891	29	2.29%	19	0.85%
Plene	27	1593	83	6.58%	52	4.41%
N.E.D.	179	1378	11		13	

Table 9. Definite Article Data

The data in Table 9 shows a preference for pluses of the definite article (123 to 84), which is consistent with the overall variation rate. Further, the *plene* scrolls contain far more pluses and minuses of the definite article than the defective scrolls (pluses - *plene*: eighty-three, defective: twenty-nine; minuses – *plene*: fifty-two, defective: nineteen). Statistical testing of this data produces some results that are difficult to interpret. First, I will analyse the pluses by utilizing a t-test. The null and alternative hypotheses are as follows:

H_0: The greater accumulation of pluses of the definite article within the *plene* scrolls happened by chance.

H_1: The greater accumulation of pluses of the definite article within the *plene* scrolls did not happen by chance.

Comparing Means [t-test assuming unequal variances (*heteroscedastic*)]			
Descriptive Statistics			
Corpus	Sample Size	Mean	Variance
Defective	52	0.02285	0.0272
Plene	27	0.0658	0.03504
One-Tailed Distribution			
P-value	0.12215	t Critical Value (5%)	1.69913

Table 10. T-Test Applied to the Definite Article (Pluses) Data

The results of the one-tailed t-test are presented in Table 10: The P-value of 12.22% tells us to accept the H_0 and thus conclude that greater accumulation of pluses of the definite article found in the *plene* scrolls happened by chance. Yet two other important pieces of data (the means and variances of each corpus) reported by the t-test cause us to reconsider this conclusion. The mean variation for the *plene* scrolls is nearly three times higher than for the defective scrolls. This difference would suggest a much lower P-value than is reported. Yet the large difference in variances between the two corpora has forced the P-value to be higher than one would expect based on the means. Because of this, I suggest the H_0 should be rejected in favour of the H_1. This conclusion needs to be taken with caution, but as I discussed in Chapter III. B. 4., when a P-value is close to the arbitrary threshold hold of five percent other factors need to be brought into the picture. I will return to the pluses of the definite article after applying a t-test to the data of the minuses.

The null and alternative hypotheses for the minuses are similar to those for the pluses and are as follows:

H_0: The greater accumulation of minuses of the definite article within the *plene* scrolls happened by chance.

H_1: The greater accumulation of minuses of the definite article within the *plene* scrolls did not happen by chance.

The results of the one-tailed t-test are presented in Table 11:

Comparing Means [t-test assuming unequal variances (*heteroscedastic*)]			
Descriptive Statistics			
Corpus	Sample Size	Mean	Variance
Defective	52	0.00849	0.0031
Plene	27	0.04412	0.0474
One-Tailed Distribution			
P-value	0.00587	t Critical Value (5%)	1.69913

Table 11. T-Test Applied to the Definite Article (Minuses) Data

The P-value for the one-tailed t-test in this case is 0.5%, which is much lower than the 5% threshold suggesting that the H_0 should be rejected in favour of the H_1 telling us that the correlation between the *plene* scrolls and the minuses of the definite article is statistically valid. The main reason the P-value for the minuses is so much lower than that for the pluses is the greater difference between the means for the minuses. In the previous comparison, the mean for the *plene* scrolls was almost three times higher than the defective scrolls. In this case, the mean for the *plene* scrolls is more than five times higher. This greater difference between the means overcame the large difference in variance resulting in a low P-value.

These results suggest that the *plene* scrolls contain significantly more pluses and minuses of the definite article than the defective scrolls. This stands in contrast to what was seen with the directive *he*. In that case, the *plene* scrolls only contain significantly more pluses of the directive *he* than the defective scrolls. When the minuses were analysed, this difference was not found. Rather, each corpus contained a similar number of such variations. Yet in the case of the definite article the *plene* scrolls contain significantly more pluses and minuses. This suggests that these variations are due more to the normal manuscript variation found in the *plene* scrolls and not a change in the use of the definite article. Yet at least two scholars have developed theories trying to explain the variation in the use of the definite article between the witnesses by appealing to changes in the Hebrew language. I will work through these theories here and will provide a deeper analysis of the data in order to ascertain the cause(s) of the pluses and minuses of the definite article.

Kutscher was one of the first scholars to grapple with the pluses and minuses of the definite article within the 'biblical' DSS. In reference to such changes within the Great Isaiah Scroll, Kutscher writes, 'One phenomenon in particular points to the scribe's [*sic*] being the author of the changes in the vast majority of these cases: of the 72 instances of substitution, 40 — i.e. 60% — are in words beginning with either pharyngeals or laryngeals; hence this cannot have been simply a matter of chance'.[20] Kutscher argues that since the scribe did not pronounce the *aleph, he, khet* or *ayin* it would have been difficult for him to know if he should write the definite article or not. This, in turn, would have caused the scribe to unintentionally add and omit the definite article more often than expected when a word began with those four letters. Indeed, at first glance Kutscher's argument seems logical. If sixty percent of the variations occur in connection with words beginning with one of these four letters, one would assume a causal relationship. This would support the conclusion that the scribe of the scroll was the author of the vast majority of these variations. Yet a thorough examination of the data and some comparative analysis shows these conclusions to be false.

The fact that sixty percent of the pluses and minuses of the definite article within 1QIsa[a] are found on words that begin with either *aleph, he, khet* or *ayin* is striking. But, once one realizes that the definite article is actually found more often on words that begin with these letters, the variation becomes less telling. The following two charts will help to show that the sixty percent variation rate is what is expected and not something that should be considered exceptional.

All the data for pluses and minuses of the definite article in conjunction with *aleph, he, khet* and *ayin* in 1QIsa[a] are presented in Table 12:

---

20 Kutscher, *Language*, 412.

	Plus Definite Article on all Words	Plus Definite Article on Words Starting with א, ה, ח, ע	Variation Rate	Minus Definite Article	Minus Definite Article on Words Starting with א, ה, ח, ע	Variation Rate	Total Variation of Definite Article with Words Beginning with א, ה, ח, ע
1QIsaª	53	27	0.51	26	19	0.73	0.58
1QIsaª I	25	15	0.60	16	12	0.75	0.66
1QIsaª II	28	12	0.43	10	7	0.70	0.50

Table 12. Definite Article and *Aleph, He, Khet* and *Ayin*: Pluses and Minuses (1QIsaª)

Table 12 shows that of the fifty-three pluses of the definite article in 1QIsaª, twenty-seven are found on words that begin with *aleph, he, khet* and *ayin*. This is fifty-one percent. Of the twenty-six minuses, nineteen are found on such words, which is seventy-three. This shows a total variation rate of fifty-eight percent for the definite article in connection with words that begin with these particular letters. By way of comparison, Table 13 shows the general distribution of the definite article:

	Definite Article and א	Definite Article and ע	Definite Article and ה	Definite Article and ח	Total Definite Article on These 4 Letters	Total Definite Article on all Other Letters	% of Definite Article with the 4 Letters out of the Total
1QIsaª I	126	24	94	26	270	457	0.59
1QIsaª II	96	20	4	14	134	225	0.60
1QIsaª	222	44	98	40	404	682	0.59

Table 13. Definite Article and *Aleph, He, Khet* and *Ayin*: By Letter (1QIsaª)

Table 13 shows that of the 682 total definite articles found in 1QIsaª, 404 are found on words that begin with *aleph, ayin, he* and *khet*. These definite articles account for fifty-nine percent of the total definite articles found in 1QIsaª. Therefore, if the adding and omitting of the definite article were to occur at random, we would expect fifty-nine percent of the variations to occur with words that begin with these specific four letters, since fifty-nine percent of all of the definite articles are found on such words. This is almost exactly what we find: fifty-eight percent of the pluses and minuses of the definite article in 1QIsaª are found on words that begin with these four letters. This data calls into question Kutscher's claim that variations involving the definite article are caused by the scribe's distinctive pronunciation of the pharyngeals and laryngeals. Kutscher's conclusion is also challenged by the data from the other 'biblical' DSS.

When the analysis is expanded to include all of the 'biblical' DSS, a similar picture emerges, although there is relatively less variation (which is consistent with the variation rate for this corpus). Table 14 contains the data for the variations involving the definite article:

	Plus Definite Article on All Words	Plus Definite Article on Words Starting with א, ה, ח, ע	Variation Rate	Minus Definite Article	Minus Definite Article on Words Starting with א, ה, ח, ע	Variation Rate	Total Variation
bDSS	173	88	0.51	113	66	0.58	0.54

Table 14. Definite Article and *Aleph, He, Khet* and *Ayin*: Pluses and Minuses ('Biblical' Dead Sea Scrolls)

Of the 286 total variations, 154 occur on words beginning with *aleph, he, khet* or *ayin*. This is a total of fifty-four percent, which is very similar to 1QIsa^a's rate of fifty-eight percent. It is also consistent with the distribution rate of the definite article on words beginning with pharyngeals and laryngeals compared with its distribution on all words as is seen in Table 15.

	Definite Article and א	Definite Article and ע	Definite Article and ה	Definite Article and ח	Total Definite Article with These Four Letters	Total Definite Article on All Other Letters	% Of Definite Article with the Four Letters out of the Total
bDSS	978	218	284	252	1732	4049	0.43

Table 15. Definite Article and *Aleph, He, Khet* and *Ayin*: Rate of Occurrence

This data shows that the definite article occurs on words that begin with *aleph, he, khet* or *ayin* 43% of the time. This is eleven percent lower than the rate of pluses and minuses on these words, but this difference does not seem to be statistically significant. Since the variation rate of definite articles on words that occur with these letters is similar between 1QIsa^a and across the 'biblical' DSS corpus, we must conclude that the pharyngeals and laryngeals did not influence the scribes' ability to reproduce their *Vorlagen* in this area.

Since the weakening of the pharyngeals and the laryngeals does not appear to have influenced the use of the definite article within the 'biblical' DSS, we must consider other possible explanations for the variation between witnesses. Muraoka has proposed two explanations that may account for a small portion of the variations of the definite article. I will briefly review his conclusions here.

Muraoka argues that by comparing the 'biblical' DSS to the MT we can better understand the nature of QH. In a summary of his work he writes, 'This study of twelve morpho-syntactic or syntactic isoglosses seems to indicate that

QH, *in grosso modo,* represents a phase of Hebrew between LBH and MH'.[21] Thus Muraoka sees a diachronic difference between QH and other phases of Hebrew. He uses this diachronic development to explain two isoglosses that deal with the definite article and its 'addition' in the 'biblical' DSS. The first of these is the placement of the definite article in a *nomen regens*. In this brief section, Muraoka claims that the 'biblical' DSS use the non-standard form (definite article on the first noun) in contrast to the standard form (no definite article on the first noun) found in the MT. Muraoka notes that '[a]lready in BH we meet with non-standard phrases such as Isa. 36:8 המלך אשור'.[22] While Muraoka does not state it directly, this quote seems to imply that he views the non-standard form to be a diachronic development, with the standard being the older form and the non-standard being representative of later stages of Hebrew. While this explanation may account for a small portion of the variations involving the definite article, a thorough analysis of the data does not reveal a significant pattern pointing to scribal intervention.

The first challenge to Muraoka's implication that the plus of the definite article in a *nomen regens* represents a diachronic development found in QH is the lack of data. Muraoka notes only six examples.[23] To those I can add eight more while also noting one minus of the definite article from a *nomen regens*. Table 16 contains these variations along with the short and long forms of לא for comparison:

Scroll Name	לא	לוא	Definite Article Plus *Nomen Regens*	Definite Article Minus *Nomen Regens*
1QIsa^a		443	2	1
1QIsa^a I		167	2	
1QIsa^a II		276		1
4QExod-Lev^f	1		1	
4QpaleoExod^m	18		1	
4QDeut^j	1	3	1	
4QKgs	2		1	
4QPhyl^c	5		2	
4QPhyl^g		10	1	
4QPhyl^j		7	2	

Table 16. Definite Article and *Nomen Regens*

---

21 Muraoka, 'An Approach', 214.
22 Ibid., 201.
23 Muraoka notes the following examples: 4Q364 frg 17:3; 4Q365 frg 12b ii 4; 4Q37 X 12; 4Q54 frg 6:11; 4Q138 i 5; 1QIsa^a 8:23. The first two of these are found in 'reworked' manuscripts and thus have not been included in the 'biblical' DSS corpus for the purposes of this study.

The limited data makes it difficult to come to any solid conclusions regarding the nature of these variations. A diachronic explanation may be valid for some of the individual variations, but no pattern emerges that implies a specific scribal practice or linguistic development that could be labelled a Qumran feature. This becomes clearer when one considers the different types of scrolls in which this variation is found. Five of the eleven manuscripts that contain an 'addition' of the definite article to a *nomen regens* are phylacteries. We also find this variation in Torah scrolls, a Kings scroll and in 1QIsa^a. Further, the diverse linguistic nature of these scrolls, as represented by the defective and *plene* spelling of לא as shown in the above table, suggests that different communities may have penned these scrolls. This feature does not seem to be a characteristic of any particular group of scrolls, but is found throughout the 'biblical' DSS corpus. Therefore, each individual variation should be considered on its own and not treated as a feature of QH.

The second use of the definite article that Muraoka discusses is its insertion after a proclitic preposition. He writes: 'In BH, and especially in LBH, though not exclusively therein, we find the definite article inserted or retained between a proclitic preposition and the substantive'.[24] Here, Muraoka again implies a diachronic development and in turn suggests that variations such as these place QH between BH and MH. He provides three examples of this variation, and I can add two more. Table 17 presents the distribution of these variations:

Scroll Name	Scroll #	P.P.
1QIsa^a	1QIsa^a	2
1QIsa^a I	1QIsa^a I	2
4QJudg^b	4Q50	1
4QIsa^n	4Q67	1
4QPhyl^m	4Q140	1

Table 17. Definite Article and Proclitic Prepositions

The lack of data, just as with the variations involving the definite article and the *nomen regens*, call into question Muraoka's suggestion that variations involving the definite article and the proclitic preposition can be used to characterize QH. And just as with the previously discussed variations, these variations may be explained as a diachronic development in Hebrew on a case-by-case basis, but no pattern of development or scribal practice can be suggested.

What then can account for the 286 variations involving the definite article? Due to the diversity of contexts in which these variations are found, including

---

24 Ibid., 202.

different types of manuscripts and different linguistic contexts, along with the lack of correlation with other known scribal practices such as *plene* spellings, we must suggest a diverse range of possible causes. Among these causes we can likely include historical development of texts, exegetical scribal intervention, linguistic development and scribal error, among others. Yet for the purposes of this study the important conclusion is that there does not seem to be any consistent pattern of scribal intervention.

4. Direct Object Marker

Table 18 presents a summary of the data for pluses and minuses of the direct object marker.

	Number of Mss	Number of Direct Object Markers	Direct Object Marker Plus	Mean Percent Change (Pluses)	Direct Object Marker Minus	Percent Change (Minus)
Defective	52	1102	26	4.37%	9	0.67%
Plene	27	959	37	3.69%	13	1.22%
N.E.D.	179	103	4		0	

Table 18. Direct Object Marker (Pluses and Minuses) Data

A review of this data shows the direct object marker to be a plus in the 'biblical' scrolls sixty-seven times and a minus twenty-two times. These variations are spread over forty different scrolls. Twenty-seven scrolls contain only pluses, four of which have more than one. Only five scrolls contain at least one minus without any pluses, and only one of those has more than one minus. The remaining scrolls contain both pluses and minuses.

Statistical analysis does not show any correlation between variations involving the direct object marker and the long and short forms of לא. The following hypotheses can be proposed for the pluses of the direct object marker:

H_0: The greater accumulation of pluses of the direct object marker within the *plene* scrolls happened by chance.

H_1: The greater accumulation of pluses of the direct object marker within the *plene* scrolls did not happen by chance.

The results of a one-tailed t-test applied to the data for the direct object marker are presented in Table 19:

Comparing Means [t-test assuming unequal variances (*heteroscedastic*)]			
Descriptive Statistics			
Corpus	Sample Size	Mean	Variance
Defective	52	0.04367	0.02135
Plene	27	0.03686	0.034
One-Tailed Distribution			
P-value	0.38608	*t Critical Value (5%)*	1.66691

Table 19. T-Test Applied to the Direct Object Marker (Pluses) Data

These results show the defective manuscripts having a slightly higher mean of pluses of the direct object marker than the *plene* manuscripts, 4.37% to 3.69%; yet the P-value of 38.61% (far above the 5% threshold of significance) forces us to accept the H_0 and conclude that this difference occurred by chance. Similar results are found for the minuses of the direct object marker.

The hypotheses for the minuses are essentially the same as for the pluses. The results of the one-tailed t-test are presented in Table 20.

Comparing Means [t-test assuming unequal variances (*heteroscedastic*)]			
Descriptive Statistics			
Corpus	Sample Size	Mean	Variance
Defective	52	0.00668	0.0035
Plene	27	0.01222	0.0053
One-Tailed Distribution			
P-value	0.1406	*t Critical Value (5%)*	1.67793

Table 20. T-Test Applied to the Direct Object Marker (Minuses) Data

Here we see the *plene* scrolls containing nearly double the mean rate of minuses than the defective scrolls. However, the P-value of 14.06% still forces us to accept the H_0 and conclude that this difference occurred due to chance.[25]

The above conclusions suggest a level of randomness to the pluses and minuses of the direct object marker. These results reflect the following statement by Tov: '[T]he *nota accusativi* is freely added or omitted in all textual sources'.[26]

---

25 When analysing the definite article, I concluded that we should reject the H_0 in favour of the H_1 even though the P-value was twelve percent. I came to this conclusion because the mean for the *plene* scrolls was three times higher than the mean for the defective scrolls. Further, the variances for each of those sub-corpora were significantly different, causing the P-value to be inflated. In the case of the direct object marker, the mean for the *plene* scrolls is only double that of the defective scrolls, and their variances are not nearly as divergent. Thus, I conclude that the H_0 should be accepted even though the P-value is relatively close to the five percent threshold.

26 Tov, *Scribal Practices*, 204.

Yet, some scholars have suggested that these variations are not simply random, but that they show some patterns of change.

Fassberg, Muraoka[27] and Abegg have all noted an increased use of the direct object marker within the DSS. Fassberg correlates this increase with Tannaitic Hebrew's requirement for את before definite direct objects.[28] Fassberg, along with Muraoka and Abegg, suggests that this increased use of the direct object marker within the scrolls is caused by its increased use within Hebrew during the Second Temple period. Yet Abegg's analysis of the data is a bit more nuanced, 'We might have expected a larger number of plusses in the whole corpus, but the global survey does indeed show a slight increase'.[29] And indeed there is an increase in direct object markers within the 'biblical' DSS, but as has already been shown, the direct object marker has a rate of variation consistent with the overall variation rate as well as the variation rates of other particles. Another look at the tables containing this data confirms this observation.

Global Variation Rate	Direct Object Marker	Definite Article	*Vav*	Directive *he*	Preps
Pluses	66	125	483	40	77
Minuses	22	84	314	27	32
Total occurrences	1914	4043	9312	207	7120
% Increase	3.45%	3.09%	5.19%	19.32%	1.08%
% Decrease	1.15%	2.08%	3.37%	13.04%	0.45%
Total Variation	4.60%	5.17%	8.56%	32.37%	1.53%

Table 21. Variations Involving Particles

Total Variations	4993
Total Words	91716
% Variation	5.44%

Table 22. Overall Variation Rate

In Tables 21 and 22 we find that the total variation rate for the pluses of the direct object marker is 3.45%. This is compared with the variation rates for the pluses of the definite article (3.09%), pluses of *vav* (5.19%), pluses of the directive *he* (19.32%), pluses of the prepositions ב, כ and ל (1.08%) and the over-all variation rate of 5.44%. The mean for these variations is 6.33%. With this mean, the only variation rate that falls outside two standard deviations is the directive *he*. This leaves all the other variation rates within the expected range of varia-

---

27 Muraoka, 'An Approach', 203.
28 Fassberg, 'The Syntax of the Biblical Documents', 103.
29 Abegg, 'The Biblical Dead Sea Scrolls', 166.

tion and thus they must be considered statistically irrelevant. In other words, the increased use of the direct object marker correlates with the overall variation rate as well as with the increased use of other particles. Because of this the increased use of the direct object marker should not be considered the result of the diachronic development of Hebrew. This increase should simply be considered a part of the 'biblical' scrolls' expanding tendencies. Thus the evidence suggests that the variations involving the direct object marker do not show signs of a distinctive scribal practice. Alternative explanations for these changes should be developed on a variation-by-variation basis. These alternatives may include diachronic change, exegetical scribal intervention, and so on, but again there does not seem to be any pattern of scribal intervention within this corpus.

5. Interchange Between על - אל

Table 23 summarizes the data for the interchange between אל – על:

	Number of Mss	על	על - אל	Mean Percent Change (Pluses)	אל	על - אל	Mean Percent Change (Minus)
Defective	52	617	26	2.30%	129	9	2.20%
Plene	27	619	37	4.12%	258	13	1.45%
N.E.D.	179	72	4		912	0	

Table 23. Interchange between אל – על

Comparisons between the 'biblical' DSS and the MT do not reveal any significant patterns of change. 1QIsa[b], which contains only defective spellings of לא, contains a total of six interchanges between these two particles. A manuscript such as 1QIsa[a] I, with the opposite orthographic character containing only *plene* spellings of לוא, shows seven shifts from על to אל and eight from אל to על. We also see manuscripts with mixed orthographic characteristics such as 4QSam[a] that have a similar pattern of variation between אל and על. This shows a lack of correlation between the orthographic character of a manuscript and interchanges between אל or על.[30] Statistical analysis of the data confirms this result. The null and alternative hypotheses for readings of MT = אל, Scroll = על are as follows:

H_0: The distribution of אל to על interchanges between the *plene* and defective 'biblical' DSS is random.

H_1: The distribution of אל to על interchanges between the *plene* and defective 'biblical' DSS is not random.

---

30 Statistical analysis confirms this lack of correlation. The P-value (when comparing scrolls with and without *plene* לוא) for shifts to אל is eighty-one percent and for shifts to על it is forty percent.

In order to test these hypotheses, I will use a two-tailed, instead of one-tailed, t-test. This is necessary, because it is not immediately obvious if there is an accumulation of this type of variation within one type of scroll.[31] The results of the two-tailed t-test for the readings of MT = אל, Scroll = על are presented in Table 24:

Comparing Means [t-test assuming unequal variances (*heteroscedastic*)]			
Descriptive Statistics			
Corpus	Sample Size	Mean	Variance
Defective	52	0.02295	0.045
Plene	27	0.04123	0.0892
Two-Tailed Distribution			
P-value	0.37074	*t Critical Value (5%)*	1.68107

Table 24. T-Test Applied to the MT = אל, Scroll = על Variations Data

These results show that the *plene* scrolls contain more MT = אל, Scroll = על than the defective scrolls with a mean of 4.12%, nearly double the defective scrolls. Yet due to the high rate of variation within both corpora, the P-value is well above the 5% threshold of significance falling at 37.07%. The data for the opposite variation, MT = על, Scroll = אל, is slightly different, but the results are the same. The following hypotheses and two-tailed t-test show this:

H_0: The distribution of על to אל interchanges between the *plene* and defective 'biblical' DSS is random.

H_1: The distribution of על to אל interchanges between the *plene* and defective 'biblical' DSS is not random.

Comparing Means [t-test assuming unequal variances (*heteroscedastic*)]			
Descriptive Statistics			
Corpus	Sample Size	Mean	Variance
Defective	52	0.02209	0.0622
Plene	27	0.01453	0.0109
Two-Tailed Distribution			
P-value	0.55637	*t Critical Value (5%)*	1.99346

Table 25. T-Test Applied to the MT = על, Scroll = אל Variations Data

---

31 As was noted in Chapter III, a one-tailed t-test is used when there is a clear accumulation of data points within one group. In these cases, the one-tailed t-test tells us whether or not that accumulation is statistically relevant or due to random chance. When there is no clear accumulation of data points within one group, a two-tailed t-test is utilized to determine if the data points fall more often in one group or another.

While the means of variation for the MT = אל, Scroll = על variations showed the *plene* scrolls having nearly twice as many variations, the opposite is true for MT = על, Scroll = אל. The above table shows the mean for the defective scrolls as 2.21% and for the *plene* scrolls 1.45%. Yet again the P-value (55.64%) tells us that this difference is not significant, likely due to the high range of variation within each corpora. However, the differences in mean between the two corpora for each variation type suggests that further analysis may reveal a statistically valid result.

The above analysis of the interchanges between על and אל has focused only on the comparison between the MT and the 'biblical' DSS. A different picture emerges when the focus of this analysis is refined to deal only with the distinctive readings found within the 'biblical' scrolls. Of the thirty-nine variations where the scrolls contain על and the MT contains אל, sixteen are distinctive to the 'biblical' scrolls. Of these sixteen, twelve are found in scrolls that contain *plene* לוא. The other four are found in 1QIsa[b]. While this is a small amount, it does suggest a leaning towards על by scrolls that use a full orthography. Statistical analysis confirms the relevance of this data, even though it is limited. A two-tailed t-test produces the following results:

Comparing Means [t-test assuming unequal variances (*heteroscedastic*)]			
Descriptive Statistics			
Corpus	Sample Size	Mean	Variance
Defective	52	0.0167	0.0014
Plene	27	0.0284	0.0407
Two-Tailed Distribution			
P-value	0.00503	*t Critical Value (5%)*	1.99167

Table 26. T-Test Applied to the MT = אל, Scroll = על Variations Data (Distinctive Readings)

Again, we see the difference in means between the *plene* and defective scrolls, but this time the variance is much lower, resulting in a statistically relevant P-value: 0.50%.[32] This suggests that the *plene* scrolls contain more readings of על where the other witnesses have אל than the defective scrolls have. Yet this conclusion needs to be taken lightly due to the limited amount of data available. A number of theories might help account for this possibility. Abegg provides a helpful summary of how scholars have considered the interchange between על and אל:

---

32 By way of comparison, the same test applied to the rates of variation for those cases where the scrolls have אל and the other major witnesses do not result in a P-value of 54.98%.

The alternation of על or אל has been attributed to various causes; Kutscher posited that the major one was the weakening of the gutturals. The lexicons suggest overlapping semantic fields. Moreover, על for אל in Late Biblical Hebrew has been understood as evidence for Aramaic influence...[33]

Identifying the exact cause or causes of the interchange between these two particles is difficult, as evidenced by the wide range of proposed explanations. Yet a basic analysis of the use of each of these words in different corpora suggests a diachronic development.

EBH	אל	3,383	על	2,648
LBH	אל	866	על	1,301
Qumran	אל	465	על	1,839
Mishnah	אל	71	על	3,860

Table 27. Interchange Between אל and על by Corpus

The general pattern does point to an increased use of על corresponding to a decrease in the occurrences of אל. However, the challenges of identifying and working with these corpora make any conclusions here tentative. If this trend does indeed point to a diachronic development in the Hebrew language,[34] then the alternation between אל and על in the 'biblical' DSS could be explained on those grounds. A witness with על instead of אל could be considered to have been linguistically modernized. This is consistent with the conclusions of Hurvitz,[35] Qimron[36] and A. Sáenz-Badillos[37] who all argued that later Hebrew corpora favoured על over אל. The diachronic development of these particles may also account for the correlation between the distinctive readings of על over אל and the use of *plene* לוא.

6. The Inseparable Prepositions – ב, כ and ל

As was noted above, these prepositions, while occurring a significant number of times in the 'biblical' DSS corpus, have a relatively low variation rate — just

---

33 Ibid., 169. Abegg references Kutscher, *Language*, 401–3 as well as F. Brown et al., *A Hebrew and English Lexicon of the Old Testament: With an Appendix Containing the Biblical Aramaic* (Oxford 1959), 41a and 757a.

34 Further analysis of these particles is undertaken in Chapter VI – 'The Linguistic Character of Individual Manuscripts'.

35 A. Hurvitz, *Ben lashon le-lashon: le-toldot leshon ha-Miḳra' bi-yeme bayit sheni* (Jerusalem 1972), 22.

36 Qimron, *Hebrew*, 93.

37 A. Sáenz-Badillos, *A History of the Hebrew Language*, trans. J. Elwolde (Cambridge 1993), 143.

1.53%. Even with this low variation rate, these particles (particularly ל) have received significant attention in secondary literature. A deeper analysis of the data and review of scholarly opinions will help to shed some light on these common words.

	Number of Manuscripts	ב Plus	ב Minus	ל Plus	ל Minus	כ Plus	כ Minus
Defective	52	10	5	9	7	2	1
Plene	27	23	3	31	13	6	2
N.E.D.	179	1	1	4	1	0	0

Table 28. The Inseparable Prepositions - ל, כ, ב

Of the forty-nine manuscripts that contain a variation involving one of the inseparable prepositions, twenty contain at least one *plene* reading of לוא. The other twenty-nine are written in a defective orthography. This data reveals there to be no correlation between variations involving these prepositions and the scribal practice of writing in a full orthography. Again, we must ask what other explanation there might be for these variations.

Kutscher,[38] Muraoka,[39] Abegg[40] and a number of others[41] have commented on variations involving the preposition ל. Early research concluded that LBH and Second Temple Hebrew had an impact upon the use of ל within the 'biblical' and nonbiblical DSS. As Kutscher writes: 'The infinitive absolute is not used at all in Mishnaic Hebrew and the infinitive construct is found only when it is preceded by a ל. Hence the marked tendency of [1QIsaᵃ] to add a ל to infinitives'.[42] The notion that ל was added in a significant way to infinitives in the 'biblical' scrolls was perpetuated by the scholars noted above, but it was not until Abegg reviewed the data that a clear picture appeared. Abegg summarizes the situation nicely: 'Of the 158 infinitives extant in the biblical scrolls without initial prepositions in the MT, in 14 instances a *lamed* has been added…In three cases the reverse occurs…'[43] Further, five of the fourteen plusses are found in 1QIsaᵃ leaving little room for this variation to be considered widespread in the 'biblical' scrolls. Just as has been concluded a number of times above, on a case-by-case basis these variations may be explained by the diachronic development of Hebrew. However, we cannot conclude based on the evidence from the

---
38 Kutscher, *Language*, 193.
39 Muraoka, 'An Approach', 194.
40 Abegg, 'The Biblical Dead Sea Scrolls', 169–70.
41 J.T. Milik, *Dix ans de découvertes dans le désert de Juda* (Paris 1957), 121.
42 Kutscher, *Language*, 41.
43 Abegg, 'The Biblical Dead Sea Scrolls', 170.

'biblical' scrolls that this was a consistent scribal practice. In fact, the relatively low variation rate involving these particles suggests that scribes avoided (consciously or unconsciously) changing occurrences of ב, כ and ל. A review of these variations does not seem to reveal a reason for this avoidance. Yet one can speculate that these particles are often syntactically and semantically required in the clauses in which they are found and thus cannot be adjusted easily. A contrasting example is found in the direct object marker which is not normally required, allowing a scribe to add or remove it based on stylistic preferences.

7. The Conjunction Vav

Goshen-Gottstein argues that '*[w]aws* are omitted and added in our versions and witnesses to such a degree, that almost anything can be proved or disproved'.[44] The following analysis of the conjunction *vav* supports this view, at least in part.

Table 29 presents a summary of the data for the pluses and minuses of the conjunction *vav* found in the 'biblical' DSS.

	Number of Mss	Number of *Vavs*	*Vav* Plus	Mean Percent Change (Pluses)	*Vav* Minus	Mean Percent Change (Minus)
Defective	52	1102	357	2.58%	197	2.88%
Plene	27	959	109	6.54%	97	7.20%
N.E.D.	179	103	12		18	

Table 29. The Conjunction *Vav*

With 478 pluses and 312 minuses, the raw numbers follow what is expected for this corpus — more pluses than minuses. In order to analyse this data to see if the raw numbers are telling the whole picture, the following hypotheses will be tested:

H_0: The distribution of pluses of *vav* between the *plene* and defective 'biblical' DSS is random.

H_1: The distribution of pluses of *vav* between the *plene* and defective 'biblical' DSS is not random.

The application of a one-tailed t-test results in the following data:

---

44 Goshen-Gottstein, 'Linguistic Structure', 129, n. 200.

Comparing Means [t-test assuming unequal variances (*heteroscedastic*)]			
Descriptive Statistics			
Corpus	Sample Size	Mean	Variance
Defective	52	0.02578	0.0091
Plene	27	0.06539	0.0588
One-Tailed Distribution			
P-value	0.0524	*t Critical Value (5%)*	1.69092

Table 30. T-Test Applied to the Conjunction *Vav* (Pluses) Data

The mean variation rate for the *plene* scrolls is nearly three-times that of the defective scrolls, a difference that is statistically valid as the P-value of 5.24% shows, which is just above the 5% threshold and thus likely reveals statistical relevancy. By itself, this result suggests that the scribes of the *plene* scrolls had a tendency to add *vav*s to their texts. However, when the minuses of *vav* are analysed a fuller picture is obtained. The hypotheses for the minuses of *vav* are similar to those for the pluses:

H_0: The distribution of minuses of *vav* between the *plene* and defective 'biblical' DSS is random.

H_1: The distribution of minuses of *vav* between the *plene* and defective 'biblical' DSS is not random.

The results of a one-tailed t-test are as follows:

Comparing Means [t-test assuming unequal variances (*heteroscedastic*)]			
Descriptive Statistics			
Corpus	Sample Size	Mean	Variance
Defective	52	0.02882	0.0183
Plene	27	0.072	0.0969
One-Tailed Distribution			
P-value	0.01436	*t Critical Value (5%)*	1.68957

Table 31. T-Test Applied to the Conjunction Vav (Minuses) Data

Again, just as with the pluses, we find nearly three-times as many variations involving a minus of a *vav* in the *plene* scrolls (2.82% variation rate) than in the defective scrolls (7.20% variation rate). The P-value of 1.44% confirms that this difference is statistically relevant. Therefore, we must conclude that the *plene* scrolls contain significantly more pluses and minuses of the conjunction *vav* when compared with the defective scrolls. This overview of the variations involving the conjunction *vav* shows that both pluses and minuses of the particle should be considered statistically significant. Further analysis reveals some significant patterns involving verbs and the conjunction *vav*, but I will discuss these in the following section on the verbal system.

8. Conclusions

The above analysis has presented a comprehensive review of every variation involving nine particles: the directive *he* with comments on מאדה, the definite article, the direct object marker, the prepositions ב, כ and ל, the interchange between אל and על and the conjunction *vav*. The purpose of this analysis, covering over 28% of the 4,993 variations between the 'biblical' scrolls and the MT, was to ascertain whether or not any patterns of scribal intervention could be identified. Statistical analysis was used to identify relevant data. The *plene* and defective readings of לא served as a control, helping to reveal correlations between a specific set of scrolls and any patterns that were identified. And scholarly views on these variations were also tested to see if those theories proved to be consistent with the statistical analysis.

The results of this analysis identified a number of patterns of scribal intervention. Most significant are the variations involving the directive *he*. Statistical analysis showed this particle to have an unusually high variation rate when compared with the other particles analysed as well as the global variation rate for the 'biblical' scrolls. Further investigation highlighted the use of this particle with שם as well as with the possibly related long reading of מאדה. Those scrolls with *plene* readings of לוא were found to have שמה as well as מאדה significantly more often than those scrolls with defective readings of לא. Further, nearly all of these variations were found to be distinctive of the 'biblical' scrolls – not being found in any of the other major witnesses.

Another pattern of scribal intervention identified by this work was the use of על instead of אל by the *plene* scrolls. While the data is limited, statistical analysis showed that those scrolls characterized by long orthography also contain significantly more shifts from אל to על (however, this is only the case for the small amount of readings distinctive to the 'biblical' DSS). And a final variation type that can be connected with *plene* manuscripts are the pluses and minuses of the conjunction *vav*.

Of equal significance are the negative conclusions reached by this analysis. Over the past sixty years of work on the variations between the scrolls and the other witnesses, scholars have developed many theories regarding the influence of the language of the scribes upon their manuscripts. Kutscher argued that many of the variations involving the definite article were caused by the scribe not pronouncing pharyngeals or laryngeals.[45] Yet a review of his conclusions and a comprehensive analysis of the data showed no correlation between these variations and that change in the Hebrew language. Similarly, Muraoka claimed that the scrolls reveal a diachronic development of Hebrew in their use of the direct object marker.[46] Yet again a comprehensive analysis showed there to be no significant pattern of variation. These conclusions point to the need for not just viewing the variations globally, but also on a case-by-case basis. As I noted above, diachronic changes to the use of the direct object marker may be apparent in individual variations even if those shifts did not cause any global pattern of change. This sort of analysis will be undertaken after a comprehensive review of the variations involving the verbal and nominal systems.

B. Global Analysis of the Verbal System

The previous section focused on variations that involved a particle and it concluded with a review of the conjunction *vav*. That analysis revealed a correlation between *plene* orthography and pluses and minuses of the conjunction *vav*. Further work on the variations involving *vav* reveal patterns related to verbs, which leads nicely into this section which will focus on the verbal system of the 'biblical' DSS.

The approach in this section will be the same as the last. Four steps will be used to identify and explain the variations within the verbal system. First I will undertake a global analysis of all the variations in the verbal system. In the second step, I will compare variation rates between manuscripts looking for any patterns that surface, such as variations that cluster in scrolls that use a *plene* orthography. For the third step, I will move beyond my default comparison of the 'biblical' DSS with the MT to placing this analysis in the larger context of other major witnesses. And finally, I will review how previous research has analysed variations that involve the verbal system.

Fifty-five scrolls contain a total of 347 variations involving a verb when compared with the MT. Of these, 250 are only found in the 'biblical' DSS. 1QIsa[a] contains the majority of these variations with 208, while three other scrolls have 10 or more: 4Q51 (25), 4Q57 (12) and 11Q5 (11). These variations are diverse in nature, with fifty-four distinct changes. Some of the more common differences are as follows:

---

45 See section IV. A. 1. above for analysis of the directive *he*.
46 See section IV. A. 4. above on the direct object marker.

Vav plus perfect to imperfect – 15

Vav plus perfect to vav plus imperfect – 31

Vav plus imperfect to imperfect – 18

Perfect to imperfect – 26

Perfect to vav plus perfect (unconverted) – 13

Imperfect to perfect – 18

Imperfect to vav plus perfect (converted) – 31

Imperfect to vav plus imperfect – 68

Preterite to vav plus perfect (unconverted) – 15

Preterite to imperfect - 11

Table 32 provides an exhaustive count of these shifts as well as others.

	Tokens	Total in bDSS	Percent	z-score
To Imperf	85	4575	1.86%	-0.399
To Perf	28	3516	0.80%	-0.564
Away Imperf	120	4575	2.62%	-0.280
Away Perf	51	3516	1.45%	-0.463
To v+imperf	110	495	22.22%	2.767
To v+perf	77	1714	4.49%	0.010
Away v+imperf	25	495	5.05%	0.097
Away v+perf	60	1714	3.50%	-0.144
To Preterite	10	1981	0.50%	-0.610
Away Preterite	35	1981	1.77%	-0.414

Table 32. Verbal System Variations

The standard deviation of this group of changes can be calculated to determine if these shifts are statistically relevant or not. The mean percent of change according to this data is 4.63%, with a standard deviation of 6.33%. The last column in Table 32 reports the z-score[47] for each change. The probability of a z-score occurring that is more than plus or minus two from the mean is five percent, which is the standard cut-off point for a relevant statistical result.[48] Therefore the only shift presented in Table 32 that is statistically relevant is the shift to vav plus imperfect, which has a z-score of 2.77 or a chance of 1.79% of occurring randomly. These statistics do not of course tell why such a variation is relatively common in the 'biblical' DSS; the standard deviation and z-score simply highlight which sets of data require further investigation. I will therefore consider explanations for the shift to vav plus imperfect below. In order to provide a contrast to the analysis of the vav plus imperfect, I will also consider variations involving vav plus perfects. Further, I will analyse less common types

---

47 The z-score presents the number of standard deviations from the mean for each change.
48 M.P. Oakes, *Statistics for Corpus Linguistics* (Edinburgh 1998), 9.

of variations that have been discussed widely in secondary literature, namely variations involving preterites and infinitives construct. But, before discussing these variation types two preliminary topics need to be considered: the impact of 1QIsa^a and distinctive readings in the Qumran 'biblical' manuscripts.

1. The Role of 1QIsa^a and its Influence on the Data

1QIsa^a accounts for 208 of the total 347 variations involving the verbal system (60%). Due to this high percentage, an overview of the data needs to be undertaken to determine if 1QIsa^a is skewing the results or if it is in line with the holistic picture. A comparison of data for three groups — all of the scrolls, all of the scrolls except for 1QIsa^a and 1QIsa^a alone — will help to determine if 1QIsa^a is consistent with or contrary to the other 'biblical' scrolls.

The 'biblical' scrolls as a group have a mean variation rate of 5.44%, 1QIsa^a has a mean of 6.11% and the remaining scrolls have a mean of 4.02%. These results show that 1QIsa^a has a slightly higher variation rate than other 'biblical' scrolls. This higher rate of variation has been interpreted as a vulgarization of the language of Isaiah, while many of the other 'biblical' scrolls do not have the same influence.[49] Yet a higher rate of variation does not necessarily mean that 1QIsa^a is vulgar while the other scrolls are not. The higher rate could potentially be interpreted as 1QIsa^a being linguistically influenced to a greater extent than the other scrolls, but it does not reveal the nature of that influence. In order to investigate whether or not there are similar variations found in 1QIsa^a and the other 'biblical' scrolls, a closer analysis of the changes is needed.

	Tokens	Total in bDSS - 1QIsa^a	Percent	z-score
To Imperf	34	1835	1.85%	-0.429
To Perf	12	1507	0.80%	-0.638
Away Imperf	40	2593	1.54%	-0.490
Away Perf	17	1178	1.44%	-0.510
To *v*+imperf	33	189	17.46%	2.655
To *v*+perf	32	647	4.95%	0.182
Away *v*+imperf	12	189	6.35%	0.459
Away *v*+perf	19	647	2.94%	-0.215
To Preterite	6	995	0.60%	-0.676
Away Preterite	23	995	2.31%	-0.338

Table 33. Verbal System Variations Excluding 1QIsa^a

Table 33 contains the data for all of the 'biblical' scrolls excluding the Great Isaiah Scroll.

49 Kutscher, *Language*, 627.

The data in Table 33 reveals that the shift to *vav* plus imperfect in the 'biblical' DSS, excluding 1QIsaᵃ, has a lower overall percentage of change when compared with the data collected for all of the scrolls, yet the z-score is only 0.112 different and it is still well within the range of statistical relevancy. Table 34 presents the data for 1QIsaᵃ.

	Tokens	1QIsaᵃ	Percent	z-score
To Imperf	51	1330	3.83%	-0.488
To Perf	16	1001	1.60%	-0.711
Away Imperf	80	572	13.99%	0.526
Away Perf	34	1330	2.56%	-0.615
To *v*+imperf	77	220	35.00%	2.624
To *v*+perf	45	487	9.24%	0.052
Away *v*+imperf	13	220	5.91%	-0.280
Away *v*+perf	41	487	8.42%	-0.030
To Preterite	4	241	1.66%	-0.705
Away Preterite	12	241	4.98%	-0.373

Table 34. Verbal System Variations 1QIsaᵃ

This data shows that 1QIsaᵃ contains a larger rate of variation towards the *vav* plus imperfect; yet its z-score is just 0.143 different than the z-score for all of the scrolls. This comparison of z-scores (overall – 2.767, 'biblical' DSS [excluding 1QIsaᵃ] – 2.655 and 1QIsaᵃ – 2.624) shows that while these corpora have different mean rates of variation, they all contain similar relative rates — that is, they all show a statistically significant shift towards the *vav* plus imperfect. Further this shift towards the *vav* plus imperfect occurs at the same level compared with other shifts across corpora. Because of this we must conclude that 1QIsaᵃ does not skew the overall data and we can move forward with our analysis considering 1QIsaᵃ as a part of a larger whole.

2. Distinctive Readings in the Qumran 'Biblical' Manuscripts

A comparison between the 'biblical' scrolls and the MT reveals that the Qumran texts use the *vav* plus imperfect significantly more than the MT. This conclusion is based only on a comparison between the Qumran texts and the MT. To determine if this is simply a difference between these two collections of manuscripts or if this is truly a distinctive feature of the Qumran 'biblical' texts, I will now examine those readings that are only found in the 'biblical' scrolls.

An overview of all of the variants shows that there are 4,993 differences (excluding orthographic and morphological variations) between the Qumran 'biblical' manuscripts and the MT. Of these differences 2,888 are only found in the 'biblical' scrolls (when compared with the LXX and the SP).[50] These numbers suggest that the Qumran scrolls inherited a significant portion of their readings from non-MT *Vorlage*. Because of this, any patterns identified by comparing the scrolls with the MT need to be further compared with the other major witnesses.

Table 35 presents the distinctive variations found in the 'biblical' scrolls according to the same categories that have been analysed thus far.

	Tokens	Total in bDSS	Percent	z-score
To Imperf	60	4575	1.31%	-0.369
To Perf	23	3516	0.65%	-0.497
Away Imperf	75	4575	1.64%	-0.306
Away Perf	35	3516	1.00%	-0.431
To *v*+imperf	87	495	17.58%	2.791
To *v*+perf	62	1714	3.62%	0.079
Away *v*+imperf	13	495	2.63%	-0.114
Away *v*+perf	41	1714	2.39%	-0.159
To Preterite	5	1981	0.25%	-0.575
Away Preterite	21	1981	1.06%	-0.418

Table 35. Distinctive Verbal System Variations in the 'Biblical' DSS

Table 35 reveals that while the percent of difference is less, which is expected, the z-scores are very similar to previous comparisons. Even when considering only the distinctive variations found in the 'biblical' scrolls, the only shift that is statistically significant is the movement towards the *vav* plus imperfect. This result validates the initial 'biblical' scroll/MT comparison and suggests that further analysis of this feature is needed.

3. Vav plus Imperfect

To begin the analysis of the verbal system of the 'biblical' DSS, I will focus on the distribution of the variations involving a shift to *vav* plus imperfect. I will then consider possible explanations for any trends that are uncovered. Table 36 contains a summary of all of these variations:

	Number of Manuscripts	Number of Verbs	Shifts to *Vav* Plus Imperfect	Mean Percent Change (Pluses)
Defective	52	7548	17	8.49%
Plene	27	8409	87	18.90%
N.E.D.	177	2548	12	

Table 36. Shifts to *Vav* Plus Imperfect

---

50 The alignment of the LXX and SP as determined by DJD was utilized to obtain this data.

Eleven *plene* scrolls contain a shift to *vav* plus imperfect, nine of which have more than one of these variations. These scrolls account for 87 of the 116 (75%) shifts to *vav* plus imperfect. Eight defective scrolls have this variation, only one of which has more than one.

The above data shows that the shifts to *vav* plus imperfect are found more often in *plene* scrolls. Statistical analysis confirms the significance of this conclusion. The hypotheses for this analysis are as follows:

H_0: The rate of distribution of *vav* plus imperfects in the 'Biblical' Scrolls is random.

H_1: The rate of distribution of *vav* plus imperfects in the 'Biblical' Scrolls is not random.

A one-tailed t-test produces the following results:

Comparing Means [t-test assuming unequal variances (*heteroscedastic*)]			
Descriptive Statistics			
Corpus	Sample Size	Mean	Variance
Defective	52	0.08485	0.04859
Plene	27	0.18902	0.08917
		One-Tailed distribution	
P-value	0.05113	t Critical Value (5%)	1.67793

Table 37. T-Test Applied to the Shifts Towards *Vav* Plus Imperfect Data

Table 37 shows the mean variation rate of the defective scrolls to be ten percent lower than that of the *plene* scrolls. Further, the t-test has produced a P-value of 5.11%. While this is slightly above the five percent threshold, it still strongly suggests we should reject the H_0 in favour of the H_1 and conclude that the higher rate of occurrences of *vav* plus imperfect variations in the *plene* scrolls did not happen by chance. That conclusion confirms our previous observation that the *plene* scrolls contain significantly more shifts to *vav* plus imperfect than the defective scrolls. Yet of course these results do not explain why the *plene* scrolls contain more of these variations. Below I will examine some possible explanations.

In a recent article, Abegg discusses variations involving *vav* plus imperfect at length. As a starting place I will explore his explanations for why this type of variation developed. Abegg notes three possible reasons for this shift including: the increased use of the conjunction *vav*, the slight decrease in the use of the *vav* plus converted perfect and the loss of the special sense of *vav* plus imperfect.[51]

---

51 Abegg, 'The Biblical Dead Sea Scrolls', 168.

Abegg argues that part of the shift to *vav* plus imperfect can be explained by the increased use of the conjunction *vav* in the 'biblical' scrolls. There are a total of 484 places where the 'biblical' scrolls have the conjunction *vav* while the MT does not. This is in contrast with 315 places where the opposite is true. This is a net increase of 169 *vav*s, which is 1.8%. This is a relatively low increase compared with the overall variation rate of around six percent. Yet Abegg's point is still clear, namely that the large number of additional *vav*s in the 'biblical' scrolls likely brought about some of the shifts to *vav* plus imperfect. This is clear from the fact that 68 of the 110 shifts to *vav* plus imperfect involve only adding a *vav* to an imperfect. Abegg's suggestion that the increase of *vav* plus imperfect may be partially due to the decrease in *vav* plus converted perfect might also shed some light on this phenomenon.

The overall increase of *vav*s by 1.8% is relatively low, as noted above, yet the large number of added *vav*s, 484, may account for some of the increase in the *vav* plus imperfect. If these additional *vav*s are to account for this shift, we would also expect to find a significant number of additional *vav*s added to perfects. Yet this is not the case. There are roughly 3,800 perfects not preceded by a *vav* in the 'biblical' scrolls; yet only 16 places where a *vav* has been added to a perfect when compared with the MT — 0.4%. In contrast, there are roughly 4,600 imperfects not preceded by a *vav*, with 68 places where the scroll has an additional *vav* — 1.5% or nearly 4 times as many as the perfects. The reduced usage of the *vav* plus converted perfect may signal a scribal tendency to avoid *vav* plus perfect in general. This theory though is not supported by all of the available evidence. As we have seen above in Table 32, there are seventy-seven shifts to *vav* plus perfect, nearly half of which include an additional *vav* (i.e. imperfect to *vav* plus converted perfect occurs thirty-one times). This theory may not explain why *vav*s are added more often to imperfects in contrast to perfects, but it may help to elucidate the thirty-one shifts from *vav* plus perfect to *vav* plus imperfect. The scribes that brought about these changes may have intentionally avoided using the *vav* plus converted perfect and replaced it with the semantically similar *vav* plus imperfect.

Abegg's third and final explanation for the shift to *vav* plus imperfect is the loss of the special sense that this form had in classical Hebrew. Abegg does not develop this explanation in great detail, but logically it makes sense. If the special sense of this form was lost, then it could be utilized in a wider range of contexts. And this could account for the relatively large increase in the usage of this form. Further analysis will show that a form of this theory is valid, but it requires some adjustment from Abegg's original suggestion.

Abegg notes one example of the special sense of the *vav* plus imperfect — the telic use. J. Baden developed this idea in his article 'The *wəyiqtol* and the Volitive Sequence'.[52] Based on the only examples that he considered relevant (totalling eleven examples), Baden argues that the *vav* plus imperfect should always be translated with a telic meaning. From this he concludes that the volitive system should be understood as having three tiers: volitive followed by volitive with a simple continued volitive meaning (but also many other meanings based on context); volitive followed by *wəqatal* with a consecutive meaning; and volitive plus *wəyiqtol* connoting purpose or result (telicity).[53] Abegg states that perhaps the telic meaning of this third tier was lost, allowing the *vav* plus imperfect to be used in places where it was not normally found in classical Hebrew. The potential loss of the telic meaning of the *vav* plus imperfect may have allowed later scribes to use this form in place of others where before the telic meaning would have made such a replacement impossible.

If the *vav* plus imperfect did have a special telic meaning and if it was lost as the Hebrew language developed, then it may account for some of the shift to *vav* plus imperfect that we find in the 'biblical' scrolls. Yet Joosten argues directly against Baden's theory in 'A Note on *wəyiqtol* and the Volitive Sequences'.[54] By critiquing Baden's gathering of data (Joosten notes nine more examples that should be included), his analysis of the examples, and his conclusions regarding the syntactic function of the *wəyiqtol* form, Joosten shows that *vav* plus imperfect should not be understood to have a telic meaning distinct from other volitive forms. Joosten states: 'Ostensible cases of *wəyiqtol* are to be regarded as instances *of wə* + jussive, in which the jussive form has been replaced by *yiqtol* due to natural evolution of the language or to modernizing by later scribes'.[55] Joosten argues that this replacement of the jussive form by the *yiqtol* is possible due to the 'well-attested fact that the distinction between *yiqtol* and the volitives is obscured in Late Biblical Hebrew and Qumran Hebrew, and disappears completely in Mishnaic Hebrew'.[56] Thus the *vav* plus imperfect form does take a telic meaning sometimes, but only because it is filling the semantic and syntac-

---

52 J. Baden, 'The *wəyiqtol* and the Volitive Sequence', *VT* 58 (2008), 147–58.
53 Ibid., 157–8.
54 J. Joosten, 'A Note on '*wəyiqtol*' and Volitive Sequences', *VT* 59 (2009), 495–8.
55 Ibid., 495.
56 Ibid., 498.

tic slot of the jussive, which also often connotes purpose or result. This blurring of the distinction between *yiqtol* and the volitives may help to account for the increase in *vav* plus imperfect in the scrolls. As Joosten argues, this change may be due to developments in the Hebrew language and the modernization of the scrolls by the scribes who produced them.

The above theories may account for some of the variations where the scrolls have *vav* plus imperfect and the MT does not; yet there may be a more straightforward explanation. Just as with the directive *he*, the correlation between *vav* plus imperfects and *plene* orthography may be the key to understanding this type of variation. If the scribes of the *plene* scrolls favoured full orthographic readings due to how they looked, then it is possible that they favoured *vav* plus imperfects for how that form looked as well. While adding a *vav* to an imperfect does not make it grammatically equivalent to a preterite, it does make it look like a preterite. This theory is supported by the fact, as will be seen below, that the only scrolls which contain a plus of a preterite are written in *plene* orthography. Therefore, the scribes may have favoured this form to give their manuscripts an archaic feel.

4. Preterite

Table 38 presents a summary of the data for the pluses and minuses of the preterite:

	Number of Manuscripts	Shift to Preterite	Shift Away from Preterite
Defective	52	0	4
Plene	27	8	27
N.E.D.	177	6	3

Table 38. Pluses and Minuses of the Preterite

Muraoka has argued that the scribes of the 'biblical' DSS had a strong aversion to the preterite.[57] Based on his conclusion we would expect a large movement away from this form. Yet, as Abegg concluded, the data presented in Table 38 reveals what should be considered a relatively minor shift in the usage of the preterite as Table 39 confirms.

As was discussed previously and is shown in Table 39, the z-score for shifts away from the preterite is -0.414. This is within one standard deviation of the mean. A z-score of -0.414 has a 47% chance of occurring when compared with the data in Table 39. So, even though 34 shifts may appear to be noteworthy and the rate of variation of 1.77% is lower than the mean, statistically speaking

---
57 Muraoka, 'An Approach', 208.

	Tokens	Total in bDSS	Percent	z-score
To Imperf	85	4575	1.86%	-0.399
To Perf	28	3516	0.80%	-0.564
Away Imperf	120	4575	2.62%	-0.280
Away Perf	51	3516	1.45%	-0.463
To *v*+imperf	110	495	22.22%	2.767
To *v*+perf	77	1714	4.49%	0.010
Away *v*+imperf	25	495	5.05%	0.097
Away *v*+perf	60	1714	3.50%	-0.144
To Preterite	10	1981	0.50%	-0.610
Away Preterite	34	1981	1.77%	-0.414

Table 39. Verbal System Variations

these results are not significant and may be explained based on random chance. Further analysis of these variations shows no correlation between the use of a *plene* orthographic style and either the plusses or minuses of the preterite. Table 40 highlights this point:

	Number of Minuses	Total Number of Preterites	Percent Change
Defective Scrolls	4	78	6.41%
Plene Scrolls	27	549	4.74%

Table 40. Preterite Variations and Orthographic Style

A simple glance at the raw number of omissions suggests that *plene* scrolls have significantly more minuses of the preterite than the defective scrolls, twenty-six to five respectively. When the number of minuses found in the above table is normalized to the total occurrences of the preterite in each corpus, we see clearly that there is no significant difference between the defective and *plene* scrolls. In fact, the defective scrolls have a slightly higher rate than the *plene* scrolls. A two-tailed t-test[58] which produces a P-value of 89.90% confirms that there is no statistically significant deference between these two corpora.

From the data in Table 41, we must conclude that the diachronic development of Hebrew did not produce any recognizable pattern of change within the 'biblical' DSS corpora where the preterite form is involved. While some individual variations[59] may have been brought about by the development of Hebrew, that development does not seem to have caused a large-scale change within these manuscripts.

---

58 A two-tailed t-test, as opposed to a one-tailed, is used here, because the means between the two corpora are very close, making it impossible to anticipate which tail of the Gaussian Curve is relevant for analysis.

59 See Chapter V below for further discussion of this point.

Comparing Means [t-test assuming unequal variances (*heteroscedastic*)]			
Descriptive Statistics			
Corpus	Sample Size	Mean	Variance
Defective	52	0.01558	0.0527
Plene	27	0.0141	0.0102
Two-Tailed distribution			
P-value	0.89901	t Critical Value (5%)	1.99167

Table 41. T-Test Applied to the Preterite (Minuses) Data

That conclusion is in direct opposition to the conclusion reached by Muraoka.

Deeper analysis further challenges Muraoka's claim that the DSS scribes had an aversion to the preterite. The most problematic piece of Muraoka's argument is that he connects every manuscript from the Dead Sea to Qumran. In Muraoka's thinking, every manuscript from the Dead Sea reflects QH. Thus he uses data from a wide range of manuscripts to support conclusions such as: 'The following cases, where a *Waw* inversive is absent in QH when the corresponding MT has one and the pc. is used as a future, are indicative of a measure of uneasiness over such a *Waw* on the part of DSS authors or scribes'.[60] The examples Muraoka uses to support this claim come from 4Q30, 4Q76, 11Q19 and 4Q56. Of these, 11Q19 is mostly likely to provide reliable evidence for the nature of QH. 4Q30, 4Q76 and 4Q56 are all 'biblical' manuscripts written in a defective orthography. While defective orthography of a scroll does not automatically disqualify it from representing QH, without it there is little possible evidence that these scrolls were copied by a scribe who lived at Qumran. An occupant of the Qumran site could just as easily have brought these three manuscripts from elsewhere, and thus they could represent any number of scribal traditions.[61]

The above statistical analysis of variations involving preterites, as well as further critique of scholarly analysis of these variations, shows that the scribes did not have any particular aversion to this form. An analysis of variations involving infinitives will also challenge previous research.

5. Infinitives

Scholars have argued that both forms of the infinitive show diachronic development within the history of the Hebrew language.[62] Kutscher, Qimron and Mura-

---

60 Ibid., 209.
61 This topic has been discussed in section I.D. above.
62 As examples see Polzin, *Late Biblical Hebrew*, 60–1. And P. Joüon and T. Muraoka, *A Grammar of Biblical Hebrew*² (Rome 2006), 135.

oka have all argued that the infinitive construct plus *lamed* was used more often in QH than it was in earlier forms of Hebrew. Yet, as I discussed above, there is very little evidence of such a change in the 'biblical' scrolls. Abegg discusses the alleged decreased use of the infinitive absolute in later forms of Hebrew and concludes that there is some evidence for such a diachronic development of this verbal form within the 'biblical' scrolls.[63] This conclusion is supported, in part, by the data, which is summarized in Table 42:

	Number of Manuscripts	Shifts Away from the Infinitive Absolute
Defective	52	9
Plene	27	19
N.E.D.	177	0

Table 42. Infinitive Absolute Data

There are 28 places where the 'biblical' scrolls contain a minus of the infinitive absolute, and there are a total of 253 occurrences of the infinitive absolute within the 'biblical' DSS, resulting in a change of 11.07%. This is notably higher than the mean rate of variation, but still within two standard deviations of the mean, suggesting that while this change is higher than normal, it is not statistically significant. Further, this variation type only occurs in eight manuscripts. This may be due to the rarity of the infinitive absolute. Alternatively, the fact that this variation type occurs in so few manuscripts may suggest that the reduced use of the infinitive absolute in Hebrew did not influence the 'biblical' scrolls in any significant way. Finally, there is no correlation between a minus of the infinitive absolute and *plene* orthography. Thus even though the infinitive absolute presents a relatively high rate of variation, the lack of data, the relatively low number of scrolls containing this variation, and the lack of correlation with *plene* orthography all suggest that this variation type does not reveal a pattern of scribal intervention.

6. Conclusions

The above review of the variations involving the verbal system of the 'biblical' DSS has shown there to be very little correlation between the *plene* scrolls and nonorthographic/morphological features. The one exception is the shift towards *vav* plus imperfect, which stands out as having a statistically significant higher rate of variation than other differences within the verbal system. While scholars have proposed a number of diachronic explanations for this variation type, I

---
63 Abegg, 'The Biblical Dead Sea Scrolls', 170–1.

have suggested a simpler view based on its link with *plene* orthography. This link suggests that the addition of the *vav* to the imperfect may have been the result of a desire for a specific, possibly archaic, style.

C. Global Analysis of the Nominal System

In this section, I will review all the variations that involve nouns, pronouns, proper nouns, independent personal pronouns and suffixes. As in previous sections, I will statistically analyse the data to identify any patterns of change that are significant. Specifically, I will consider any correlation between differences in the nominal systems of the major witnesses and the use of *plene* orthography.

Table 43 breaks down the 636 nominal variations by category:

Type of Variation	Tokens
Noun Masculine to Feminine	17
Noun Feminine to Masculine	19
Noun Absolute to Construct	23
Noun Construct to Absolute	5
Suffix Masculine to Feminine	14
Suffix Feminine to Masculine	16
Noun Singular to Plural	97
Noun Plural to Singular	81
Suffix Singular to Plural	21
Suffix Plural to Singular	12
Noun Singular to Dual	25
Noun Dual to Singular	9
Pronoun Singular to Plural	5
Pronoun Plural to Singular	0
Pronoun Feminine to Masculine	1
Suffix Plus	64
Suffix Minus	58
Suffix Number Shift	54
Suffix to Independent Pronoun	2
Adjective Singular to Plural	9
Adjective Plural to Singular	2
Adjective Masculine to Feminine	3
Adjective Absolute to Construct	2
Changes to God's Name	93
Changes to other Proper Nouns	5
Total	636[64]

Table 43. Nominal Variations

---

[64] Some variations may fall into more than one category, such as a shift from a 3ms absolute noun to a 2fp construct noun. This variation would receive one token in four different categories.

Shifts in number and gender, pluses and minuses of suffixes and changes to God's name are the most common variations, and I will focus mainly on these here.

1. Shifts in Number

Shifts in number represent the most common variation type in the nominal system of the 'biblical' DSS. Table 44 breaks down these variations by type as well as by group of manuscripts:

	Tokens	*Plene*	Defective
Singular to Dual/Plural	193	141	42
Dual/Plural to Singular	88	47	35

Table 44. Shifts in Number Data

This table shows that there are more than twice as many shifts from singular to dual/plural (s to d/p) than the shifts from dual/plural to singular (d/p to s). Further, we see that the *plene* scrolls contain about 3.5 times the number of shifts from s to d/p than the defective scrolls. The same trend is not seen in shifts from d/p to s, where the *plene* and defective scrolls contain nearly the same amount of variations. Statistical analysis confirms, as the following results show, that the *plene* scrolls have significantly more shifts from s to d/p than the defective scrolls.

Hypotheses:

H_0: There is no statistically significant difference between the *plene* scrolls and the defective scrolls in the rate of shifts from s to d/p.

H_1: There is a statistically valid difference between the *plene* scrolls and the defective scrolls in the rate of shifts from s to d/p, and this difference is not likely to have been caused by chance.

T-test results:

Comparing Means [t-test assuming unequal variances (*heteroscedastic*)]			
Descriptive Statistics			
Corpus	Sample Size	Mean	Variance
Defective	52	0.00547	0.0021
Plene	27	0.01956	0.0078
One-Tailed Distribution			
P-value	0.00709	*t Critical Value (5%)*	1.68595

Table 45. T-Test Applied to the Shifts from S to P/D Data

Table 45 shows that the mean for the *plene* scrolls is 1.96%, which is nearly

4 times higher than the 0.54% mean for the defective scrolls. The one-tailed t-test shows that these means are statistically different with a P-value of 0.70%. Since this is below the five percent threshold of significance, we reject the null hypothesis and accept the alternative hypothesis and conclude that there is a statistically relevant difference between the *plene* and defective scrolls in this area.

In order to provide a point of comparison, I will also statistically analyse the data for shifts from d/p to s. The hypotheses are as follows:

H_0: There is no statistically significant difference between the *plene* scrolls and the defective scrolls in the rate of shifts from d/p to s.

H_1: There is a statistically valid difference between the *plene* scrolls and the defective scrolls in the rate of shifts from d/p to s, and this difference is not likely to have been caused by chance.

The t-test results are:

Comparing Means [t-test assuming equal variances (*homoscedastic*)]			
Descriptive Statistics			
Corpus	Sample Size	Mean	Variance
Defective	52	0.0055	0.0009
Plene	27	0.00537	0.0009
One-Tailed Distribution			
P-value	0.4767	*t Critical Value (5%)*	1.66412

Table 46. T-Test Applied to the Shifts from P/D to S Data

Here we see that the means for these two groups of scrolls are nearly the same, 0.55% for the defective scrolls and 0.54% for the *plene* scrolls. The one-tailed t-test confirms that this small difference is not statistically relevant by producing a P-value of 47.67%, which is well above the 5% threshold of statistical significance. The results for shifts from d/p to s stand in contrast to those found for s to d/p, which clearly shows that the *plene* scrolls contain significantly more shifts to dual/plural nominal forms than the defective scrolls, while these two groups contain a relatively close number of shifts from d/p to s.

One possible explanation for this trend is the large number of shifts from יד to ידי. There are a total of forty-four shifts from יד to ידי in the 'biblical' DSS, and all but one are found in *plene* scrolls (there are only five shifts from ידי to יד). Such variations may have been caused by a diachronic development in the usage of this noun. A number of scholars have noted a preference for plural forms of certain nouns in LBH as opposed to EBH.⁶⁵ יד may also fall into this category as Table 47 suggests:

	יד	ידי	Ratio
EBH	570	57	10 to 1
LBH	192	24	8 to 1
bDSS	227	83	2.73 to 1
Qumran	345	75	4.60 to 1
Mishnah	411	290	1.42 to 1

Table 47. Comparison of the Use of יד and ידי in Hebrew Corpora

In EBH, the ratio of יד as a singular to יד as a plural noun is ten to one. The ratio drops (although not consistently) from EBH to the Mishnah where it is 1.42 to 1. The trend towards the plural form of this noun may have contributed to its heavy usage within the *plene* scrolls. Yet a possible diachronic change in the way this word is used does not account for the overall movement from s to d/p.

Further evidence suggests this shift may be diachronic in nature. The defective spelling of a preposition or third masculine plural noun with a third masculine singular suffix is found in some early Hebrew inscriptions,⁶⁶ while the full form became more common in later texts.⁶⁷ F.I. Andersen and Forbes argue that the 'יו' form was introduced to help differentiate between the two possible meanings of a phrase such as בנו (his son or his sons).⁶⁸ With the introduction of the *yod*, the plural attains a distinctive form — בניו. The evidence presented above suggests that the scribes of the *plene* scrolls may have over applied this use of the *yod*. Instead of utilizing the long form to mark plurals, it seems that they exploited it simply out of preference for fuller readings.⁶⁹ This conclusion is consistent with the overall trend of fuller readings in the *plene* scrolls.

65 See Qimron, *Hebrew*, 68. Also see: I. Young, ''*Am* Construed as Singular and Plural in Hebrew Biblical Texts: Diachronic and Textual Perspectives', *Zeitschrift für Althebraistik* 12 (1999), 29–63 and idem ''*Edah* and *Qahal* as Collective Nouns in Hebrew Biblical Texts', *Zeitschrift für Althebraistik* 14 (2001), 68–78.
66 Lachish 3:18 (three – אנשו mp noun plus 3ms suffix) and Yavneh-Yam line 13 (אלו – preposition plus 3ms suffix).
67 Joüon and Muraoka, *A Grammar of Biblical Hebrew*, 287 n. 2.
68 F.I. Andersen and A.D. Forbes, *Spelling in the Hebrew Bible: Dahood Memorial Lexture* (BibOr 41, Rome 1988), 324–6.
69 The possibility that the scribes simply preferred the longer form or the shorter form is consistent with Goshen-Gottstein's observation that 'the alternation of the pronominal suffixes, commonly spelled ו - / יו -, seems to belong to morphology'. Goshen-Gottstein, 'Linguistic Structure', 116. Also see F.M. Cross, 'Some Problems in Old Hebrew Orthography with Special Attention to the Third Person Masculine Singular Suffix on Plural Nouns (-âw)', *ErIsr* 27 (2003), 19–20.

2. Pluses and Minuses of Suffixes

In this section, I will analyse the variations that involve a plus or minus of a suffix. First, I will review the data, then I will use significance tests to see if there are any statistically relevant patterns, and finally I will present some possible explanations for any such patterns.

Pluses and minuses of suffixes are the second most common type of variation involving the nominal system. There are a total of sixty-four pluses and fifty-eight minuses of suffixes found in the variations between the 'biblical' DSS and the MT. The variations cover pluses and minuses of all types of suffixes and involve singular and plural nouns.

Forty-eight of the sixty-four (seventy-five percent) pluses of suffixes are found in the *plene* scrolls, thirteen (twenty percent) are in the defective scrolls and three are in those scrolls containing insufficient data to determine alignment.[70] That data is summarized in Table 48:

	Number of Manuscripts	Number of Suffix - Plus
Defective	52	13
Plene	27	42
N.E.D.	179	3

Table 48. Suffix Pluses Data

From the raw data in Table 48, we can make the observation that the *plene* scrolls have more pluses of suffixes than the defective scrolls, which leads to the following two hypotheses that will be tested using the t-test:

H_0: The *plene* scrolls do not have significantly more pluses of suffixes than the defective scrolls.

H_1: The *plene* scrolls have significantly more pluses of suffixes than the defective scrolls, and this difference is not due to random chance.

A one-tailed t-test results in the following data:

---

70 As before, this data is normalized for statistical analysis. Here I am using the number of suffixes per scroll to attain means of pluses to the number of suffixes.

Comparing Means [t-test assuming unequal variances (*heteroscedastic*)]			
Descriptive Statistics			
Corpus	Sample Size	Mean	Variance
Defective	52	0.00681	0.0011
Plene	27	0.00922	0.0033
One-Tailed Distribution			
P-value	0.25559	*t Critical Value (5%)*	1.68385

Table 49. T-Test Applied to the Suffix (Pluses) Data

The mean variation rate for the *plene* scrolls is 0.76%, while it is only 0.32% for the defective scrolls and the P-value for this data is 10.64%. Since the P-value is higher than the five percent threshold, we should accept the null hypothesis. Thus we conclude that the *plene* scrolls do not have significantly more pluses of suffixes than the defective scrolls. The difference in means may suggest that there is a significant difference between these two corpora, but the relatively small amount of data (only fifty-four tokens total found in only twenty manuscripts) makes accepting the null hypothesis the safer conclusion.

Similar results are found for the minuses of suffixes. I will test the following hypotheses, which are essentially the same as for the pluses:

H_0: The *plene* scrolls do not have significantly more minuses of suffixes than the defective scrolls.

H_1: The *plene* scrolls have significantly more minuses of suffixes than the defective scrolls, and this difference is not due to random chance.

The following data is obtained through a one-tailed t-test:

Comparing Means [t-test assuming unequal variances (*heteroscedastic*)]			
Descriptive Statistics			
Corpus	Sample Size	Mean	Variance
Defective	52	0.00681	0.0011
Plene	27	0.00922	0.0033
One-Tailed Distribution			
P-value	0.25559	*t Critical Value (5%)*	1.68385

Table 50. T-Test Applied to the Suffix (Minuses) Data

The mean for the *plene* scrolls is 0.92%, while the mean for the defective scrolls is only slightly lower at 0.68%. This leads to a P-value of 25.56%, which is well above the threshold for statistical significance. Thus we accept the null hypothesis and conclude that there is no statistically valid difference between these two corpora when minuses of suffixes are the focus. While the scrolls contain a large number of pluses and minuses of suffixes (compared with other variations in the nominal system), statistical analysis does not reveal any correlation between these variations and the orthographic character of the manuscripts.

3. Shifts in Gender

For this section, I will review the shifts in gender found in the variations between the 'biblical' DSS and the MT.

Table 51 contains the data for shifts from feminine to masculine and masculine to feminine in the nominal system.

	Fem to Masc	Masc to Fem
Plene	26	24
Defective	7	9
Other	1	0

Table 51. Shifts in Gender Data

The 'biblical' DSS contain a feminine nominal form in thirty-four places where the corresponding passage in the MT has a masculine form. The opposite is found in thirty-three places. The raw numbers show the *plene* scrolls containing far more of these variations than the defective scrolls, but when the data is normalized and analysed using a statistical significance test, this difference is minimal. The following data supports this conclusion:

	Mean Difference Fem to Masc[71]	Mean Difference Masc to Fem[72]
Plene	0.36%	0.11%
Defective	0.74%	0.11%

Table 52. Shifts in Gender Compared with Orthographic Style

As can be seen in Table 52, the means for the *plene* and defective scrolls are nearly the same. A one-tailed t-test confirms that the small difference between the two corpora is not statistically significant. The P-value for feminine/masculine variations is 15.13%, and for masculine/feminine it is 46.94%. Both of these P-values suggest there is no statistically valid difference between the *plene* and defective scrolls.

---

71 This column is normalized to the number of feminine nouns in the scrolls.
72 This column is normalized to the number of masculine nouns in the scrolls.

4. Names for God

There are ninety-two differences in the names of God[73] between the 'biblical' DSS and the MT. This high number makes this the third most common type of variation in the nominal system of the 'biblical' DSS. In this section, I will briefly present the types of variations in the names of God, followed by an analysis.

There are five types of variations that involve a name of God that occur at least nine times: 1) Scroll – אלוהים, MT – יהוה: fourteen times; 2) Scroll – יהוה, MT – אלוהים: eleven times; 3) Scroll – אדני, MT – יהוה: nine times; 4) Scroll – יהוה, MT – אדני: fifteen times; 5) Scroll – יהוה אלוהים, MT – יהוה:[74] nineteen times.[75] There are twenty-six other types of variations in this category. Most of these only occur once.

A thorough analysis of these variations reveals that the *plene* scrolls have more than twice as many variations involving a name of God than the defective scrolls (sixty one to twenty six respectively). The application of a t-test confirms that this higher rate of variation is statistically valid.[76] While this difference could be attributed to the higher rate of variation within the *plene* scrolls, further analysis suggests four alternative factors that were likely contributors. Three of these factors can be connected to individual scribal preference.

The first factor is 1QIsa͏ᵃ I's high number of readings of יהוה where the MT has אדני. Of the fifteen variations of this type, eight are found in 1QIsa͏ᵃ I. On the other hand, the opposite variation, Scroll – אדני, MT – יהוה, is only found in 1QIsa͏ᵃ I once. Also of significance is the fact that the term אדני only occurs in 1QIsa͏ᵃ I nineteen times, while the parallel passages in MT Isaiah have אדני twenty-seven times. Thus 1QIsa͏ᵃ I has thirty percent less occurrences of אדני than the MT. Finally, 1QIsa͏ᵃ I only has four other variations that involve a name of God, one of which is a reading of יהוה, where the MT has אדני יהוה.[77] All of this suggests that either the scribe of 1QIsa͏ᵃ I preferred יהוה over אדני or he inherited this preference from his *Vorlage*.

The second factor that is pertinent stands in direct contrast to the first. In every place that 11Q5 contains a variation that involves a name of God, the MT reads יהוה while 11Q5 does not. Yet there are only 4 such variations found in this

---

73 For this category, I have included any variation that involves one or more of the following words when used to refer directly to the Hebrew God: יהוה, אלאהים, אדני.
74 The opposite of this type of variation only occurs once. This will be discussed below.
75 These counts group together variations such as יהוה אלוהיך and יהוה אלוהים.
76 The P-value for this one-tailed t-test is 4.7%.
77 1QIsa͏ᵃ 22:30

Chapter IV Global Analysis of the Linguistic Character of the 'Biblical' Dead Sea Scrolls

scroll out of 131 occurrences of the Tetragrammaton in this scroll.

The third factor is the mixed character of 4Q51. In three places, 4Q51 contains אלוהים where the MT has יהוה. In three places, we find the opposite. Also, this is the only scroll that does not have אלוהים where the MT has the phrase יהוה אלהים. This mixed set of variations is consistent with the mixed orthography and morphology found in this scroll.

The fourth factor does not speak to any one scroll, but to one specific word. אלוהים is a plus in the scrolls eighteen times, Scroll – יהוה אלוהים, MT – יהוה, (eleven *plene*, seven defective), while it is a plus in the MT only once,[78] Scroll – יהוה, MT – יהוה אלוהים.

These four factors likely played a role in the higher rate of variations in the *plene* scrolls involving a name of God. Those factors, and in particular three scrolls, seem to have brought about the higher rate of variation within the *plene* scrolls in this category. Because of that, we should not consider variations in the use of names for God to be linked with *plene* orthography. Instead, we should look to individual scribal practices to understand those variations.

5. Conclusions

Of the four types of variations analysed above, only one showed a correlation with the *plene* scrolls — shifts from singular to plural, and more specifically the shift from the short form of the suffix 'ו' to the long form 'יו'. In the above discussion, I concluded that the scribes of the *plene* scrolls likely preferred 'יו' due to its longer form as opposed to a preference for plural nouns. The remaining three categories of variations did not show any correlation with the *plene* scrolls. However, the different uses of the names for God did reveal some individual scribal patterns that are of note.

D. General Conclusions

In this chapter, I have analysed the linguistic character of the 'biblical' DSS, focusing upon the particle, verbal and nominal systems. Within each of the categories, I presented an overview of the variations while noting significant patterns and their implications for past research on this topic. In my introductory chapter, I hypothesized that a complete review of the variations between the 'biblical' DSS and other witnesses would not yield any correlations between

---

78 4Q51 7a:1

the orthographic character of a manuscript and other grammatical variations. In my review of past literature on this topic, I showed that scholars have both agreed and disagreed with this hypothesis. In this chapter, I have presented a complete analysis of all the major variation types found within the 'biblical' scrolls in order to test this hypothesis. After reviewing more than forty variation types (sixteen comprehensively), I have concluded that only five of these show any correlation with the *plene* scrolls, one of which, the shift from על to אל, can only be considered loosely correlated due to the limited data. The four remaining variation types are pluses of the directive *he*, pluses and minuses of the conjunction *vav*, shifts toward *vav* plus imperfect and shifts from singular to plural nouns. From here forward I will refer to these variation types as *Plene* Linked Variations (PLVs). The correlation between these variation types and the *plene* character of the manuscripts suggest that the scribes who produced these readings favoured them more for their stylistic feel as opposed to any diachronic change in the Hebrew language that may have impacted their copying. This conclusion fits particularly well for three of these types of variations. Above I have shown that the directive *he* was a plus on שם in the *plene* scrolls far more often than any other word. This suggests that the scribes favoured the long form of שמה. If the pluses of the H.L. had been more spread across a diverse range of nouns, then a diachronic explanation would be more plausible, but this is not what was found. The preference simply for the long form of שמה is consistent with the use of other long forms, particularly long suffixes such as המה. Further, the movement towards plural nouns seems to have been caused by a preference for the long form of the third masculine singular suffix. These two variation types should probably be considered simple orthographic variations as opposed to representing specific syntactic shifts in Hebrew. Finally, the shift toward *vav* plus imperfect may have also been caused by a preference for the look and/or sound of the form over a shift in the grammar of the language. If this conclusion is valid, which is admittedly difficult to demonstrate, then we must conclude that the vast majority of variations that show any patterned link with a specific orthography were likely produced due to a preference for a specific style as opposed to linguistic modernization.

This study has found only four variation types that can be linked to a *plene* orthographic style. Two of these should probably be considered orthographic variations, and another can possibly be explained based on a preference for the look or sound of a specific form. With these results in mind we can now return to the starting hypothesis presented at the beginning of this project: The 'biblical' DSS do not contain any distinctive linguistic characteristics beyond orthography and morphology. By and large the results presented in this chapter prove this hypothesis to be correct. These results then present a direct challenge to those, such as Muraoka, who have argued we can learn about the nature of QH through an analysis of the 'biblical' scrolls. Before delving deeper into this conclusion, I will analyse five individual manuscripts in order to test if this global analysis holds up on a case-by-case basis. This analysis will provide an alternative angle at which to view the data and will allow for some testing of the conclusions presented above.

Chapter V

The Linguistic Character of Individual Scrolls

In Chapter IV, I provided a comprehensive analysis of the variations found in the 'biblical' DSS. This analysis showed that most types of variations do not correlate with specific types of scrolls or with specific scribal practices, namely *plene* and defective orthography. Yet a handful of variation types clearly stood out as connected to the *plene* scrolls. Variations such as shifts to *vav* plus imperfect/preterite, plural nouns instead of singular and the increased use of the directive *he* all proved to be related to a full orthographic style. I labelled these *Plene* Linked Variations (PLVs).

Those conclusions were generalized over all of the 'biblical' scrolls by placing similar scrolls into groups and then analysing those groups. In this chapter, I will analyse individual manuscripts in order to test whether or not the correlation between these types of variations and the orthographic nature of a scroll holds true on a scroll-by-scroll basis. The conclusions from the previous section suggest the following hypotheses for this chapter. In scrolls with a *plene* orthographic style, we will find consistent use of PLVs. In scrolls with a mixed orthographic style, we will find a mixed use of PLVs. And finally, in scrolls with a defective orthographic style, we will not find many PLVs. In order to test these hypotheses, I will analyse five different manuscripts with varying orthographic styles — 1QIsa[a] I, 1QIsa[a] II, 1QIsa[b], 4QNum[b] and 4QSam[a]. These scrolls were selected to provide a range of orthographic styles, representatives from different sections of the Hebrew Bible and a mix of genres. This diversity will aid in testing the hypotheses of this chapter.

Before beginning the analysis of these five scrolls, a brief discussion of three issues is needed. First, in this chapter, I will be focusing mainly on those variations found to be PLVs by the work in Chapter IV. This will provide the best data to test the correlation between the orthographic character of a scroll and its overall linguistic nature. Yet I will also include analysis of variations that may have a diachronic explanation. This will help to gain a fuller picture of the linguistic character of each of the five manuscripts being analysed. I will also discuss some linguistic features that have been considered characteristic of QH, but are not found in large numbers within the 'biblical' scrolls.

The second methodological issue that is specifically relevant for this chapter involves the selection of variations for analysis. One of the most challenging aspects of analysing the linguistic nature of manuscripts is the issue of *Vorlage*. We can almost never know for certain if the scribe of a manuscript caused a specific reading or if he simply copied that reading from his *Vorlage*. In this chapter, I will focus my analysis upon readings found only in the manuscript at hand and not in any other major witnesses. While we cannot completely control *Vorlage* issues, we mitigate such complexities as much as possible by only analysing distinctive readings.

Third, in the results presented in the previous chapter, I have shown a connection between a small number of variation types and the main characteristics of QH, *plene* orthographic style and long morphological forms. While some of these variation types can be explained based on syntactical shifts, the more likely explanation rests on morphological and semantic considerations.[1] The following analysis of five individual scrolls will reinforce this finding. We will see that PLVs are found in manuscripts with a full orthographic character, but we will also find that the remaining variations do not reflect any consistent pattern of syntactical change. This point will be returned to throughout the following analysis.

A. 1QIsa[a]

The linguistic character of The Great Isaiah Scroll has been studied more than any other Dead Sea Scroll. From Kutscher's monumental work[2] to Abegg's recent analysis in DJD 31,[3] we have exhaustive descriptions of the language found in 1QIsa[a]. Even with this work in place, I have decided to analyse 1QIsa[a] here for two reasons. First, the analysis in the above chapters has identified features from the verbal system, nominal system and the use of particles that can be correlated with the use of a *plene* orthographic style. These have not, as far as I am aware, been fully recognized by others. These findings will help us to more fully understand the linguistic character of this scroll. And second, since we find one of the fullest orthographic styles in 1QIsa[a], we would also expect a high concentration of PLVs in this scroll. Thus this manuscript represents one extreme that

---

1   See Chapter IV.
2   Kutscher, *Language*.
3   M.G. Abegg, Jr., 'Linguistic Profile of the Isaiah Scrolls', in E. Ulrich and P.W. Flint (eds), *Qumran Cave 1. II: The Isaiah Scrolls, Part 2: Introductions, Commentary, and Textual Variants* (DJD 32, Oxford 2010), 25–42.

needs to be included in this discussion if the entire picture is to be put into focus.

My analysis of each scroll will be divided into six sections: 1. orthography; 2. textual character; 3. verbal system; 4. nominal system; 5. particles; and 6. conclusions. In sections one and two, I will briefly review the orthographic and morphological character of the manuscripts as well as the textual character of each scroll. These reviews will be based mainly on the discussions found in DJD, but will also bring in other sources as they prove to be helpful. These two sections will set the context in which the analysis of the variations will be considered. The brief conclusions for each scroll will summarize the results and provide a basis for a discussion of the implications for the larger thesis of this project.

1. Orthography

The orthographic character of the DSS varies greatly. While some scrolls contain full readings in most possible cases, others are just as conservative as the MT. The following quote from Abegg places 1QIsa[a] in this context:

> Taken as a whole, the nonbiblical manuscripts from Qumran incorporate the *waw* with near consistency in these roles; *waw* for *o/ō* occurs over 80% of the time. By comparison, in the corpus of biblical manuscripts from the Judaean Desert, *waw* for *o/ō* is used in less than 50% of possible instances. Along this spectrum, 1QIsa[a] is at the far upper end of the scale at 94% *plene* forms where possible...[4]

1QIsa[a], then, falls toward one end of the spectrum. Yet there is a noticeable difference between the two halves of this manuscript. The first half is more conservative, while '[t]he tendency in the second half of the scroll [is] toward later orthographic and morphological forms...'.[5] The distinct character of each half will be discussed at length below. The very full orthographic character of both parts of this manuscript suggests that this scroll should also contain a high percentage of PLVs. Further, the difference in orthographic character between the two halves suggests that there should be more PLVs in columns 28–54 then in the previous columns. The following analysis of the variations found in 1QIsa[a] will demonstrate these points.

---

4   Ibid., 26.
5   Ulrich and Flint (eds), *The Isaiah Scrolls*, 243.

2. Textual Character

While all the Isaiah manuscripts seem to have developed from one textual tradition, there appear to be a number of textual families.[6] E. Ulrich and P.W. Flint conclude that 1QIsa^a and the LXX are 'distant enough from each other and from the [MT] tradition that they must each be assigned to different text families'.[7] This distance between 1QIsa^a and the other major witnesses to the book of Isaiah reinforces the need to avoid MT-centred analysis. As is mentioned above, the following analysis of 1QIsa^a will focus only on readings distinctive to this manuscript. This approach is taken to minimize, as much as possible, considerations of the interrelationship between these text families.

3. One Text or Two

In Chapter III. B. 2. b. 2, I compared the variation rates of the two halves of 1QIsa^a within the context of statistical representativeness. Here I will revisit that discussion, but will recontextualize the results within the linguistic profile of this manuscript. This analysis will focus on all types of variations, with the following sections providing comparative data for the verbal system, nominal system and use of particles within each half of the scroll.

1QIsa^a clearly exists in two halves: columns 1–27 and 28–53. Yet scholars have long debated how these two halves came to be.[8] Some argue that there were two main scribes who produced this manuscript, one for each section.[9] Others propose that one scribe copied the manuscript from two different *Vorlagen*.[10] Whether one or two main scribes produced this manuscript, we clearly need to analyse it in two halves. A brief comparison of the variation rates between the two parts supports this conclusion.

Figure 11 presents a comparison of the variations rates for 1QIsa^a I and II by column:

---

6   Ibid., 91.
7   Ibid., 92.
8   For a full discussion and selected bibliography, see Tov, *Scribal Practices*, 20.
9   Idem, 'The Text of Isaiah at Qumran', in C. Broyles and C. Evans (eds), *Writing and Reading the Scroll of Isaiah: Studies of an Interpretive Tradition*, vol. 2 (VTSup 70, Leiden 1997), 8–9.
10 Kutscher, *Language*, 564–6. Ulrich and Flint (eds), *The Isaiah Scrolls*, 63–4.

Chapter V The Linguistic Character of Individual Scrolls

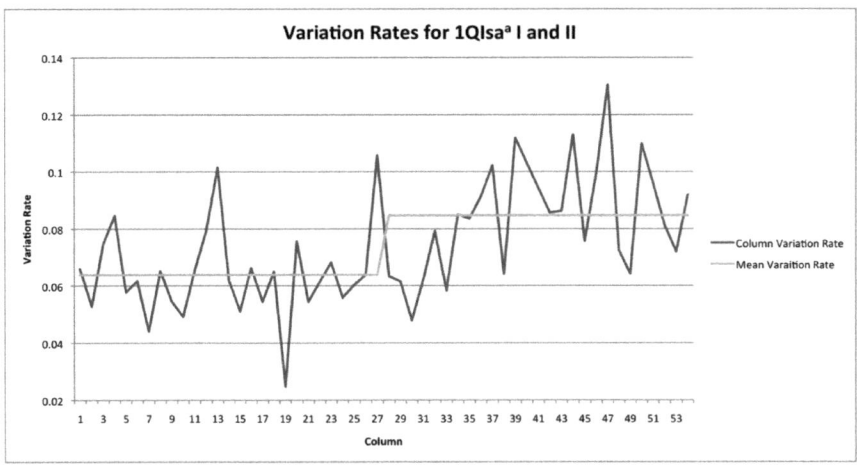

Figure 11. Variation Rates for 1QIsa^a I and II

The light grey line shows the running variation rate for each column in this manuscript. The dark grey line represents the mean variation rate for each half of 1QIsa^a by column. While the variation rates within each half of this scroll vary widely, with there being overlap between columns from each section, a comparison of the means reveals a significantly lower rate of variation for columns 1–27 than the rate for columns 28–54.

1QIsa^a I has a range of variation rates from 2.5% (column 19) to 10.6% (column 27). Overall this section of the Great Isaiah Scroll has a mean variation rate of 6.4%. In contrast, 1QIsa^a II has a range of variation rates from 4.8% (column 30) to 13% (column 47). This half has a mean variation rate of 8.5%. The mean variation rates for the two halves appear to be different, but with the wide range of variation even within each part, this difference may have come about by chance. As was developed in Chapter III. B. 4., we can use a t-test to analyse these variation rates in order to determine if the mean variation rates found in these two halves are significantly different or not.

Table 53 shows the results of a two-tailed t-test applied to the variation rates for 1QIsa^a I and II:

Comparing Means [t-test assuming equal variances (*homoscedastic*)]			
Descriptive Statistics			
Corpus	Sample Size	Mean	Variance
Defective	27	0.06387	0.0027
Plene	27	0.08468	0.004
Two-Tailed Distribution			
P-value	0.001	*t Critical Value (5%)*	2.00665

Table 53 T-Test Applied to Variation Rates of the Two Halves of 1QIsa^a

The two-tailed t-test produces a P-value of 0.1%, which is far lower than the 5% threshold for statistical significance. Thus the chance of these two means coming about by random chance is highly unlikely. This confirms the need to analyse the two halves of this manuscript separately.

Beyond the main scribe(s), recent scholarship has demonstrated that there are likely other scribes who made small changes and short additions.[11] If we take D. Longacre's conclusions at face value, the following passages should be considered secondary additions: Isa. 34:17–35:2; 36:11–12; 37:4–7; 37:31–3; 38:19–22; 40:14–16; 41:11–12; 43:3; 45:8; 51:6; 53:8; 54:17; 56:6; 57:13–14; 63:3; 65:3; 65:15–16. As can be seen, all of these passages occur in the second half of the manuscript. Of the 875 distinctive readings found in 1QIsa^a, 59 are located in these 'added' passages. These numbers reveal variation rates (distinctive readings per word) of: 1QIsa^a II overall — 7.4%; 'added' passages — 6.9%.[12] These mean variations are not significantly different, which allows us to conclude that these 'added' passages will not skew our overall analysis of 1QIsa^a. However, it should be noted here that a general overview of the variations found in the 'added' passages shows that they are of similar type and frequency as those found elsewhere in 1QIsa^a II.

4. Verbal System

The first aspect of the linguistic character of 1QIsa^a that I will analyse is the verbal system. 1QIsa^a I contains 179 distinctive readings that involve a change to a verb (10.1%)[13] while in 1QIsa^a II we find 277 such variations (12.3%). These

---

[11] D. Longacre, 'Developmental Stage, Scribal Lapse, or Physical Defect? 1QIsa^a's Damaged Exemplar for Isaiah Chapters 34–66', *DSD* 20 (2013), 17–50.

[12] A one-sample two-tailed t-test has been used to compare the variation rate of the 'added' portions with the mean variation rates of 1QIsa^a, resulting in a P-value of twenty percent, which is well over the five percent threshold for statistical significance.

[13] Normalized to the total number of verbs in columns 1–27.

numbers are consistent with the overall trend of 1QIsa^a I containing less variation than 1QIsa^a II. In this section, I will focus on the one verbal system reading that I have identified as a PLV — *vav* plus imperfect. I will also briefly discuss the lack of QH characteristics within the verbal system of this manuscript.

In Chapter IV. B. 3., I argued that the *plene* scrolls, in contrast to the defective scrolls, contain significantly more readings of *vav* plus imperfect where the MT has a different form. Thus I concluded that *vav* plus imperfect is a PLV. 1QIsa^a I and II represent the *plene* scrolls well in this regard. 1QIsa^a I contains twenty-one distinctive readings of *vav* plus imperfect.[14] Just these distinctive readings account for 31% of all the *vav* plus imperfects in columns 1–27 of the Great Isaiah Scroll,[15] clearly a large increase in this form.

1QIsa^a II reveals a similar picture as the first half of this manuscript. In this section, there are thirty-nine distinctive readings of *vav* plus imperfect. While this is nearly double those that are in 1QIsa^a I, they still only account for 31% of the total occurrences of *vav* plus imperfect in columns 28-54.[16]

A helpful contrast to these findings is provided by a brief look at the distinctive readings of *vav* plus perfect. There are seventeen distinctive readings of *vav* plus perfect in 1QIsa^a I and twenty in 1QIsa^a II. These raw numbers do not appear to be significantly different than those presented for *vav* plus imperfect, especially for the first half of this manuscript. But, when this data is normalized to the number of *vav* plus perfects found in the scroll, the difference becomes apparent. 1QIsa^a I contains 313 total *vav* plus perfects and 1QIsa^a II has 89. Thus the distinctive readings found in each half of this scroll only account for 5.4% for the first half and 22% for the second half of the total *vav* plus perfects. The contrast between distinctive readings of *vav* plus imperfect and *vav* plus perfect is particularly striking in the first twenty-seven columns. The difference for the second half of this manuscript, while still showing more *vav* plus imperfect readings, is not as pronounced. One related comparison stands out as instructive. 1QIsa^a II contains twenty-nine *vav* plus imperfect readings where the MT does not have *vav*; yet this portion of 1QIsa^a only has *vav* plus perfect in contrast with the MT's perfect four times. This shows a clear trend towards 'adding' *vav*s to imperfects as opposed to perfects, which suggests a scribal preference for *vav* plus imperfect over other forms. These findings for 1QIsa^a are consistent with

---

14 On the other hand, we only find two places were 1QIsa^a has a different reading where the MT has *vav* plus imperfect.
15 There are a total of 61 occurrences of *vav* plus imperfect in columns 1–27 of 1QIsa^a.
16 There are a total of 124 occurrences of *vav* plus imperfect in columns 28–54 of 1QIsa^a.

the conclusions presented in Chapter IV. B. 3. where I showed that *vav* plus imperfect is a variant that can be linked to *plene* orthography manuscripts.

5. QH Characteristics and the Verbal System of 1QIsa^a

Kutscher, Qimron and Muraoka, along with others, have discussed developments in the verbal system of the Hebrew language that are seen in QH. Yet, the features that they discuss seem to have had very little influence upon the 'biblical' scrolls. Abegg argues just this point by saying: 'Surprisingly, an initial study that I undertook using the 20 syntactical categories in Qimron's Hebrew of the DSS revealed no discernible influence among the biblical scrolls'.[17] Qimron's work primarily centred upon the nonbiblical scrolls (although he used 'biblical' examples often), but Kutscher and Muraoka focused almost entirely on 'biblical' texts. Yet Abegg found that a number of their conclusions are not actually supported by the data. Both Kutscher and Muraoka concluded that 'the scribe of 1QIsa^a preferred the conjunctive *Waw* to the inversive *Waw* and tended to use the sc. (suffix conjugation) as a preterital tense and the pc. [prefixed conjugation] as a future tense'.[18] This conclusion seems to make sense as we would predict just such a movement away from the preterite based on its lack of use in the Mishnah, but there is actually little evidence for this avoidance in the 'biblical' scrolls. Abegg writes: 'The scribes of the biblical manuscripts, in general, show evidence of guarding rather than abandoning [the preterite]'.[19] The data from 1QIsa^a generally supports Abegg's argument, as will be seen here.

1QIsa^a I and II contain a combined six distinct variations away from the preterite and two towards it. This is out of the 207 total preterites found in 1QIsa^a. Those six readings against a preterite may have been caused by an avoidance of this form, but clearly 1QIsa^a does not contain any significant trend away from the preterite as Kutscher and Muraoka suggest.

There is more evidence for an avoidance of the conversive *vav* plus perfect than there is for the imperfect. There are thirty-two places in 1QIsa^a where the MT has a conversive *vav* plus a perfect where the scroll does not. The opposite seems to occur twenty-one times.[20] These variations can be placed in the context of 1QIsa^a containing a total of 1,232 perfects, thus showing just a 0.9%[21]

---

17 Abegg, 'The Biblical Dead Sea Scrolls', 165.
18 Muraoka, 'An Approach', 209.
19 Ibid., 167–8.
20 These numbers are only counting distinctive readings within 1QIsa^a. For a global analysis, see Chapter IV. 3. B.
21 21 pluses – 32 minuses = a decrease of just 11 perfect forms out of the total 1,232 found in this scroll.

'decrease' in the use of this form. These numbers do show a slight trend away from *vav* conversive plus perfect, but it is hardly as dramatic as one would have predicted based on trends found in nonbiblical literature.

Of the features of post-biblical Hebrew that might have influenced the language of the 'biblical' scrolls, we would have expected the shift away from the preterite to be the most pronounced. In fact, this prevalent postbiblical feature is hardly found at all in the 'biblical' scrolls, including 1QIsa[a]. It is then no surprise that other verbal system features discussed by Kutscher, Qimron and Muraoka also seem to have had little influence upon the 'biblical' scrolls. Here I will discuss three features: a) *qatal* expressing the future perfect in conditional sentences; b) the infinitive construct; and c) the infinitive absolute.

a. Qatal Expressing the Future Perfect in Conditional Sentences

Qimron argues that in QH the perfect takes the place of the imperfect in the apodosis of conditional sentences introduced by אם. He writes: 'The prevalence of this construction in DSS Hebrew is best demonstrated by the fact that when citing a biblical verse, Qumran scribes sometimes changed the verb in the protasis from imperfect to perfect'.[22] Qimron cites TS 66:4–5 and 4Q158 7:10 as examples of this phenomenon. Yet none of the eighteen places in the 'biblical' scrolls where the MT has an imperfect and the scroll has a perfect are found in conditional sentences beginning with אם. While this may be a feature of the linguistic character of the nonbiblical scrolls, it is clearly not distinctive of the 'biblical' scrolls.

b. The Infinitive Construct

Both Kutscher[23] and Muraoka[24] argue that the infinitive construct plus *lamed* was characteristic of the texts that they examined.[25] Yet, a comprehensive analysis reveals the 'biblical' scrolls only having slightly more *lamed* plus infinitives than the other witnesses. The 'biblical' scrolls contain seventeen *lamed* plus infinitives where the MT has a different form, twelve of which involve a plus of the *lamed* in the scroll. The Isaiah Scroll contains four of these variations, three of which are distinctive and all of which are found in the second half of the manuscript. By placing these numbers in the context of the 522 total (88 in 1QIsa[a]) infinitives

---

22 Qimron, *Hebrew*, 84–5.
23 Kutscher, *Language*, 193.
24 Muraoka, 'An Approach', 194.
25 For more on this topic, see Abegg, 'The Biblical Dead Sea Scrolls', 170.

construct that are not preceded by a *lamed* in the 'biblical' scrolls, we see how few *lamed*s are actually 'added' to infinitives. Again, this feature may be found in nonbiblical manuscripts, but it is clearly not characteristic of the 'biblical' scrolls.

c. The Infinitive Absolute

Standing in contrast to the supposed increase in the use of *lamed* plus infinitive construct, is the claim that the occurrences of the infinitive absolute decreased over time.[26] Abegg concludes that there is indeed a decrease in the use of the infinitive absolute within the 'biblical' scrolls when compared with the MT, specifically a 9.4% drop in the occurrences of this form.[27] A review of the data supports this conclusion. We do find a decrease in the use of infinitives absolute in the 'biblical' scrolls compared with other witnesses. Yet a closer analysis of the data shows that this fact does not support Muraoka's main thesis, which I will quote again here: 'The basic point of departure of my presentation is that one should be able to learn about the nature of Qumran Hebrew…by analysing cases where the Qumran Biblical texts differ and deviate from the standard biblical text, namely the MT'.[28] As I have argued above, not all the 'biblical' DSS reflect characteristics of QH. Since a mix of different groups likely produced these documents, we cannot claim that a decrease in the use of the infinitive absolute throughout the 'biblical' scrolls reflects on the language of one specific group. If the decrease in this form was found only or predominantly within *plene* orthography scrolls, we might be able to conclude that the language of one group or scribal school was being reflected, but that is not the case with the infinitive absolute. There are twenty-three occurrences of the MT having an infinitive absolute where the scroll has a different form (eighteen of which are distinctive). These variations are spread over four *plene* scrolls and three defective scrolls. This distribution suggests that the reduced usage of the infinitive absolute is a common scribal feature that might be connected to Second Temple scribal practices, but not specifically QH.[29]

This review of the linguistic character of the verbal system of the Isaiah Scroll, while brief, has highlighted the use of the *plene* linked variant *vav* plus imperfect. The higher rate of occurrence of this feature within this scroll is con-

---

26 Muraoka, 'An Approach', 195.
27 Abegg, 'The Biblical Dead Sea Scrolls', 170.
28 Muraoka, 'An Approach', 193.
29 Abegg suggests this with his title 'The Biblical Dead Sea Scrolls and Second Temple Hebrew Syntax', but he also draws the same connection between those scrolls and QH that Muraoka makes. See the introductory paragraphs in Abegg, 'The Biblical Dead Sea Scrolls', 164.

sistent with its *plene* orthographic nature. The use of this PLV stands in contrast to the lack of use of other features that some scholars have argued are characteristic of QH, such as an avoidance of the conversive *vav* and an increased use of *lamed* plus infinitive construct. These conclusions are consistent with the findings developed in Chapter IV. B. Individual variations between this scroll and other witnesses may have been caused by developments in the Hebrew language, but only the *vav* plus imperfect stands out as a consistent characteristic of this scroll.

6. Nominal System

The linguistic character of the nominal system of 1QIsa^a, like its verbal system character, is consistent with this scroll's full orthography. 1QIsa^a I and II both contain large numbers of the major nominal PLV identified in Chapter IV. C., plural nouns in place of singulars. Further, as I discussed in Chapter IV. C. 4., 1QIsa^a I presents a distinctive scribal practice amongst the 'biblical' scrolls in that it contains a significant number of readings of יהוה where the MT has a different reading. I will develop the interchange between plural and singular nouns below. The distinctive use of the divine name has been discussed in Chapter IV. C. 4.

As I discussed in the previous chapter, the *plene* 'biblical' scrolls contain significantly more variations than the defective scrolls where the scroll reads a plural noun while the MT has a singular, and thus I labelled this variation type a PLV. In relationship to this variation type, I discussed the significant number of occurrences of the long form of the 3ms suffix (יו) within the *plene* scrolls. The distinctive readings in 1QIsa^a I and II are consistent with these findings. In columns 1–27, we find 30 occurrences of this PLV and in columns 28–54 there are 34. The opposite variation, scroll plural — other witnesses singular, only occurs eight times in each half of this manuscript. This data shows a significant difference between 1QIsa^a and the other witnesses in their use of plural and singular nouns.

As I also discussed in Chapter IV. C. 1., this PLV is characterized, in most cases, by simply having a *yod* or *vav* where the MT does not. This trend is seen in 1QIsa^a. A *yod* or *vav* is the only difference in twenty-six out of the thirty places where this PLV occurs in 1QIsa^a I. The same is true for twenty-five out of the thirty-four instances of this PLV in 1QIsa^a II. Yet these two halves of this manuscript have differing characteristics when it comes to this feature.

The two most common forms of this variation type are found in these examples:

Long Form of the 3ms Suffix

1QIsa^a 40:29

ידיו

MT Isaiah 49:2

ידו

3fp Construct Noun in Place of 3fs Construct Noun

1QIsa^a 3:13

הכרות

MT Isaiah 3:9

הכרת

1QIsa^a I contains fifteen 3ms suffixes spelled יו and eleven 3fp construct nouns where the other witnesses have a 3fs construct noun. 1QIsa^a II stands in stark contrast to this. Columns 28–54 contain twenty 3ms suffixes spelled יו, which is similar to the first 27 columns. But, the interchange between 3fp construct noun and 3fs construct noun is not found at all in the second half of the Isaiah Scroll. There are 198 intact occurrences of a 3fs construct noun in 1QIsa^a II, so there appear to have been plenty of places where this variation type could have found its way in, but it did not. A second distinction between the two halves of 1QIsa^a is the distribution of the long form of the 3ms suffix. In 1QIsa^a, this spelling does not occur when suffixed to feminine nouns, while we find it six times on such nouns in the second half. Those distinctions between the two halves of 1QIsa^a are difficult to account for, but probably can be attributed to scribal preference.

This review of the nominal system has shown that the one nominal PLV is present in 1QIsa^a — plural nouns in the place of singular. That result, as was seen with the verbal system above, is consistent with the conclusion developed in Chapter IV. C. This high rate of PLV occurrence in 1QIsa^a continues into the final part of speech to be analysed here – the particle system.

7. Particles

Three PLVs are found in the particle system of the *plene* scrolls: a. distinctive use of the directive *he*, b. including מאדה; c. increased use of the conjunction *vav*; and d. the use of על in place of אל. In this section, I will analyse the occurrences of these PLVs in the Great Isaiah scroll, along with the following variation types that are not correlated with *plene* orthography; e. אל and ל; f. definite article; g. direct object marker; and h. paragogic *nun*.

a. Directive he

In Chapter IV. A. 1., I discussed the increased use of the directive *he* within the *plene* scrolls. This increase is most prominent with the word שם. Yet the opposite is actually true for proper nouns with which we find a decrease in the use of this particle. Both of these trends are found in 1QIsa[a].

1QIsa[a] I contains five directive *he*s that are not found in other witnesses. Two of these are attached to שם and two others are found on ממעל, which was also discussed in the previous chapter as being a fossilized lexeme common in Mishnaic Hebrew. This half of 1QIsa[a] only contains a total of twenty-one directive *he*s. Thus the five pluses represent a twenty-four percent increase over the parallel passages in the MT. These columns of the Isaiah Scroll do not have any distinctive minuses of the directive *he*.

In 1QIsa[a] II, we find eight occurrences of this PLV, six of which are on שם and another is attached to ממעל. These pluses account for forty-four percent of the total directive *he*s within the second half of 1QIsa[a]. These columns also contain three minuses of this particle, two of which are found on a proper noun. These pluses and minuses are consistent with the findings in Chapter IV. A. 1., and could be anticipated based on the full orthographic nature of this manuscript.

b. מאדה

While מאדה may only be a long morphological form of מאד, some have considered it to be the adverb מאד plus a directive *he*. Because of this I will included a brief review of its use in 1QIsa[a]. This construction is only found in *plene* scrolls, with one exception,[30] and therefore is strongly linked to full orthography. מאדה is found in 1QIsa[a] I two times and five times in 1QIsa[a] II. The short form of this adverb is only found once in this scroll (1QIsa[a] 13:23). As this data and the full review in Chapter IV. A. 2. shows, the occurrence of מאדה in a manuscript is strongly correlated to full orthography.

c. Conjunction Vav

As was argued in Chapter IV. A. 7., the *plene* scrolls contain significantly more pluses and minuses of the conjunction *vav* than the defective scrolls. This conclusion has led to labelling the conjunction *vav* a PLV. Thus the large number

---
30 4QpaleoExod[m]

Statistics, Linguistics and the 'Biblical' Dead Sea Scrolls

of pluses and minuses of this particle within both halves of 1QIsaᵃ is consistent with its full orthographic character. First I will review the data for pluses of the conjunction *vav*, and then I will consider the minuses.

In 1QIsaᵃ I, we find 81 pluses of the conjunction *vav*, and in 1QIsaᵃ II, there are 170.[31] These numbers result in variation rates of 6.5%[32] and 18%, respectively.[33] These rates can be compared with the mean variation rates of the defective scrolls — 2.7% — and the *plene* scrolls — 6.4%. The first half of 1QIsaᵃ is consistent with other *plene* manuscripts, and the second half contains nearly three times the average for this category. As would be expected, both halves are well above the average for the defective scrolls. Also of note is the high rate of distinctive readings of this type. Fifty-eight of the 81 pluses of *vav* in the first half and 131 of the 170 in the second half are distinctive to this scroll. Even focusing just on these readings, the variation rate for both halves are well above the mean for the defective scrolls, 4.6% and 13.8% respectively.

Similar to the data found for the pluses of the conjunction *vav*, there are a large number of minuses of this conjunction. The first half of 1QIsaᵃ contains forty-one minuses, and the second half contains sixty. This results in variation rates of 3.49% and 4.71%, respectively. These numbers are lower than the overall variation rate for the *plene* scrolls, which is 7.53%, but still above the average for the defective scrolls — 2.89%. These findings, as well as those for the pluses, are consistent with its very full orthographic character and the link found above between pluses and minuses of the conjunction *vav* and the *plene* scrolls.

d. אל *and* על

The 'biblical' scrolls present a mix of readings between אל and על, yet the *plene* scrolls contain more distinctive readings of על where the other witnesses have אל. As I discussed in Chapter IV. A. 5., there are sixteen such variations in the 'biblical' scrolls, and twelve of them are found in *plene* manuscripts. Of these twelve variations, four are located in 1QIsaᵃ I and three in II. This data is very limited, but it does suggest a possible link between *plene* scrolls and the preposition על.

The same link is not found between *plene* scrolls and the preposition אל. This variation is found spread across both *plene* and defective scrolls.[34] Yet 1QIsaᵃ

---

31 These numbers include all variations, not just distinctive readings to this scroll, allowing for a clearer comparison with other manuscripts.
32 There are 1,256 total conjunction *vav*s in columns 1–27 of 1QIsaᵃ.
33 There are 947 total conjunction *vav*s in columns 28–54 of 1QIsaᵃ.
34 See Chapter IV. A. 5. for a full review of this variation type.

contains nearly an equal number of interchanges from אל to על and על to אל. In both halves of 1QIsaᵃ, we find four places where the scroll reads אל where the other witnesses have על. Thus the interchange between על to אל does not reveal much about the linguistic character of 1QIsaᵃ, except for the possible link between על readings and *plene* orthography.

e. אל *and* ל

The interchange between אל and ל is relatively rare.[35] A comparison between the 'biblical' DSS and the MT reveals only twelve occurrences of a scroll having אל with the MT having ל. The opposite is found nine times. This is a very low variation rate considering that there are a total of 4,303 intact ל in the 'biblical' Scrolls and 1,288 occurrences of אל, resulting in variation rates of 0.3% and 0.7% respectively. Yet as is seen in Table 54, the usage of these prepositions throughout Ancient Hebrew may suggest a possible diachronic shift.[36]

	אל	ל	Ratio
EBH	292	215	1 to 0.74
LBH	17	56	1 to 3.29
Qumran	20	143	1 to 7.15
Mishnah	3	684	1 to 228

Table 54. The Use of אל and ל in the Phrase 'and He Said to Him'

In the EBH books, אל is used more often than ל in the phrase 'and he said to him' at a ratio of 1 to 0.74. The LBH books have a ratio of 1 to 3.29 and by the time of the Mishnah the preposition ל has become the dominant choice for use in this phrase, while אל is only used three times. This data suggests a shift away from using אל in favour of ל. If this brief review is correct, then the three occurrences of the preposition ל in 1QIsaᵃ, where other witnesses have אל, may be explain based on a diachronic shift in the use of these particles.

The three variations involving a shift from אל to ל might be explained diachronically, but they cannot be connected to the *plene* orthography of the scroll, as a review of the data will show. This variation occurs twelve times in the 'biblical' scrolls. These variations are found in 1QIsaᵃ and 4QSamᵃ (*plene* scrolls) and 2QRuthᵃ, 4QGen-Exodᵃ, 4QpaleoExodᵐ and 4QPsᵇ (defective scrolls). The fact that this variation is found in both *plene* and defective scrolls suggest that the interchange between these two prepositions is not correlated to

---

35 Variations between ל and אל were not specifically covered in section IV. A. due to this rarity.
36 Sáenz-Badillos, *A History*, 117.

the orthographic nature of the scroll. Yet it still speaks to the general linguistic character of 1QIsaᵃ.

f. Definite Article

In Chapter IV. A. 3., I argued that variations involving the definite article are not correlated with the orthographic character of a scroll. Further, I noted that Kutscher was likely in error when he argued that the definite article is added and omitted more often on words beginning with *aleph, he, khet* or *ayin*. At the end of this analysis, I concluded that a wide range of factors might be responsible for the pluses and minuses of the definite article such as historical development of texts, exegetical scribal intervention, linguistic development, scribal error, as well as other possible factors. Yet no patterns of scribal intervention are clear. Two examples from 1QIsaᵃ will help to demonstrate the inconsistent use of this particle.

Five of the twenty pluses of the definite article found in 1QIsaᵃ I are on the noun ארץ. In the ninth column of this manuscript, we find a good example of this variation:

1QIsaᵃ 1:2

שמעו שמים והאזיני הארץ

MT Isaiah 1:2

שמעו שמים והאזיני ארץ

In this passage we find 1QIsaᵃ reading הארץ, while the other witnesses (represented here by the MT) do not have the definite article. This type of variation might lead one to conclude that the scribe of this manuscript preferred to precede 'land' with 'the'. Yet the opposite variation is found twice in 1QIsaᵃ I. A good illustration of this is found just two columns after the previous example:

1QIsaᵃ 11:17–18

הנה יום יהוה בא אגזרי ועברה וחרון אף לשום ארץ

MT Isaiah 13:9

הנה יום־יהוה בא אכזרי ועברה וחרון אף לשום הארץ

The contrast between these two examples represents well the inconsistent use of the definite article article within the first half of 1QIsaᵃ. A similar situation is found in the second half of this scroll, demonstrated by the following two examples:

1QIsaᵃ 28:3

ונמסו ההרים מדמם

MT Isaiah 34:3

מדמם הרים ונמסו

1QIsaᵃ 52:5–6

קטור[ו] על הרים

MT Isaiah 65:7

קטרו על־ההרים

In these two passages, we find 1QIsaᵃ reading ההרים first and then הרים. In both cases, the other witnesses disagree with the scroll. These examples are consistent with the overall use of the definite article within the second half of 1QIsaᵃ, which contains both pluses and minuses of this particle. However, these columns contain more than twice as many pluses as opposed to minuses, twenty three and nine respectively. This is likely due to this scribe's expanding tendencies. The above examples and this brief review of the data reinforce the inconsistent nature of this manuscript with regard to the definite article.

g. Direct Object Marker

Scholars such as Kutscher[37] and Fassberg[38] argue that late writers of Hebrew increasingly used the direct object marker. In Chapter IV. A. 4., I argued that this characteristic of later stages of Hebrew did not consistently influence the 'biblical' scrolls, but might be the cause of specific variations or trends within manuscripts. This seems to be the case with 1QIsaᵃ. A brief review of the data suggests that the scribe of this manuscript (or his *Vorlage*) used the direct object marker more often than the other witnesses. Since, as I concluded previously, this variation type is not correlated with *plene* orthography, a diachronic explanation seems plausible.

1QIsaᵃ I contains five pluses of the direct object marker all of which are distinctive to this witness. 1QIsaᵃ II has eleven pluses and three minuses. All of the pluses in this half of the scroll are distinctive, while this is true for only one of the minuses. This data represents a particular linguistic style found in this scroll, which might be explainable based on the diachronic development of this particle within the Hebrew language.

h. Paragogic Nun

In reference to the paragogic *nun*, Qimron states: 'The biblical texts from Qumran differ from MT in the use of this form; in most cases they prefer the form ו (even where MT has ן), as do the late biblical books and the Samaritan Penta-

---

37 Kutscher, *Language*, 412–23.
38 Fassberg, 'The Syntax of the Biblical Documents', 103.

teuch'.³⁹ Yet, this conclusion is not supported by the data. In eighteen places, the 'biblical' scrolls do not contain a paragogic *nun* where the MT does, while the opposite is found eight times. This appears to suggest a tendency on behalf of the 'biblical' scrolls to avoid this form, but closer analysis shows that one particular manuscript heavily skews the data, 1QIsa^a II. Columns 28–54 of 1QIsa^a contain ten of the eighteen minuses of the paragogic *nun* found in the scrolls.⁴⁰ On the other hand, 1QIsa^a II does not contain any pluses of the paragogic *nun*. As the quote from Qimron above suggests, these variations may have been caused by the influence of diachronic changes in Hebrew.⁴¹

8. Conclusion

This analysis of the particle system, as well as the nominal and verbal systems, in 1QIsa^a I and II has shown a connection between the full orthographic style of these texts and the occurrences of PLVs such as *vav* plus imperfects, plural over singular nouns and increased use of the directive *he*. These findings are consistent with the conclusions of Chapter IV. A., which found a global connection between the orthographic character of a manuscript and PLVs. The above discussion also highlights the many variation types that are not correlated with *plene* orthography (the use of definite articles and direct object markers) as well as the lack of some variation types that we would have expected based on the discussion in the secondary literature such as the avoidance of the preterite. Thus the review of 1QIsa^a I and II has supported the conclusions reached in the previous chapter. Now I will turn to analysing the linguistic nature of our next scroll, 1QIsa^b.

B. 1QIsa^b

I will now analyse 1QIsa^b, which uses a defective orthographic style, in order to provide a contrast with 1QIsa^a I and II, both of which use a full orthographic style. This analysis will be similar to above, proceeding in six parts: 1. orthography; 2. textual character; 3. verbal system; 4. nominal system; 5. particle system; and 6. conclusions.

---

39   Qimron, *Hebrew*, 45.
40   Only five other manuscripts contain a minus of the paragogic *nun*: 1QIsa^a I, 11Q5, 4Q14, 4Q30, 4Q86.
41   This conclusion holds if the lack of paragogic *nun*s is to be considered a late feature of Hebrew, as a number of scholars argue. See Ehrensvärd, 'Biblical Texts', 181–2, as well as Sáenz-Badillos, *A History*, 142.

Chapter V The Linguistic Character of Individual Scrolls

1. Orthography

The orthographic nature of 1QIsa[b] is similar to that which is found in the MT, as Ulrich, Flint and Abegg describe: '[T]he orthographic practice of 1QIsa[b] displays widespread agreement with that transmitted in MT[L] ... The fuller spelling is found now in 1QIsa[b], now in MT, in roughly equal measure'.[42] In comparison with a manuscript such as 1QIsa[a] which has a relatively full orthographic style, this manuscript should be considered to be on the defective side of the spectrum. In the previous chapter, I concluded that defective manuscripts in general contain less PLVs than *plene* manuscripts. Therefore, we should expect 1QIsa[b] to contain relatively few PLVs based on its orthographic style.

2. Textual Character

Ulrich, Flint and Abegg conclude that '[o]n the whole, 1QIsa[b] shows close agreement with MT[L], MT[Q], MT[mss] and Targum, which classifies it as belonging to the textual group that eventually emerges as the Masoretic family'.[43] Yet even with this close connection to the MT tradition, there are still a large number of variations that are useful for analysis. In total, there are 198 variations between 1QIsa[b] and the MT. Of these I will focus on the 103 readings that are only found in 1QIsa[b]: 30 from the verbal system, 26 from the nominal system and 47 from the particle system.

3. Verbal System

In Chapter IV. B. 3., I concluded that *vav* plus imperfect qualified as a PLV. That result suggests that 1QIsa[b], as a defective scroll, should contain very few of these readings when compared with other witnesses, and this is exactly what is found. 1QIsa[b] contains three readings of *vav* plus imperfect where the other witnesses have a different reading.[44] This is out of a total of 49 *vav* plus imperfects found in this manuscript resulting in a variation rate of 6.12%. This is far lower than the 39.35% variation rate for this category found in 1QIsa[a], which supports the conclusion developed in Chapter IV. B. 3.

---

42 Ulrich and Flint (eds), *The Isaiah Scrolls*, 200.
43 Ibid., 208.
44 1Q8 20:3; 1Q8 20:4; 1Q8 f10:8

4. Nominal System

a. Singular and Plural

Plene scrolls contain one nominal system characteristic that the defective scrolls lack, namely readings of plural nouns where the other witnesses have singular nouns. This is particularly true when the difference between the two is simply a *vav* or a *yod* such as ידיו instead of ידו or הכרות in place of הכרת. In the previous section, I showed that 1QIsaᵃ contains a large number of this PLV, just as would be expected based on its *plene* orthographic character. In contrast, we find very few of these variations in 1QIsaᵇ. This manuscript has four variations that involve a change from a singular noun to a plural noun. In only one of these cases do we find the plural noun in 1QIsaᵇ. This is of course consistent with the conclusion of Chapter IV. C. 1. above.

b. Names for God

Also in Chapter IV. C. 4., I found that the *plene* scrolls contain significantly more variations involving a name for God than the defective scrolls. The data from 1QIsaᵇ supports this conclusion. In this manuscript, there are only two variations of this type, including: 1Q8 16:3, where the scroll reads יהוה and the MT has אדני, and 1Q8 26:33, with a reading of יהוה אלהים in the scroll and אדני יהוה in the MT.

5. Particle System

In Chapter IV. A., I concluded that variations involving the directive *he*, shifts toward על away from אל, as well as pluses and minuses of the conjunction *vav* can be considered PLVs. 1QIsaᵇ contains forty-five distinct variations involving particles; yet it does not contain any pluses of the directive *he*. Further, this manuscript is mixed in its readings of אל and על. It reads אל in four places where other manuscripts have על. The opposite is found in three places. Finally, 1QIsaᵇ has a variation rate of 3.13% for pluses of the conjunction and 2.98% for minuses, close to the mean variation rates for the defective scrolls of 2.6% and 2.89%, respectively. This data is consistent with the defective orthographic character of this scroll.

6. Conclusions

The above analysis of the variations found in 1QIsaᵇ has shown there to be very few PLVs in this manuscript. This analysis has proven to be a good contrast to

1QIsaᵃ, in which many PLVs are found. These results are consistent with the conclusions from Chapter IV, which predicts that defective scrolls will contain few PLVs, while PLVs will be found consistently in *plene* scrolls. In order to further test the results of Chapter IV, I will now turn to another *plene* scroll, 4QNumᵇ. This analysis is particularly necessary as 1QIsaᵃ may simply be distinctive in its use of PLVs. However, the conclusions of Chapter IV will be strengthened if PLVs are also found in other *plene* scrolls.

C. 4QNumᵇ

In this section, I will analyse the distinctive readings found in 4QNumᵇ. This analysis will show that the types of variations found in this manuscript (three of which are PLVs) correlate closely with its full orthographic profile. I will start with a brief review of the orthographic and textual character of 4QNumᵇ and then I will analyse the distinctive readings found in this scroll in three sections: the verbal system; the nominal system; and the particle system.

1. Orthography

According to Ulrich and Cross, the orthography of 4QNumᵇ is 'very full, including such forms as לוא, כול, ויואמר and is quite consistent'.[45] As has been shown in Chapter IV above, many scrolls that contain a full orthographic style also contain specific readings that are not found often in defective scrolls. 4QNumᵇ is one of those *plene* scrolls.

2. Textual Character

4QNumᵇ has a rather varied textual character. Ulrich and Cross state that '[t]he array of readings in 4QNumᵇ sets up a remarkable pattern of correlations with the other textual witnesses of the book of Numbers'.[46] Ulrich and Cross develop the textual character of this manuscript further by saying:

> If the variants are counted rather than weighed, 4QNumᵇ appears to be roughly equidistant from each of the other traditions…. If the variants are weighed, however, rather than merely counted, it becomes clearer that 4QNumᵇ, the SP, and the LXX share more significant secondary readings than 4QNumᵇ and the MT and thus are more closely related.[47]

---

45 E. Ulrich et al. (eds), *Qumran Cave 4, Volume 7: Genesis to Numbers* (DJD 12, Oxford 1994), 212.
46 Ibid., 213.
47 Ibid., 215.

The varied textual character of 4QNum^b reinforces the advantages of analysing only distinctive variations.

3. Verbal System

4QNum^b contains nine, possibly ten, variations involving the verbal system. This is out of the 333 intact verbs found in this manuscript. These variations highlight the relationship that this manuscript has with the other textual witnesses, especially the SP and LXX. In two places, 4QNum^b agrees with SP and LXX against MT. In three places, this manuscript agrees with SP against the other witnesses, and in three other places it agrees with the LXX against the SP and MT. We only find one distinctive reading in 4QNum^b that involves a verb — נסע for נסעו in Num. 11:35. If one assumes a genetic relationship between these witnesses based on these shared readings, then there is little room to analyse the linguistic nature of the verbal system of 4QNum^b. Even if one sets aside *Vorlage* issues and assumes the scribe of this manuscript caused these readings, there is little evidence of a pattern of change. In two places, 4QNum^b has a plural verb against a singular, and in two others we find the opposite. In one place, 4QNum^b has a perfect against an imperfect, in two places a verb is added, and the final variation simply has a conjunction *vav* attached to a perfect where the other witnesses only have the verb.

The increase of *vav* plus simple imperfects, the only pattern of variation within the verbal system of the 'biblical' DSS that was found to be a PLV, is not found at all in this manuscript. While the scribe of this scroll seems to have intentionally used a very full orthographic and morphological style, it seems that he did not change the linguistic character of the verbal system found in his *Vorlage*.

4. Nominal System

In contrast to the verbal system of 4QNum^b, the nominal system has far more distinctive readings. Nine of the twenty-five variations found in the nominal system of this manuscript are not paralleled in any other witness. However, these variations do not include any PLVs. Yet, a brief discussion of 4QNum^b's use of suffixes helps us to better understand the linguistic character of this scroll.

Of the nine distinctive nominal system variations found in 4QNum^b, three involve pluses of pronouns and suffixes. I will briefly analyse each here.

Numbers 13:18 and in 13:20 contain very similar constructions involving pronouns. In both cases, 4QNum^b contains a pronoun where the other witnesses do not.

Num. 13:18
4Q27 f3ii+5:7–5:8
החזק הוא]ה ואם[רפה ה]ו[אה

MT
החזק הוא הרפה

Num. 13:20
4Q27 f3ii+5:10
ומה הארץ השמנה היאה ו]אם רזה היאה

MT
ומה הארץ השמנה הוא אם־רזה

In both of these examples, 4QNum^b contains a pronoun in the parallel phrase, while the MT only has a pronoun in the first phrase. Thus the scroll reads, 'whether it is strong or it is weak' and 'whether it is fat or it is lean' with two pronouns, while the MT reads 'whether it is strong or weak' and 'whether it is fat or lean' with only one pronoun.

If the scribe of 4QNum^b added these pronouns to the text, it is difficult to identify the motivation behind the changes. However, it appears that the scribe may have simply been smoothing out the text by making the two halves of the clause consistent. The third example involves a plus of a suffix:

Num. 30:5
4Q27 f3ii+5:10
...]יק[ימנו

MT
וכל־אסר אשר־אסרה על־נפשה יקום

This variation is found at the beginning of a line that is preceded by two missing lines in 4QNum^b. Those missing lines may have provided some clues as to how this phrase should be understood, but since that context is lost, any conclusion must be considered tenuous. With that said, this suffix may have been the result of a difference between the scribe's language and the language of his *Vorlage*. Yet the possible *hifil*[48] form of the verb would require an object, which is provided by the suffix. Further, a parallel passage in verse fourteen may have influenced the scribe's copying of this section. Numbers 30:14 reads as follows in

---

48 'The reading ימנו]יק[is not certain. The traces would fit an erroneous form ומם]יק[. Such a form might have been produced by a scribe who committed a dittography of one letter with two forms (medial and final *mem*), perhaps influenced by the alternate readings יקומו and יקום'. Ibid., 249.

the MT (it is not intact in 4QNum^b): וכל־שבעת אסר לענת נפש אישה יקימנו. Because of this parallel passage and the possible *hifil* form of the verb, this suffix is not likely to have been added based on linguistic pressures.[49]

This review of the nominal system of 4QNum^b reveals that the scribe likely added pronouns and suffixes in order to linguistically smooth out his text. Linguistic smoothing does not appear to be connected to the orthographic character of this manuscript, but the above discussion does elucidate the general linguistic character of 4QNum^b. In contrast to the verbal system and nominal system of 4QNum^b, which do not contain any PLVs, the particle system of this manuscript does.

5. Particles

The use of particles within this manuscript reflects more upon the linguistic character of 4QNum^b than the verbal system or the nominal system. I will focus on six types of variations where a linguistic cause is a possible explanation: a. plus of the directive *he*; b. the form מאדה; c. pluses of the conjunction *vav*; d. לא – אל, e. ל – אל; and f. pluses of the direct object marker. The first three of these types of variations have been identified as PLVs, while the other three may have a diachronic explanation.

a. Directive he

The directive *he* is a plus in 4QNum^b twice, once at f3ii+5:13 where the scroll reads שמה while the MT has שם. The second occurrence is found at f75_79:27 with the scroll reading ימה and the MT having ים. The form שמה may be explained based on linguistic factors. As is discussed above in section IV. A. 1., *plene* scrolls contain significantly more pluses of the directive *he* than the defective scrolls. More specifically, the variation שמה versus שם is not found in any defective scroll while occurring twenty-one times in *plene* scrolls. Thus this form can be considered a PLV. Further, 4QNum^b's reading of שמה here is paralleled in 4QRP, which also has a full orthographic style. This suggests that the long form שמה, as found in 4QNum^b, is correlated with its full orthography.

b. מאדה

In section IV. A. 2., I discussed the long form of מאדה and its correlation with the *plene* scrolls. This long form is found almost exclusively in *plene* scrolls.

---

49 Three further variations could possibly be explained based on parallel passage in Numbers: 27:22 – יהושע בן נון 4Q27, יהושע - MT (see 20:13, 26:65; 27:18; 32:12, 28; 34:17; and 36:4 - 4Q27); 35:21 – הו[א] הדם 4Q47, הדם - MT (see 35:19); 36:6 (see 30:7).

Chapter V The Linguistic Character of Individual Scrolls

Further, the short form is found predominately in defective scrolls, seventeen times to six occurrences in *plene* scrolls. This correlation between the long form of מאדה and full orthography suggests that the two occurrences of this form in 4QNum[b] were caused by linguistic factors and are likely linked to this manuscript's full orthographic style.

c. Conjunction Vav

4QNum[b] contains two pluses of the conjunction *vav*:

Num. 13:19

4Q27 f3ii+5:9–10

הב[מחנים] ואם במב[צ]ר[י]ם

MT

הבמחנים אם במבצרים

Num. 26:15

4Q27 3ii_40:14

ובניגד

MT

בני גד

In section IV. A. 7., I discussed the variations involving *vav* and concluded that the *plene* scrolls contain statistically more pluses and minuses of *vav* than the defective scrolls. This pattern may account for the two pluses of *vav* seen in 4QNum[b]. In both of these cases, it seems that the scribe was utilizing the *vav* as a form of punctuation. The *vav* in the first example is functioning with the conjunction אם to differentiate between two prepositional phrases that are being presented as options. The *vav* in the second example serves to mark the beginning of a new clause.[50] This use of the conjunction *vav* can be considered a PLV. Therefore, the variations in 4QNum[b] involving *vav* can be linked to its orthographic character.

d. לא - אל

In two places 4QNum[b] has the negation אל where the MT has לא. Both are found in Num 22:12 which reads as follows:

4Q27 f20_22:6a

אל] תלך ע[ם האנשים ואל [תאו]ר את העם

---

50 For a full discussion of the conjunction *vav* being used as punctuation, see W.H. Brownlee, *The Meaning of the Qumran Scrolls for the Bible* (Oxford 1964), 180.

MT

לא תלך עמהם לא תאר את־העם

These variations are distinctive for two reasons. First, these are the only two variations of their type[51] in the entire 'biblical' DSS corpus, and second, research on the interchange between these two terms in QH would have predicted a lot more variation between these two negations. I will briefly develop both of these points here.

The low rate of variation between אל and לא is rather surprising. We find only 3 such variations in the scrolls; yet these 2 words occur a total of 1,557 times. This is a variation rate of only 0.2%. This is far lower than the overall variation rate of 5.44%. As a comparison we can consider the interchange between the prepositions אל and על. There are a total of 71 such variations out of 1,286 occurrences of these prepositions resulting in a variation rate of 5.5%. This is far closer to the overall variation rate than the rate observed with the two negations אל and לא. This would seem to suggest a level of stability in the usage of these two terms.

This stability stands in contrast to the diversity observed by Qimron in the nonbiblical DSS. Qimron writes: 'Characteristic of DSS Hebrew is the use of the negative particle אל where לא might have been expected'.[52] A comparison of the use of אל and לא in EBH, LBH, the nonbiblical DSS and the Mishnah supports Qimron's conclusion (although it does not support a diachronic interpretation).

	אל	לא	Ratio
EBH	200	1628	1 to 8.1
LBH	45	449	1 to 10
DSS	397	1690	1 to 4.3
Mishnah	113	3920	1 to 34.7

Table 55. The Use of אל and ל in Hebrew Corpora

The data in Table 55 reveals two things. First, there does not seem to be a diachronic trend towards using אל in place of לא. In fact, the Mishnah uses אל significantly less than any other corpus. Second, and this supports Qimron's conclusion, the nonbiblical DSS use אל nearly twice as much as EBH books and 2.5 times as much as LBH books. Yet this characteristic does not seem to have impacted the overall linguistic character of the 'biblical' DSS. While there is little evidence that this aspect of QH impacted the 'biblical' DSS, it is possible that these two variations in 4QNum[b] were brought about by the influence of this development.

---

51 The opposite variation is found in 4Q56 f2:7.
52 Qimron, *Hebrew*, 80.

e. ל - אל

Another variation that involves prepositions found in 4QNum^b is the interchange between אל and ל. The one variation of this type in 4QNum^b is found at Num 22:16:

4Q27 f20_22:9

ויבואו אל בלעם[ו]יואמרו אליו

MT

ויבאו אל־בלעם ויאמרו לו

As was discussed above in section V. A. 7. e., the interchange between אל and ל may have developed due to a diachronic shift in the Hebrew language. This shift, while apparently not having a large impact upon the 'biblical' scrolls, may account for the one variation between אל and ל found in 4QNum^b. At some point in the history of this text, a scribe may have come across ו[יואמרו אליו, decided that אל was not the appropriate preposition to use, and substituted ל. Another possible explanation is archaization. A scribe may have wanted to use what he believed to be an archaic form in order to make his manuscript more 'biblical'. There are likely other possible explanations, but whatever the case is, the data presented above suggests that it is the MT that has the newer form, not 4QNum^b.

f. Direct Object Marker

4QNum^b contains four[53] pluses of the direct object marker where it is not found in other witnesses. This is 5.8% more direct object markers than are found in the parallel passages in the MT. This scroll also has one place where it is lacking a direct object marker where the MT has one, which is 1.5% of the total number of direct object markers in this scroll. These variation rates are consistent with the overall rates for this term in all the 'biblical' DSS, with 66 pluses (3.45%) and 22 omissions (1.15%). The thorough analysis of these variations presented in section IV. A. 4. demonstrated that the variations involving the direct object marker do not correlate with full or defective orthography, and thus each variation should be considered on a case-by-case basis.

Linguistic pressures may have caused these variations. As was noted in section IV. A. 4., some scholars have argued that the use of the direct object marker increased over time in ancient Hebrew.[54] Yet if this diachronic approach was

---

53 Two of the four cases of pluses are also paralleled in other witnesses, so they will be excluded for the purposes of this study, except for in the general comments on the data.

54 See section IV. A. 4. for full discussion and references.

accepted in the variations found in 4QNum^b, one would have to argue that this manuscript contains two new features and one older feature. If there was a clear pattern in either direction, a diachronic explanation might be plausible, but as the data stands, we must agree with Tov when he states that 'the *nota accusativi* is freely added or omitted in all textual sources'.[55]

6. Conclusion

The above analysis of the linguistic character of 4QNum^b has demonstrated that this scroll does not contain variations reflecting linguistic changes in the verbal system or nominal system. On the other hand, this analysis does show distinct shifts in 4QNum^b's use of particles, some of which can be correlated with its orthographic and morphological nature. Some of the variations found in 4QNum^b do not align with a *plene* orthographic style, such as the plus of the direct object marker and the use of אל instead of לא. Pluses of the direct object marker as well as interchanges between אל and לא, as found in 4QNum^b, could have developed due to diachronic changes in the Hebrew language. But, some readings such as שמה and מאדה, as well as pluses of *vav*, are found in significant proportions in *plene* scrolls. All three of these types of variations are found in 4QNum^b and can likely be correlated with this scroll's full orthographic character. At the beginning of this chapter, I hypothesized that scrolls with full orthography would also use PLVs. The appearance of three PLVs in 4QNum^b supports that hypothesis.

D. 4QSam^a

In the above sections, I analysed 4QNum^b, which has a full orthographic style, and concluded that it also uses three PLVs. This supports the hypothesis proposed at the beginning of this chapter, which predicted that *plene* scrolls would contain PLVs. In this section, I will analyse 4QSam^a to see if the proposed hypothesis continues to hold true.

The linguistic character of 4QSam^a can be characterized as 'mixed'. Its orthography, as discussed below, stands somewhere between that of the MT and the Mishnah, being full at times, while at others not containing those 'late' features found in other Qumran documents. The linguistic evidence for this mixed nature goes beyond that of orthography and morphology. This manuscript contains numerous examples of mixed readings, from the verbal system to the nom-

---

55 Tov, *Scribal Practices*, 204.

Chapter V The Linguistic Character of Individual Scrolls

inal system to its use of particles. In the following section, I will review these three aspects of the linguistic character of 4QSam[a] after providing a brief description of its orthographic and textual character.

1. Orthography

The orthography of 4QSam[a] can be considered mixed as Cross develops when stating: 'The orthographic usage exhibits what has been called late orthography, a fuller notation than that of the MT of the Pentateuch — or Masoretic Samuel — but not so full as the orthography of the Mishnah'.[56] This varied orthographic style of 4QSam[a] is demonstrated by the mixed use of לוא and לא, כוא and כי, and כול and כל as well as a number of other forms.

2. Textual Character

Ulrich summarizes the textual character of 4QSam[a] by stating: 'Above all, the study of the full manuscript has reinforced our early conclusion that 4QSam[a] stands in the same general tradition as the Hebrew text upon which the Old Greek translation was based'.[57] This correlation reinforces the need to work only with those readings that are distinctive to this manuscript. If we relied upon only a comparison between 4QSam[a] and the MT, our understanding of the linguistic character of this scroll would be missing a large piece of the picture. By only focusing upon distinctive readings we are able to separate, to some extent, the examination of linguistic elements from considerations of *Vorlagen*.

3. Verbal System

The character of the verbal system of 4QSam[a], just as its orthographic character, is mixed. While this manuscript contains some features that can be correlated with the *plene* scrolls, such as *vav* plus imperfects in the place of other verbal forms, 4QSam[a] also contains readings that present the opposite characteristics. The verbal system of 4QSam[a] contains two examples of this mixed character: a. the interchange between *vav* plus imperfects and preterites for other verb forms; and b. the interchange between singular and plural verbs.

a. Interchanges Between Vav Plus Imperfects and Preterites for Other Verb Forms

4QSam[a] contains three places where the scroll has a *vav* plus imperfect or a pret-

---

56 Ulrich et al. (eds), *Qumran Cave 4, Volume 7: Genesis to Numbers*, 6.
57 Ibid., 25.

erite and the MT has a different verb form. The opposite is seen in four places. The following examples demonstrate this mixed character well.

2 Sam. 8:2

4Q51 f80_83:2

ומדד] שני חבלים

MT

וימדד שני־חבלים

In 2 Sam. 8:2, 4QSamᵃ contains the reading ומדד, a *vav* plus perfect, while the MT reads וימדד, a preterite. The following example presents the opposite.

1 Sam. 2:22

4Q51 3a_e:13

וישמע] את [אשר [עו]שים

MT

ושמע את כל־אשר יעשון

In 1 Sam. 2:22, 4QSamᵃ reads וישמע, a preterite, while the MT reads, ושמע, a *vav* plus perfect. This is just the opposite of what was seen above in 2 Sam. 8:2. In total, 4QSamᵃ contains two preterites and one *vav* plus imperfect where the MT has a different reading. This is paralleled by the opposite situation, where this manuscript has a different verbal form where in three places the MT has a preterite and one place where it has *vav* plus imperfect. Again, this reveals a mixed linguistic character.

As was shown above in section IV. B. 3., the *plene* scrolls contain significantly more *vav* plus imperfect/preterite readings against the MT's reading than are seen in the defective scrolls. This shows that a *plene* orthographic style can be correlated with shifts to *vav* plus imperfect and shifts to preterites. Logically then, the mixed character of 4QSamᵃ is consistent with these findings. Since this scroll contains a mix of *plene* and defective readings, we would also expect it to contain a mix of shifts to and shifts away from *vav* plus imperfect and preterites. This is exactly the situation that we find.

b. Interchange Between Singular and Plural Verbs

4QSamᵃ also shows some inconsistency in its use of singular and plural verbs when compared with the other witnesses.[58] This manuscript contains six singular verbs where the MT has plural verbs. This can be seen in the following example:

---

58 However, any conclusions in this section need to be taken with caution as some of the readings are uncertain and some of the subjects of the verbs could be either plural or singular.

Chapter V The Linguistic Character of Individual Scrolls

2 Sam. 3:2
4Q51 f55_57a_b+58:7
ויולד לדויד בנים

MT
וילדו לדוד בנים

In this passage, we find the MT construing the subject 'sons' as plural by using a plural verb, while 4QSam^a uses a singular verb. In contrast, we also find two places where 4QSam^a has plural verbs where the MT has singular. The following is one of those places:

2 Sam. 8:2
4Q51 f80_83:1[59]
ויה]יו מואב [ל]דויד לעבדים

MT
ותהי מואב לדוד לעבדים

Even though 4QSam^a's reading is reconstructed, it seems likely that this scroll contains the plural and thus construes מואב as plural while the MT has a singular verb. Some scholars have argued that the construal of collective nouns as plurals is a late feature of Hebrew.[60] If this is the case, then 4QSam^a contains six 'early' features (singular verb with plural subject) and two 'late' features (plural verbs with plural subjects).

The interchanges between *vav* plus imperfect and preterites with other verbal forms has been identified as a PLV in Chapter IV. B. 6. 4QSam^a's mixed use of this PLV, supports the hypothesis that scrolls with mixed orthography will also contain mixed linguistic features in other parts of speech. The mixed character of 4QSam^a is also seen in its construal of singular and plural subjects.

4. Nominal System

The nominal system of 4QSam^a also presents a mixed linguistic character. This is seen in the following two types of variations: a. singular and plural interchanges; and b. pluses and minuses of suffixes. I will review each of these here.

a. Interchanges Between Singular and Plural

In section IV. C. 1., I argued that the *plene* scrolls contain significantly more

---

59 Cross notes: '4QSam^a reads either יו[היה or, less likely, י[ויה'. Ibid., 133.
60 See Hurvitz, A Linguistic Study, 165; Polzin, Late Biblical Hebrew, 40–2, and Young, ''Am Construed as Singular and Plural', 29–63, idem ''Edah and Qahal as Collective Nouns', 68–78.

shifts to plural nouns than the defective scrolls. This is especially true for shifts to plurals that require only an additional *yod* or *vav*, such as when a masculine singular noun plus suffix is shifted to a masculine plural noun plus suffix. A single *yod* makes the difference between these two forms. This type of shift is found throughout many *plene* manuscripts. In 4QSam[a], though, we find some places where the scroll has a plural while the MT has a singular and other places where the scroll has a singular while the MT has a plural. This is consistent with the mixed orthographic character of this scroll as well as the mixed readings found in the verbal system presented above. A couple of contrasting examples will help to develop this point further. 4QSam[a] contains two nouns that are singular where the MT reads plural. One of these occurrences is given here.

1 Sam. 14:48

4Q51 f6:2

ויצל את ישראל מיד] ש[סיו

MT

ויצל את־ישראל מיד שסהו

In this passage, the scroll has an additional *yod*, making שסה plural in the scroll while the MT has the singular. In contrast to this, we find two other places in this manuscript where the opposite is true, one of which is seen in this example:

2 Sam. 7:28

4Q51 f78_79:9

ודברך]יהיה אמת

MT

ודבריך יהיו אמת

In 2 Sam. 7:28 we find that 4QSam[a] has a singular noun where the MT has a plural. These examples highlight the mixed nature of this manuscript.

b. Pluses and Minuses of Suffixes

The mixed linguistic character of 4QSam[a] can also be seen in its use of suffixes. Overall, we find four minuses and two pluses of suffixes in this scroll. Here I give two contrasting examples.

2 Sam. 13:31

4Q51 f102ii+103_106i+107_109a_b:29

וכול עבדיו קרעו איש] בגדיו

MT

וכל־עבדיו נצבים קרעי בגדים

In this example, 4QSamᵃ has an additional suffix attached to בגד. The contrasting example is found in 1 Samuel:

1 Sam. 6:5

4Q51 6a_b:14

ועשיתם צלמי העפ[ל]י[]ם

MT

ועשיתם צלמי עפליכם

In this passage, it is the MT that has the additional suffix, which is found on עפל. These two examples help to draw attention to the mixed linguistic character that is found in the nominal system of 4QSamᵃ. This result is consistent with the findings in the analysis of 4QSamᵃ's verbal system as well as with what was predicted based on the mixed orthographic nature of this manuscript.

5. Particles

The linguistic character of 4QSamᵃ's use of particles is also consistent with the picture developed thus far. 4QSamᵃ contains six types of variations involving particles: a. pluses and minuses of the directive *he*; b. interchanges between על and אל; c. pluses and minuses of the conjunction *vav*; d. interchanges between ל and אל; e. pluses and minuses of the direct object marker; and f. interchanges between מ and מן. These six types of variations will be considered here.

a. Pluses and Minuses of the Directive he

In section IV. A. 1., I concluded that pluses of the directive *he* are much more common in *plene* scrolls than defective scrolls. In fact, the defective scrolls only contain five pluses of this particle, while the *plene* scrolls have fifty-nine. Further, only five of the thirty-eight manuscripts that contain either a plus or minus of the directive *he* have one or more of each. 4QSamᵃ is one of those five, containing two pluses and two minuses. The following two examples help to shed light on this mix of variation types found in 4QSamᵃ.

2 Sam. 4:3

4Q51 f61i+62:31

ו[]יברחו הברתים גת[]י[]ם

MT

ויברחו הבארתים גתימה

2 Sam. 15:29
4Q51 f116:4

וישב צדוק ואביתר את ארון [האלוהים ירו]שלימה

MT

וישב צדוק ואביתר את־ארון האלהים ירושלם

In the example from 2 Sam. 4:3, we find Beeroth fleeing to Gittaim, and Gittaim is marked with a directive *he* in the MT, while it is not in the 4QSam^a. In 2 Sam. 15:29, the ark is being brought to Jerusalem, but this time it is the scroll that marks the location with a directive *he*, while it is missing in the MT. This lack of consistency highlights the mixed linguistic nature of 4QSam^a.

b. על - אל

In section IV. A. 5., I discussed the variations involving the interchange between על and אל. In that section, I concluded that overall these two prepositions are interchanged freely and do not correlate with any particular type of scroll. But, further analysis revealed a link between על and the *plene* scrolls.[61] When the data for this type of variation was restricted to only distinctive readings found in the scrolls, the *plene* manuscripts strongly favoured על over אל, while the defective manuscripts did not gravitate towards either in particular. Therefore, it is again not a surprise that 4QSam^a contains a mix between על and אל. In this scroll, we find three places where it reads על while the MT reads אל and the opposite is found two times. Only one example is necessary to demonstrate this inconsistency.

1 Sam. 27:10
4Q51 f43:3–4

ויאמר דויד על נגב יהודה] ואל נגב ירח[מ]אל ועל נגב] הקנזי

MT

ויאמר דוד על־נגב יהודה ועל־נגב הירחמאלי ואל־נגב הקיני

1 Sam. 27:10 presents a mix of readings, both between 4QSam^a and the MT as well as within each witness. In this passage, David recounts where he has raided and says: 'Against the South of Judah, and against the South of the Jerahmeelites, and against the South of the Kenites'.[62] In the MT the first two occurrences of 'against' are rendered with על while the final one is אל. 4QSam^a only has the last two intact. In both of these, the scroll switches the reading. This

---

61 The use of על in place of אל has been seen as a characteristic of Late Biblical Hebrew. See Sáenz-Badillos, *A History*, 117. As well as Qimron, *Hebrew*, 93.

62 American Standard Version.

example highlights the inconsistent use of this particle in 4QSam^a as well as in the MT. This inconsistency serves as a stark contrast to the significantly more stable trend towards על within the *plene* scrolls.

c. Pluses and Minuses of the Conjunction Vav

As was discussed in section IV. A. 7., the *plene* scrolls contain significantly more pluses and minuses of *vav* than the defective scrolls. This trend is especially true for *vav*s in conjunction with verbs. Just as has been seen above, trends that are prevalent within the *plene* scrolls tend to be mixed in 4QSam^a, which we can also see with the pluses and minuses of *vav*. In this manuscript, we find two pluses and two minuses of the conjunction *vav*; one of the pluses and two of the minuses are connected to verbs. These variations have been developed in detail above (V. 3. a.), but highlighting them here helps to confirm 4QSam^a's diverse use of particles.

d. אל - ל

Interchanges between אל and ל are relatively rare in the variations between the 'biblical' DSS and the MT. This type of variation is only found twenty-one times. Considering that these prepositions are used a combined total of 5,592, this is a very low rate of variation (0.4% compared with the overall variation rate of 5.44%). This low variation rate is also surprising considering that a number of scholars see the use of ל in place of אל as a well-known diachronic development in Hebrew.[63] Whether this interchange is a mark of a diachronic shift in Hebrew or whether it is simply a stylistic feature does not change the fact that 4QSam^a makes inconsistent use of these prepositions. In two places, 4QSam^a has ל where the MT has אל and in three places the opposite is true. Contrasting examples of this interchange are found in the following examples.

2 Sam. 11:8
4Q51 f89_92:9
ו[יאמ]ר דויד אל[ ]אוריה

MT
ויאמר דוד לאוריה

1 Sam. 28:2
4Q51 f43:12[64]

---

63 See Joüon and Muraoka, *A Grammar of Biblical Hebrew*, 117.
64 Cross notes: '[I]t is probable that the manuscript did not contain sufficient room for the *'aleph* of the אל found in [MT]'. Ulrich et al. (eds), *Qumran Cave 4, Volume 7: Genesis to Numbers*, 95.

ויאמר [אכי]ש [ל]דויד

MT

ויאמר דוד אל־אכיש

In these two examples we see differing ways of saying 'and he said to ...'. There is evidence that the reading with ל was more prevalent in 'late' forms of Hebrew (see section V. C. 5. e. above), which if true would suggest that both 4QSam[a] and the MT contain some late and some early features.

e. Direct Object Marker

As is noted in section IV. A. 4. above, Tov argues that 'the *nota accusativi* is freely added or omitted in all textual sources'.[65] This conclusion is support by the data presented in section IV. A. 4. where I show that there is no statistically relevant pattern between pluses and minuses of the direct object marker and the *plene* or defective scrolls. Thus the mixed use of this particle in 4QSam[a] is probably not due to the inconsistent linguistic nature of this scroll. The four pluses and three minuses of the direct object marker are more likely due to the mixed use of this particle throughout many different scribal traditions.

6. Conclusion

The above analysis of 4QSam[a] and its use of PLVs is consistent with the results presented in the previous chapter. In that section, I argued that manuscripts that contain a *plene* orthographic style use PLVs far more often than defective manuscripts. 4QSam[a] shows that this conclusion is not a simple black and white picture. This manuscript contains a thoroughly mixed orthographic style. Because of this we would expect a mixed use of PLVs, and that is exactly what has been seen above. All five PLVs (shifts toward *vav* plus imperfect, shifts from singular to plural nouns, pluses and minuses of the conjunction *vav*, shifts toward על and pluses of the directive *he*) are found in 4QSam[a], but their opposites are also found at about the same rate (such as shifts away from *vav* plus imperfect and minuses of the directive *he*). Again, this is exactly what is predicted from the conclusions present in Chapter IV. B. 6., thus lending support to results of the global analysis developed in that chapter. Before developing these conclusions further, I will discuss some broader implications of these results for how we understand QH and the texts from the Dead Sea.

---

65 Tov, *Scribal Practices*, 204.

Chapter VI

Qualitative Analysis of the Linguistic Character of the 'Biblical' DSS: Some Broader Implications

In this section, I will discuss connections between the linguistic character of the 'biblical' DSS and the sociohistorical context in which they were produced. I will analyse the influence of social and historical factors upon the language found in these texts, exploring three main views: A. antilanguage; B. holy language and C. linguistic stability and textual authority.

Sociolinguistic studies have focused on two main theories regarding the function of Hebrew at Qumran. One view, beginning with C. Rabin[1] and developed by W.M. Schniedewind[2] as well as G.A. Rendsburg,[3] argues that QH was an antilanguage. The second main theory, championed by M.L. Grossman[4] and C. Newsom,[5] focuses on the creating of self and community identity. I will label this view secondary socialization — a term described by the sociologists P.L. Berger and T. Luckmann,[6] but not used by Qumran scholars as far as I am aware. Finally, I will discuss Tigchelaar's suggestion that the linguistic character of the 'biblical' DSS is rooted in linguistic stability and textual authority.

A. Antilanguage

M.A.K. Halliday developed the dual concepts of 'anti-society' and 'antilanguage' in 1976.[7] He defines the former as 'a society that is set up within another

---

1. C. Rabin, 'The Historical Background of Qumran Hebrew', in C. Rabin and Y. Yadin (eds), *Aspects of the Dead Sea Scrolls* (ScrHier 4, Jerusalem 1958), 144–61.
2. W.M. Schniedewind, 'Qumran Hebrew as an Antilanguage', *JBL* 118 (1999) 235–52.
3. G.A. Rendsburg, 'Qumran Hebrew (With a Trial Cut [1QS])', in L.H. Schiffman and S. Tzoref (eds), *The Dead Sea Scrolls At 60: Scholarly Contributions of New York University Faculty and Alumni* (STDJ 89, Leiden 2010), 217–46.
4. M.L. Grossman, 'Cultivating Identity: Textual Virtuosity and 'Insider' Status', in F. García Martínez and M. Popović (eds), *Defining Identities: We, You, and the Other in the Dead Sea Scrolls* (STDJ 70, Leiden 2008), 1–12.
5. C. Newsom, *The Self as Symbolic Space: Constructing Identity and Community at Qumran* (STDJ 52, Leiden 2004).
6. P.L. Berger and T. Luckmann, *The Social Construction of Reality: A Treatise in the Sociology of Knowledge* (Garden City, NY 1991).
7. For a thorough review of Halliday's antilanguage theory and its application to New Testament studies, see D.A. Lamb, *Text, Context and the Johannine Community: A Sociolinguistic Analysis of the Johannine Writings* (LNTS 477, London 2014), 103–44.

society as a conscious alternative to it. It is a mode of resistance, resistance which may take the form either of passive symbiosis or of active hostility and even destruction'.[8] These anti-societies are based on a shared history, cultural norms, as well as a shared language, but develop on top of these in order to bring about distinctiveness. Halliday shows that anti-societies often develop a corresponding antilanguage. Halliday argues that at its core an antilanguage 'is the acting out of a distinct social structure; and this social structure is, in turn, the bearer of an alternative social reality'.[9] Antilanguages, and their corresponding anti-societies, are characterized by their 'otherness' to the primary society. So, just as an anti-society is based upon the corresponding society, an antilanguage is based upon its parallel language. The differences between the two languages bear out the distinctiveness and the alternativeness that is characteristic of the anti-society. Thus it is common for antilanguages to introduce changes into the parallel language that emphasize the 'otherness' of the anti-society. Halliday notes examples from Calcutta's underworld language — metathesis: e.g. *kodan* (shop) from *dokan*, *karca* (servant) from *cakar*; back formation: e.g. *khum* (mouth), from *mukh*.[10] From these examples we see that the antilanguage is not creating an entirely new language; it is modifying the existing language. Those examples also serve to highlight not only the function of secrecy that many antilanguages have, but also the altering of the prevailing society by the anti-society. This altering functions as a reminder that the antilanguage stands in opposition to the prevailing society.

On the surface, QH does seem to function as an antilanguage. The Qumran community clearly stood in opposition to the prevailing Jewish society, thus it could be called an 'anti-society'. And their language is distinct from other forms of Hebrew, thus it could possibly be called an 'antilanguage'. But QH does not fulfil the role of an antilanguage. One of the reasons QH does not fulfil this role is because the Qumran community would not have viewed their language that way. They would more likely have viewed their form of Hebrew as either just another type of Hebrew or as the only true God-given language. Yes, QH served to separate them from the prevailing society, yet it does not seem likely that they intentionally used it for that reason. At least some from this community may have viewed Hebrew as the holy tongue, created in the beginning, and given to Abraham so that he could understand God's wisdom. And through this form of Hebrew,

---

8   M.A.K. Halliday, 'Anti-Languages', *AA* 78 (1976), 570.
9   Ibid., 572.
10 Ibid., 576.

they had access to God's wisdom and true understanding of their scriptural texts.

Another reason that QH does not fit the definition of antilanguage is that the self-identity of the Qumran community did not rely upon its opposition to the dominate Jewish culture. That is to say, if the other Jewish groups did not exist, the Qumran community would still view themselves in the same way — the one true Israel. But, true anti-societies exist because of the opposition that they have with the dominant society. If the mainstream society ceased to exist, the anti-society would lose its primary source of self-identification. As another example of an antilanguage, Halliday discusses the subculture of Polish prisons. The inmates in these prisons developed their own society in order to separate themselves (not just physically, for that had been forced upon them, but also in many other ways) from the prevailing society. If Polish society in general no longer existed, the prisoners would lose their identity and the main reason for their continued functioning as an anti-society. Further, these ex-prisoners would no longer have a use for their antilanguage. Their forty-one words for 'police',[11] as an example, would become useless if the police no longer existed. On the other hand, if Jewish society ceased to exist and non-Qumran forms of Hebrew vanished, the Qumran community would still continue as they had and they would still speak their form of Hebrew.

Thus the theory of antilanguage, as used by Schniedewind and Rendsburg, has been misapplied to QH. Tigchelaar clearly and forcibly makes this point when critiquing its use by Schniedewind: '[He] provides nothing that warrants calling Qumran Hebrew an antilanguage. When referring to antilanguage, he was not using a theoretical model, and not applying it appropriately to the ancient data'.[12] For this reason, and those developed above, the construct of antilanguage should be set aside in favour of other possible sociological understandings of QH.

B. Secondary Socialization

How did the communities that made up the *Yaḥad* view their language? S. Weitzman argues that they would have viewed Hebrew as the one true language of God.[13] Some evidence for this view is found in Jubilees (a book used extensively by the *Yaḥad* as well as those who gathered together the Qumran texts) when

---

11 Ibid., 571.
12 E.J.C. Tigchelaar, 'Sociolinguistics and Which Dead Sea Scrolls?' (Paper presented at IOQS, München, 6 July 2013), 6.
13 S. Weitzman, 'Why Did the Qumran Community Write in Hebrew?', *JAOS* 119 (1999), 35–45.

it refers to Hebrew as 'the language of creation'.[14] We find similar themes in 4QExposition on the Patriarchs (4Q464).[15] 4Q464 calls Hebrew לשון הקודש ('the holy language').[16] Those two passages reflect a linguistic ideology that separates Hebrew from other languages. Yet Weitzman rightly cautions that '[a]t best…we might only use these documents to reconstruct the beliefs of the unknown group from which the Qumran community emerged'.[17] However, the important place that Jubilees held within the *Yaḥad*, especially the D community, and apparently also within the Qumran community itself, suggest that these groups may have adopted the ideological beliefs presented in Jubilees and the thematically parallel text, 4Q464.

Thus one possible answer for why the *Yaḥad* community chose to write its documents in Hebrew is that they may have viewed it as the one true language of God. But, apparently some within that community did not view all forms of Hebrew as equal. 4QExposition on the Patriarchs seems to claim that God purified the language of the community. This text, an admittedly very fragmentary scroll, quotes Zeph. 3:9 — 'For I will give] purified lips [שׂפה ברורה] to the people'.[18] Because this phrase is found in close proximity[19] to the 'holy language' reference mentioned a moment ago, it may be interpreted as God cleansing the language of the community so that they could speak in the holy tongue. This view finds some support from other texts found at Qumran, which speak of an 'uncircumcised'[20] and 'strange'[21] language used by those who were not part of the community. Thus some within the *Yaḥad* not only believed they were a purified nation physically; they may have also viewed themselves as speaking a pure language. I will return to this point after looking more closely at Jubilees 12 and 4Q464.

---

14 Jubilees 12:25–7. Unfortunately, this passage of Jubilees has been lost in the manuscripts found at Qumran, and thus the Hebrew is unknown.

15 However, the background of this text is unclear; it was apparently utilized by those who gathered together the Qumran scrolls. See Ibid., 37.

16 4Q464 f3i:8; translation from M.O. Wise, M.G. Abegg, Jr. and E.M. Cook, *The Dead Sea Scrolls: A New Translation*, Rev. ed. (San Francisco 2005).

17 Weitzman, 'Why Did the Qumran Community Write in Hebrew?', 37.

18 4Q464 f3i:9

19 לשון הקודש is found near the middle of line eight, while שׂפה ברורה is found near the middle of line nine.

20 1QH^a 10:20 'You placed it in his heart to open up the source of knowledge to all who understand. But they have changed them, through uncircumcised lips [בערול שׂפה] and a strange message, into a people with no understanding, that they might be ruined in their delusion'. Wise, Abegg and Cook, *The Dead Sea Scrolls: A New Translation*.

21 1QH^a 12:17b 'With mocking lips and a strange tongue [ולשון אחרת] they speak to Your people …' Ibid., 96.

The *Yaḥad* may have conceptualized Hebrew as the one true holy language and potentially a specific form of Hebrew as the pure form of that language, a view of their language that may have been influenced by Patriarchal ideology.[22] I quoted briefly above from Jubilees 12 as making reference to the 'holy language', but a fuller examination of the passage also reveals the influence of Abraham. Just after God called Abram to leave Ur we find the following passage:[23]

> Then the Lord God said to me, 'Open [Abram's] mouth and his ears so that he might hear and speak with his tongue in the revealed language. For from the day of the collapse, it had disappeared from the mouth of all mankind'. I opened his mouth and his ears and his lips and began to speak with him in Hebrew, in the language of the creation. He took his father's books (they were written in Hebrew) and he copied them. From that time he began to study them while I was telling him everything that he was unable (to understand)... Jubilees 12:25–7[24]

In this passage, we find Abram using Hebrew for the first time, which allowed him to understand a collection of books that he received from his father. 4Q464 seems to echo some of these themes. '[...] servant [...] on the first [...] confused [...] to Abraham [...] forever, for he [... re]ad the holy language [... 'For I will give] purified lips to the people' (Zeph. 3:9).[25] While we cannot be certain that 4Q464 and Jubilees contained identical views, they likely shared the common themes of the Patriarch's connection to Hebrew, and the distinctiveness of that language. These parallels, and others, would have likely resonated with many members of the *Yaḥad*. While these connections are not expounded upon in Qumran literature, as far as I know, it is possible that parallels such as these would have had an influence upon their ideological views of themselves.

Sociologically, it may be better to view QH functioning less as an antilanguage and more as a vehicle for what Berger and Luckmann have called secondary socialization.[26] They define this as 'the internalization of institutional or in-

---

22 The impact of Abraham on the Qumran community's ideological views of their language is discussed in the following articles: Schniedewind, 'Qumran Hebrew as an Antilanguage', 235–52. Idem, 'Linguistic Ideology in Qumran Hebrew', in *Diggers*, 245–55. Weitzman, 'Why Did the Qumran Community Write in Hebrew?', 35–45.

23 While Jubilees likely predates the Qumran settlement, it was clearly an important work in that community. See especially chapter 3, 'The 'Canon Within the Canon' at Qumran and in the New Testament', in G.J. Brooke, *The Dead Sea Scrolls and the New Testament* (Philadelphia 2005), 27–51.

24 Wise, Abegg and Cook, *The Dead Sea Scrolls: A New Translation*.

25 4Q464 f3i:3, Wise, Abegg and Cook, *The Dead Sea Scrolls: A New Translation*, 402.

26 Berger and Luckmann, *The Social Construction of Reality*, 157–66. For relevant articles per-

stitution-based "sub-worlds"'.[27] Berger and Luckmann show that all people are primarily socialized as children, but as we enter new roles and new communities we undergo a process of secondary socialization by internalizing the self-identity of the group. This often requires us to learn a new form of our current language (e.g. when one joins the military) and sometimes it requires us to learn an entirely new language (e.g., when a person moves to a new country). This learning of a new language helps with the socialization of the person and provides that person with a way to express their newfound identity. By observing this language, we can learn about the sub-culture into which the speaker (or writer) has been socialized. Newsom highlights this by reflecting upon an imagined conversation with a Qumran sectarian. In her words: 'As the sectarian continued to speak, it would become apparent that a distinctive form of self-understanding and distinctive patterns of community were embedded in his language, not only in the direct assertions of his statements but also in his choice of figures of speech, metaphors and even verbal style'.[28] As we are socialized into a new group we internalize the ideology of that group and our expressions become flavoured by it. Even the language that we use becomes characterized by the community's self-identity. As a basic example, conservative religious people will often avoid swear words, considering them 'dirty' and disrespectful, while gang members use swear words regularly. In fact, a gang member who refused to swear would likely be considered atypical and weak. Learning the particular forms of speech of the sub-culture acts as a right-of-passage to enter the group and continued use allows the new member to function within the group efficiently.

New members of the Qumran community might have been required to internalize that group's style of Hebrew as a form of secondary socialization. This process might have required shunning other forms of Hebrew that may have been part of the new member's primary socialization as a child. These new members would not only be required to learn this language, they would also internalize the community's ideological views regarding Hebrew, particularly their form of Hebrew. As I noted earlier, this process can be (and might have been) paralleled to Abram's 'resocialization' as recounted by Jubilees. Abram left his land, learned a new language, and was then able to understand his father's books. This may have been the path of the new member as well.

---

taining to the self-identity of the Qumran community, see F. García Martínez, *Defining Identities: We, You, and the Other in the Dead Sea Scrolls* (STDJ 70, Leiden 2008).

27 Berger and Luckmann, *The Social Construction of Reality*, 158.
28 Newsom, *The Self as Symbolic Space*, 91.

C. Linguistic Stability and Textual Authority

An alternative to antilanguage and holy language ideologies may be found in theories of linguistic stability and textual authority. In previous chapters, I have discussed Tigchelaar's article that assesses Tov's scribal school theory. Towards the end of that article Tigchelaar tentatively proposes a theory that he believes may explain the diversity of linguistic characteristics found in the scrolls (both 'biblical' and nonbiblical). Tigchelaar briefly discusses his theory, which can be summarized with a few questions that he poses:

> Were scribes of [apocryphal or pseudo-compositions] only imitating what they thought to be the scribal practice of biblical texts, or can we go further and ask, speculatively, whether they expressed their attitude towards those texts by writing them in 'biblical' orthography? Was spelling, at least for some scribes, part of the strategies of authorization? Did defective spelling reflect that the scribes held the texts to be authoritative and of a different character than those which they copied in the more distinctive spelling and morphology...?[29]

In this quote, Tigchelaar is discussing those sectarian manuscripts that are exceptions to Tov's Qumran scribal school theory. He hypothesizes that the scribes of the defective apocryphal and pseudo-compositions may have chosen not to use the so-called Qumran scribal practice for those manuscripts because of their relationship to the biblical texts Jeremiah and Ezekiel. Thus Tigchelaar envisions two parallel scribal practices, one that the scribes may have used on 'authoritative' texts (or to give texts authority) and another used for texts with less authority. This theory is in direct contrast to the 'Holy Language' theory developed above. The 'Holy Language' theory argues that the Qumran style might have been used to purify or sanctify texts. Tigchelaar argues that defective spelling could be connected to the 'authorization' of texts. That is to say, scribes may have 'expressed their attitude towards those texts by writing them in 'biblical' orthography'.[30] If a defective orthography is to be connected to 'sacred' texts, then one could possibly connect the use of distinctive Qumran characteristics and a fuller orthographic and morphological style with texts intended for practical purposes.

The three theories discussed above can be summarized as follows. The antilanguage approach argues that the distinct linguistic forms found in the DSS were utilized in order to differentiate 'us' from 'them'. The holy language ap-

---
29 Tigchelaar, 'Assessing', 204–5.
30 Ibid., 204.

proach argues that the distinctive features found in the DSS documents where used in order to purify the language of the texts. And finally, the textual authority view focuses on the use of defective features (as opposed to Qumran features) to authorize specific texts. While the results of the study presented in the previous five chapters do not necessarily conflict with any of these theories, the data is most consistent with the textual authority approach. In order to develop this, I will highlight a few places where my results are in conflict with the antilanguage and holy language approaches and then will move into a discussion of the textual authority view.

One of the results of the current study highlights the diversity of linguistic character found in the 'biblical' scrolls. There is a wide range of orthographic and morphological styles, as well as other grammatical elements. As Tigchelaar notes, the different styles found in the scrolls should be characterized as a spectrum, as opposed to two distinct groups.[31] Further, individual scrolls contain significant diversity. A prime example of this is 4QSam^a, which was discussed above in Chapter V. D. This diversity of styles is not what we would expect from a society which utilized an antilanguage. The use of an antilanguage requires intentionality due to its artificial nature. If a scribe was intentionally employing an antilanguage to distinguish his manuscript from others, it seems likely that his conscious effort would have resulted in a more consistent application.

Another aspect of antilanguages that is not found in the 'biblical' DSS is an element of secrecy or encoding. A primary conclusion presented in the above chapters is that the only patterns of difference between the 'biblical' DSS and the other major witnesses are orthographic and morphological in nature. These patterns along with the other QH features, which are also mostly orthographic and morphological in nature, do nothing to hide the meaning of the text. On the contrary, fuller orthography is generally very helpful when one is reading an unpointed Hebrew text. The longer morphological forms may have appeared unusual to some in the Second Temple period, but they likely would not have obscured the meaning of the text.

Finally, as discussed above, the communities represented by the Qumran documents likely would not have viewed themselves as an anti-society and thus would not have viewed their language as an antilanguage. An antilanguage and anti-society is only useful as long as the primary language and primary society

---

31 Ibid., 195.

exist. This is because an anti-society and the language that it produces is essentially a response to normative society. The Qumran movement(s) was characterized by more than just being different than the norm. Therefore, if the norm did not exist, the identity of the Qumran group(s) would still be intact. In fact, the diversity found in the linguistic character of the 'biblical' scrolls suggest that those who used these texts were comfortable with various styles of Hebrew and did not shun one in favour of another. The holy language view helps to solve this problem, but it raises others.

While the holy language approach may be more consistent with how the Qumran communities viewed themselves, it still contains problems. The main issue is the same as the antilanguage argument and that is the problem of diversity and intentionality. If a scribe viewed his language as the only pure and holy form of Hebrew and he wanted to somehow purify his manuscript with it, we would expect a more consistent application of the features that make it pure and holy. Further, if this linguistic ideology was pervasive within a community we would expect a more homogeneous collection of texts. What we have is wide scale diversity, both within individual manuscripts as well as within the corpus as a whole.

Of the three theories discussed above, my data and conclusions are most consistent with the textual authority view for a number of reasons. I will discuss the five main ones here. First, the fact that most of the 'biblical' manuscripts are written in a defective orthographic style may suggest a link between 'biblical' and defective. However, this is by no means the only possible explanation. Second, the diversity of styles found in the scrolls does not present a problem for the textual authority view. While some scribes may have utilized a defective orthographic style because they found it to be more 'biblical', others may have chosen a fuller orthographic style for other reasons. Further, the diversity of orthography even in the MT, which is often considered to be very defective, may account for the scribes' willingness to utilize various styles. Third, using defective orthography to instil some sort of authority to a text does not presuppose a high level of intentionality, such as is required for the antilanguage and holy language perspectives. Scribes could have both subconsciously and consciously recognized a specific type of orthographic and morphological style as more authoritative than another. Fourth, presumably a completely defective form of the text is behind some of those texts with fuller orthography. This may have given the scribes the impression that defective orthography is older and thus more authoritative. However, this connection between old and authoritative may simply be a modern construct that does not pertain to the Second Temple period. Finally, and possibly most significantly, is the distribution of *plene* manuscripts among different text types. The full reading of לוא is found far less often in Torah scrolls than other types of scrolls. The mean occurrences of לוא to the total occurrences of this term for the Torah scrolls is 12.57%, while the mean for the non-Torah scrolls is 40.06%. A one-tailed t-test confirms that this difference is statistically valid by producing a P-value of 0.1%. This data suggests that scribes of the Torah scrolls were less inclined to use *plene* orthography than scribes of non-Torah scrolls. This may have been due to the authoritative place of the Torah scroll within Second Temple Jewish communities.

D. Conclusions

The results of this study do not single out any one of the above (or other possible) sociohistorical approaches to the linguistic character of the Qumran documents. Yet the main results of general diversity and a small number of PLVs is most consistent with the textual authority view. These results strongly support Tigchelaar when he states: 'We should expand the discourse that Tov has started and introduce different parameters apart from the sectarian versus nonsectarian one'.[32] The methodology, global analysis and work on the representative individual scrolls, presented in this study, all call for a reanalysis of QH and its social and historical place within the history of the Hebrew language and the Second Temple period.

---

32   Ibid., 205.

Chapter VII

Conclusion

For a long time, scholars have debated the usefulness of the 'biblical' scrolls for understanding Second Temple period Hebrew. A cursory look at the DSS reveals a distinct, although inconsistent, orthographic and morphological practice. And this orthographic character has been studied in detail. Yet research on non-orthographic and non-morphological features of the scrolls has been limited. Therefore, I set out to provide a comprehensive analysis of the linguistic character of the 'biblical' scrolls. In these concluding remarks, I discuss the aims of this project, the various conclusions reached in the preceding chapters and the next steps toward producing a complete picture of the linguistic character of the DSS.

A. Addressing the Problems with Past Research

As outlined in the introduction, this project set out to comprehensively analyse the linguistic nature of the 'biblical' DSS. While a general analysis is presented throughout, one of the project's main foci was upon distinctive linguistic features within the scrolls, particularly those that correlate with *plene* orthographic style. Further, I intended to test previous scholarly claims regarding the connection between the 'biblical' scrolls and QH in general. In order to fulfil these goals, I tested the following hypothesis: The 'biblical' DSS do not contain any distinctive linguistic characteristics beyond orthography and morphology. As I have outlined in previous chapters, a number of scholars have considered this issue. However, these scholars have come to little agreement. Some see many distinctive characteristics of QH within the 'biblical' scrolls, while others do not. In my review of scholarly work, I concluded that much of the disagreement is due to a lack of sound linguistic methodology. Because of that, I extensively utilized current linguistic theories throughout this project to provide a solid basis for my conclusions. I will briefly review how this methodology addresses the main problems with past research.

The lack of principled corpora was the first issue with past research that I highlighted in Chapter II. I argued there that many scholars worked with a manuscript or a set of manuscripts that were not appropriate for the questions they were trying to answer. This was in part due to the small number of available manuscripts in the early years of scrolls research. A second contributing factor was some scholars' tendency to work with all available manuscripts without considering which would help to answer their questions and which would result in inadequate answers (such as manuscripts too small for statistically valid analysis). Through the use of statistical tools and theories such as representativeness, standard deviations and histograms, I was able to identify the best manuscripts for statistical analysis. Though I reviewed variations from all available 'biblical' DSS, I only included in my statistical analysis manuscripts with a sufficient number of words. I also worked to make sure this corpus contained a sufficient number of representative manuscripts of different types, such as phylacteries, narrative and poetic manuscripts, Torah and prophetic manuscripts, among others. Using statistical tools and representative manuscripts, I have been able to design a principled corpus appropriate for the project at hand.

A second shortcoming of past research is the absence of current linguistic methodology. Though Kutscher used the historical comparative methodology current at his time, others have not engaged with linguistic theory in significant ways. Throughout this project, the application of corpus linguistics, especially inferential statistics, and cross-textual variable analysis have proven to be valuable. Rigorous linguistic methodology, such as that used in this study, is necessary when analysing texts. Without it scholars are in danger of either coming to false conclusions or missing valuable pieces of information.

The third shortfall of past research addressed throughout this project is the use of deficient data. Often scholarly work on the linguistic character of the scrolls is plagued by missing data, reliance on very little or bad data or inclusion of data that heavily skews results. By undertaking a thorough comparison of witnesses, using multiple methodologies of comparison, engaging scholars to check my results, and comparing my datasets to others, I have been able to collect the most comprehensive and accurate set of variations available. However, large sets of data are bound to have a small number of errors. Potential errors in the data necessitate the use of robust statistical tools to avoid basing conclusions on perceived patterns. Small differences between witnesses (including those caused by errors in data collection) can appear to be significant at first, but the proper statistical tests avoid these small differences by highlighting only statistically relevant variations. I have a high level of confidence in my conclusions by basing them on the most comprehensive dataset available and by using powerful statistical tools to analyse that data.

The final two issues with past research are an MT-centred analysis and the lack of focus on non-orthographic and morphological features. In order to move away from having the MT be the starting point for this study, I included the SP and the LXX in my work. I also focused at times only on those readings distinctive to the 'biblical' DSS. Similarly, instead of focusing only on the orthographic or morphological character of the scrolls, I moved beyond those aspects of language to include more than forty features from other parts of Hebrew grammar. Moving away from an MT centred analysis and broadening the focus beyond orthography and morphology has resulted in a more comprehensive and less biased study than much of past research.

B. Review of Conclusions

After reviewing past research, both its shortcomings and strengths, I developed the methodology to address those issues and build upon previous research. Next, a detailed analysis of the many variations found between different witnesses focused upon the hypothesis stated at the beginning: The 'biblical' DSS do not contain any distinctive linguistic characteristics beyond orthography and morphology. My analysis of the 'biblical' scrolls found only four features that can be considered distinctive of the 'biblical' scrolls: pluses of the directive *he*, pluses and minuses of the conjunction *vav*, shifts toward *vav* plus imperfect and shifts from singular to plural nouns. The pluses of the directive *he* and the shifts to plural nouns probably should be considered orthographic or morphological in nature. The high occurrence of pluses and minuses of the conjunction *vav* point to heightened scribal activity within these scrolls. The shifts toward *vav* plus imperfect may be the only true variation type distinctive of the 'biblical' DSS. However, those shifts to *vav* plus imperfect may have come about simply due to scribal preference for a form that looked or sounded archaic. If this shift did develop because of that preference, this variation type should be considered not a grammatical variation but a scribal style variation.

The four variations found to be distinctive of the 'biblical' DSS, especially the scrolls with *plene* orthography, are significant in their own right. But more telling is what was not found. My analysis did not reveal any large-scale patterns of change within the 'biblical' scrolls connected to diachronic development, dialect, or, more specifically, to QH in general. We can conclude, then, that the language of the scribes who produced the 'biblical' scrolls had very little impact upon the production of their manuscripts. This lack of linguistic impact profoundly speaks to the scribal culture in which the 'biblical' scrolls were produced. The scribes likely knew 'biblical Hebrew' well and intentionally avoided letting other forms of Hebrew influence their work. Clearly, some of the scribes were open to various orthographic and morphological styles, as well as numerous other scribal interventions, but linguistic updating does not appear to have been widely spread.

As I discussed in the methodology chapter, quantitative statistical analysis is only part of producing sound linguistic research. The next step is qualitative analysis. Thus, in Chapter VI, I discussed the broader implications of my conclusions. I drew upon sociological and historical analyses of the Qumran communities and the Second Temple period in order to place my conclusions in a larger context. I discussed three main views scholars have developed regarding the linguistic ideology of the Qumran communities: antilanguage, holy tongue and linguistic stability. While my conclusions in the previous chapter do not exclude any one of these theories, my data and analysis are most consistent with the view that the scribes intentionally avoided modifying the language of their text, thus producing linguistic stability.

C. Steps Toward a Comprehensive Picture of the Linguistic Character of the DSS

In the above analysis, I have shown that a rigorous methodology founded in current linguistic theory is essential when analysing the language of ancient witnesses to the 'biblical' text. Further, due to the very small amount of consistent patterns of linguistic change, I concluded that the 'biblical' scrolls should not be one of our main sources for understanding the language of QH. A final conclusion revealed that linguistic stability was a priority in the scribal culture of the Second Temple period. While the 'biblical' DSS do have numerous variations that involve language, it appears that the scribes avoided allowing their language to consistently impact the copying of their texts.[1] These conclusions should be tested and built upon through further research. The methodology, especially the inferential statistical tools, can and should be widely applied

---

1 There are of course relatively rare grammatical elements not discussed in this study that do speak to the nature of QH, but those features are by far the exception.

in linguistic analyses of ancient Hebrew. Future work on QH should take into account the findings in this study by prioritising nonbiblical manuscripts; only looking to the 'biblical' scrolls in rare cases. And studies related to Second Temple scribal culture should further investigate the motivations that may have caused the linguistic stability behind the Qumran manuscripts. These general directives will improve future research on the scrolls, while the above analysis can be a stepping stone for further investigations of the Hebrew used in the Dead Sea Scrolls.

Bibliography

Abegg, M.G., Jr., 'The Hebrew of the Dead Sea Scrolls', in P.W. Flint and J.C. VanderKam (eds), *The Dead Sea Scrolls after Fifty Years: A Comprehensive Assessment* (Leiden 1998), 325–58
—— *Qumran Non-biblical Manuscripts (Qumran)*. Version 2.5. (Altamonte Springs, FL 1999)
—— 'Linguistic Profile of the Isaiah Scrolls', in E. Ulrich and P.W. Flint (eds), *Qumran Cave 1. II: The Isaiah Scrolls, Part 2: Introductions, Commentary, and Textual Variants* (DJD 32, Oxford 2010) 25–42
—— 'The Biblical Dead Sea Scrolls and Second Temple Hebrew Syntax', in P.W. Flint, J. Duhaime and K.S. Baek (eds), *Celebrating the Dead Sea Scrolls: A Canadian Collection* (SBLEJL 30, Atlanta 2011), 163–72
Abegg, M.G., Jr. and C. Toewes, *Qumran Biblical Texts*. Version 1.0. (Altamonte Springs, FL 2007)
Abegg, M.G., Jr., J.E. Bowley, E.M. Cook, E. Tov and E. Ulrich, *The Dead Sea Scrolls Concordance*. 3 vols (Leiden 2003)
Altman, D.G., *Practical Statistics for Medical Research* (New York 1991)
Andersen, F.I. and A.D. Forbes, *Spelling in the Hebrew Bible: Dahood Memorial Lexture* (BibOr 41, Rome 1988)
Auer, A. and A. Voeste, 'Grammatical Variables', in J.M. Hernández Campoy and J.C. Conde Silvestre (eds), *The Handbook of Historical Sociolinguistics* (Blackwell Handbooks in Linguistics, Malden, MA 2012), 253–70
Baden, J., 'The *wəyiqtol* and the Volitive Sequence'. *VT* 58 (2008), 147–58
Bailey, C.-J. N., *Variation and Linguistic Theory* (Arlington, TX 1973)
Berger, P.L. and T. Luckmann, *The Social Construction of Reality: A Treatise in the Sociology of Knowledge* (Garden City, NY 1991)
Biber, D., *Dimensions of Register Variation: A Cross-Linguistic Comparison* (Cambridge 1995)
—— 'Representativeness in Corpus Design', *LLC* 8 (1993), 243–57
Biber, D. and S. Conrad, *Register, Genre, and Style* (Cambridge 2009)
Biber, D., S. Conrad and R. Reppen, *Corpus Linguistics: Investigating Language Structure and Use*. (Cambridge 1998)
Brooke, G.J., *The Dead Sea Scrolls and the New Testament* (Philadelphia 2005)
Brown, F., E. Robinson, S.R. Driver, W. Gesenius and C.A. Briggs, *A Hebrew and English Lexicon of the Old Testament: With an Appendix Containing the Biblical Aramaic* (Oxford 1959)
Browner, W.S., *Publishing and Presenting Clinical Research* (Philadelphia 2006)
Brownlee, W.H., *The Meaning of the Qumran Scrolls for the Bible* (Oxford 1964)
Burrows, M., 'Orthography, Morphology, and Syntax of the St. Mark's Isaiah Manuscript', *JBL* 68 (1949), 195–211
Cantos Gómez, P., 'The Use of Linguistic Corpora for the Study of Linguistic Variation and Change: Types and Computational Applications', in J.M. Hernández Campoy and J.C. Conde Silvestre (eds), *The Handbook of Historical Sociolinguistics* (Blackwell Handbooks in Linguistics, Malden, MA 2012), 99–122
Collins, J.J., 'Sectarian Communities in the Dead Sea Scrolls', in J.J. Collins and T.H. Lim (eds), *The Oxford Handbook of the Dead Sea Scrolls* (Oxford Handbooks in Religion and Theology, Oxford, 2010), 151–72
Cook, J.A., 'Detecting Development in Biblical Hebrew using Diachronic Typology', in C.L. Miller-Naudé and Z. Ziony (eds), in *Diachrony in Biblical Hebrew* (LSAWS 8, Winona Lake, IN 2012), 83–95
Cross, F.M., 'Some Problems in Old Hebrew Orthography with Special Attention to the Third Person Masculine Singular Suffix on Plural Nouns (-âw)', *ErIsr* 27 (2003), 18–24

——— 'The History of the Biblical Text in the Light of Discoveries in the Judaean Desert', in F.M. Cross and S. Talmon (eds), *Qumran and the History of the Biblical Text* (Cambridge, MA 1975), 177–95

Cross, F.M. and S. Talmon (eds), *Qumran and the History of the Biblical Text* (Cambridge, MA 1975)

Crystal, D., 'Style: The Varieties of English', in W.F. Bolton and D. Crystal (eds), *The English Language* (London 1987), 199–222

Ehrensvärd, M., 'Why Biblical Texts Cannot Be Dated Linguistically?', *HS* 47 (2006), 177–89

Everitt, B., *The Cambridge Dictionary of Statistics* (Cambridge 1998)

Fassberg, S.E., 'The Syntax of the Biblical Documents from the Judean Desert as Reflected in a Comparison of Multiple Copies of Biblical Texts', in T. Muraoka and J.F. Elwolde (eds), *Diggers at the Well: Proceedings of a Third International Symposium on the Hebrew of the Dead Sea Scrolls and Ben Sira* (STDJ 36, Leiden 2000), 94–109

——— 'Dead Sea Scrolls: Linguistic Features', *EHLL* 1:673–84

Feagin, C., 'Entering the Community: Fieldwork', in J.K. Chambers, P. Trudgill and N. Schilling-Estes (eds), *The Handbook of Language Variation and Change* (Blackwell Handbooks in Linguistics, Malden, MA 2001), 20–39

Fischer, O., *Morphosyntactic Change: Functional and Formal Perspectives* (Oxford 2007)

Forbes, A.D., 'The Diachrony Debate: A Tutorial on Methods', Paper presented at the Annual Meeting of the SBL, Atlanta, GA, 20–24 November 2015.

García Martínez, F., *Defining Identities: We, You, and the Other in the Dead Sea Scrolls* (STDJ 70, Leiden 2008)

García, J. and C. Quintana-Domeque, 'The Evolution of Adult Height in Europe: A Brief Note', *EHB* 5 (2007), 340–9

Geiger, G., *Das hebräische Partizip in den Texten aus der judäischen Wüste* (STDJ 101, Leiden 2012)

Goshen-Gottstein, M., 'Linguistic Structure and Tradition in the Qumran Documents', *ScrHier* 4 (1958), 101–37

Grintz, J.M., 'Hebrew as the Spoken and Written Language in the Last Days of the Second Temple', *JBL* 79 (1960), 32–47

Grossman, M.L., 'Cultivating Identity: Textual Virtuosity and "Insider" Status', in F. García Martínez and M. Popović (eds), *Defining Identities: We, You, and the Other in the Dead Sea Scrolls* (STDJ 70, Leiden 2008), 1–12

Halliday, M.A.K., 'Anti-Languages', *AA* 78 (1976), 570–84

Hernández-Campoy, J.M. and N. Schilling, 'The Application of the Quantitative Paradigm to Historical Sociolinguistics: Problems with the Generalizability Principle', in J.M. Hernández Campoy and J.C. Conde Silvestre (eds), *The Handbook of Historical Sociolinguistics* (Blackwell Handbooks in Linguistics. Malden, MA 2012), 63–79

Holmstedt, R.D., 'Historical Linguistics and Biblical Hebrew', in C.L. Miller-Naudé and Z. Ziony (eds), *Diachrony in Biblical Hebrew* (LSAWS 8, Winona Lake, IN 2012), 97–124

Holmstedt, R.D. and J. Screnock, 'Whither Esther? A Linguistic Profile of the Book of Esther'. Paper presented at the Annual Meeting of the SBL, Baltimore, 20–24 November 1994.

Hurvitz, A., *Ben lashon le-lashon: le-toldot leshon ha-Miḳra' bi-yeme bayit sheni* (Jerusalem 1972)

——— *A Linguistic Study of the Relationship Between the Priestly Source and the Book of Ezekiel: A New Approach to an Old Problem* (CahRB 20, Paris 1982)

——— 'Was QH a 'Spoken' Language? On Some Recent Views and Positions: Comments', in T. Muraoka and J.F. Elwolde (eds), *Diggers at the Well: Proceedings of a Third International Symposium on the Hebrew of the Dead Sea Scrolls and Ben Sira* (STDJ 36, Leiden 2000), 110–14

—— 'The Recent Debate on Late Biblical Hebrew: Solid Data, Experts' Opinions, and Inconclusive Arguments', *HS* 47 (2006), 191–210

—— 'Can Biblical Texts be Dated Linguistically? Chronological Perspectives in the Historical Study of Biblical Hebrew', in A. Lemaire and M. Saebø (eds), *Congress Volume, Oslo 1998* (VTSup 80, Leiden 2000), 143–60

Jacobs, J. and M.G. Abegg, *Dead Sea Scrolls and Masoretic Text Variants*. Version 1.0. (Altamonte Springs, FL 2013)

Jacobs, J., 'A Comprehensive Analysis of the Conjunction *Waw*: Variants and Their Implications', M.A. thesis (Trinity Western University, 2008)

Joosten, J., 'A Note on '*wəyiqtol*' and Volitive Sequences', *VT* 59 (2009), 495–8

—— 'Hebrew, Aramaic and Greek in the Qumran Scrolls', in J.J. Collins and T.H. Lim (eds), *The Oxford Handbook of the Dead Sea Scrolls* (Oxford Handbooks in Religion and Theology, Oxford 2010), 351–74

Joüon, P. and T. Muraoka, *A Grammar of Biblical Hebrew*² (Rome 2006)

Kim, D.-H., *Early Biblical Hebrew, Late Biblical Hebrew, and Linguistic Variability: A Sociolinguistic Evaluation of the Linguistic Dating of Biblical Texts* (VTSup 156, Leiden 2013)

Kutscher, E.Y., *The Language and Linguistic Background of the Isaiah Scroll (1QIsaᵃ)* (STDJ 6, Leiden 1974)

—— 'Hebrew Language: The Dead Sea Scrolls', *EncJud* 8:634–8

Labov, W., 'Some Principles of Linguistic Methodology', *LS* 1 (1972), 97–120

—— *Social Change* (Malden, MA 2001)

Lamb, D.A., *Text, Context and the Johannine Community: A Sociolinguistic Analysis of the Johannine Writings* (LNTS 477, London 2014)

Longacre, D., 'Developmental Stage, Scribal Lapse, or Physical Defect? 1QIsaᵃ's Damaged Exemplar for Isaiah Chapters 34–66', *DSD* 20 (2013), 17–50

Lumley, T., P. Diehr, S. Emerson and L. Chen, 'The Importance of the Normality Assumption in Large Public Health Data Sets', *ARPH* 23 (2002), 151–69

Mansoor, M., 'Some Linguistic Aspects of the Qumran Texts', *JSS* 3 (1958), 40–54

Marantz, A., 'No Escape from Syntax: Don't Try Morphological Analysis in the Privacy of Your Own Lexicon', in A. Dimitriadis, L. Siegel, C. Surek-Clark and A. Williams (eds), *University of Pennsylvania Working Papers in Linguistics: Proceedings of the 21st Annual Penn Linguistics Colloquium* (Philadelphia 1997)

Milik, J.T., *Dix ans de decouvertes dans le desert de Juda* (Paris 1957)

Milik, J.T. (ed.), *Qumran Grotte 4, Volume 6: II. Teffillin, Mezuzot et Targums (4Q128–4Q157)* (DJD 12, Oxford 1977)

Morag, S., 'Qumran Hebrew: Some Typological Observations', *VT* 38 (1988), 148–64

—— מחקרים בלשון המקרא (Jerusalem 1995)

Muraoka, T., 'An Approach to the Morphosyntax and Syntax of Qumran Hebrew', in T. Muraoka and J.F. Elwolde (eds), *Diggers at the Well: Proceedings of a Third International Symposium on the Hebrew of the Dead Sea Scrolls and Ben Sira* (STDJ 36, Leiden 2000), 193–214

Neuman, W.L., *Social Research Methods: Qualitative and Quantitative Approaches* (Boston 1997)

Newsom, C., *The Self as Symbolic Space: Constructing Identity and Community at Qumran* (STDJ 52, Leiden 2004)

'Normal Distribution'. Six-Sigma-Material.com. http://www.six-sigma-material.com/Normal-Distribution.html

Oakes, M.P., *Statistics for Corpus Linguistics* (Edinburgh 1998)

Polzin, R., *Late Biblical Hebrew: Toward an Historical Typology of Biblical Hebrew Prose* (HSM 12, Missoula, MT 1976)

Pulikottil, P., *Transmission of Biblical Texts in Qumran: The Case of the Large Isaiah Scroll 1QIsa*ᵃ (JSPSup 34, Sheffield 2001)

Qimron, E., *The Hebrew of the Dead Sea Scrolls* (HSM 29, Atlanta 1986)

Rabin, C., 'The Historical Background of Qumran Hebrew', C. Rabin and Y. Yadin (eds), *Aspects of the Dead Sea Scrolls* (Scripta Hierosolymitana IV, Jerusalem 1958), 144–61

Rendsburg, G.A., 'Qumran Hebrew (With a Trial Cut [1QS])', in L.H. Schiffman and S. Tzoref (eds), *The Dead Sea Scrolls at 60: Scholarly Contributions of New York University Faculty and Alumni* (STDJ 89, Leiden 2010), 217–46

—— 'Northern Hebrew Through Time: From the Song of Deborah to the Mishnah', in C.L. Miller-Naudé and Z. Zevit (eds), *Diachrony in Biblical Hebrew* (LSAWS 8, Winona Lake, IN 2012), 339–60

Renouf, A., 'Lexical Resolution', in W. Meijs (ed.), *Corpus Linguistics and Beyond: Proceedings of the Seventh International Conference on English Language Research on Computerized Corpora* (Costerus 59, Amsterdam 1987), 121–32

Reymond, E.D., *Qumran Hebrew: An Overview of Orthography, Phonology, and Morphology* (SBLRBS 76, Atlanta 2014)

Rezetko, R., 'The Qumran Scrolls of the Book of Judges: Literary Formation, Textual Criticism, and Historical Linguistics', *JHS* 13 (2013), http://www.jhsonline.org/Articles/article_182.pdf

—— 'Evaluating a New Approach to the Linguistic Dating of Biblical Texts', review of *Early Biblical Hebrew, Late Biblical Hebrew, and Linguistic Variability: A Sociolinguistic Evaluation of the Linguistic Dating of Biblical Texts*, by D.-H. Kim, *JHS* 13 (2013), http://jhsonline.org/reviews/reviews_new/review678.htm

Rezetko, R. and I. Young, *Historical Linguistics and Biblical Hebrew: Steps Toward an Integrated Approach* (ANEM 9, Atlanta 2014)

Romaine, S., *Socio-Historical Linguistics: Its Status and Methodology* (Cambridge Studies in Linguistics 34, Cambridge 1982)

Rubinstein, A., 'Singularities in Consecutive-Tense Constructions in the Isaiah Scroll', *VT* 5 (1955), 180–8

Sáenz-Badillos, A., *A History of the Hebrew Language*. Translated by J. Elwolde. (Cambridge 1993)

Schneider, E., 'Investigating Variation and Change in Written Documents', in J.K. Chambers, P. Trudgill and N. Schilling-Estes (eds), *The Handbook of Language Variation and Change* (Blackwell Handbooks in Linguistics, Malden, MA 2001), 67–98

Schniedewind, W.M., 'Qumran Hebrew as an Antilanguage', *JBL* 118 (1999), 235–52

—— 'Linguistic Ideology in Qumran Hebrew', in T. Muraoka and J.F. Elwolde (eds), *Diggers at the Well: Proceedings of a Third International Symposium on the Hebrew of the Dead Sea Scrolls and Ben Sira* (STDJ 36, Leiden 2000), 245–55

Talmon, S., 'The Old Testament Text', in P.R. Ackroyd and C.F. Evans (eds), *The Cambridge History of the Bible* (Cambridge 1970), 159–99

Tigchelaar, E.J.C., 'Sociolinguistics and which Dead Sea Scrolls?'. Paper presented at IOQS, Munich, 6 July 2013

—— 'Assessing Emanuel Tov's "Qumran Scribal Practice"', in S. Metso, H. Najman and E. Schuller (eds), *The Dead Sea Scrolls: Transmission of Traditions and Production of Texts* (STDJ 92, Leiden 2010), 173–208

Tov, E., 'The Text of Isaiah at Qumran', in C. Broyles and C. Evans (eds), *Writing and Reading the Scroll of Isaiah: Studies of an Interpretive Tradition* (VTSup 70, Leiden 1997), 491–511

—— *Scribal Practices and Approaches Reflected in the Texts Found in the Judean Desert* (STDJ 54, Leiden 2004)

—— 'Scribal Features of Two Qumran Scrolls', in S.E. Fassberg and M. Bar-Asher (eds), *Hebrew in the Second Temple Period: The Hebrew of the Dead Sea Scrolls and of other Contemporary Sources* (Leiden 2013), 241–58

Tov, E. and N.B. Reynolds (eds), *The Dead Sea Scrolls Electronic Library* (Leiden 2006)

Ulrich, E., *The Biblical Qumran Scrolls: Transcriptions and Textual Variants*. (Leiden 2009)

Ulrich, E., F.M. Cross, J. Davila and N. Jastram (eds), *Qumran Cave 4, Volume 7: Genesis to Numbers* (DJD 12, Oxford 1994)

Ulrich, E. and P.W. Flint (eds), *Qumran Cave 1. II: The Isaiah Scrolls, Part 2: Introductions, Commentary, and Textual Variants* (DJD 32, Oxford 2010)

Weitzman, S., 'Why Did the Qumran Community Write in Hebrew?', *JAOS* 119 (1999), 35–45

White Crawford, S., 'The "Rewritten" Bible at Qumran: A Look at Three Texts', in J.H. Charlesworth (ed.), *The Bible and the Dead Sea Scrolls, Volume One: Scripture and the Scrolls: The Second Princeton Symposium on Judaism and Christian Origins* (Waco, TX, 2006), 131–48

Wise, M. O., M.G. Abegg, Jr. and E.M. Cook, *The Dead Sea Scrolls: A New Translation*. Rev. ed. (San Francisco 2005)

Yadin, Y., 'The Excavation of Masada—1963/64: Preliminary Report', *IEJ* 15 (1965), 1–120

Young, I., '`Am Construed as Singular and Plural in Hebrew Biblical Texts: Diachronic and Textual Perspectives', *Zeitschrift für Althebraistik* 12 (1999), 29–66

—— '`Edah and Qahal as Collective Nouns in Hebrew Biblical Texts', *Zeitschrift für Althebraistik* 14 (2001), 68–78

—— 'Late Biblical Hebrew and Hebrew Inscriptions', in I. Young (ed.), *Biblical Hebrew: Studies in Chronology and Typology* (JSOTSup 369, London 2003), 276–311

—— 'Biblical Texts Cannot be Dated Linguistically', *HS* 46 (2005), 341–51

Young, I., R. Rezetko and M. Ehrensvärd, *Linguistic Dating of Biblical Texts*. 2 vols. (London 2008)

Appendices

A. Pluses and Minuses of the Directive *he*

Scroll Name	Scroll #	לא	לוא	Directive *he*s	Directive *he* Plus[1]	Percent Change	Directive *he* Minus[2]	Percent Change	שמה[3]	שם[4]
1QGen	1Q1			0	0	0	0	0		
1QExod^d	1Q2	1		0	0	0	0	0		
1QpaleoLev-Num^a	1Q3	1		0	0	0	0	0		
1QDeut^a	1Q4		1	0	0	0	0	0		
1QDeut^b *	1Q5	10		0	0	0	0	0		
1QJudg	1Q6			1	0	0	0	0		
1QSam	1Q7	2		0	0	0	0	0		
1QIsa^b *	1Q8	89		6	0	0	0	0		
1QEzek	1Q9			0	0	0	0	0		
1QPs^a	1Q10			0	0	0	0	0		
1QPs^b	1Q11			0	0	0	0	0		
1QPs^c	1Q12			0	0	0	0	0		
1QPhyl *	1Q13	8		0	0	0	0	0		
1QDan^a	1Q71	1		0	0	0	0	0		
1QDan^b	1Q72	2		0	0	0	0	0		
1QIsa^a	1QIsa^a		443	45	21	0.41	6	0.12		
1QIsa^a I	1QIsa^a I		167	31	8	0.26	3	0	2	
1QIsa^a II	1QIsa^a II		276	14	13	0.93	3	0	9	
2QExod^a	2Q1			0	0	0	0	0		
2QExod^b	2Q2	1	1	1	0	0	0	0		
2QGen	2Q3			0	0	0	0	0		

---

1 1QIsa^a 5:22, 9:17, 10:15, 11:28, 11:28, 11:29, 12:15, 28:12, 28:14, 28:15, 28:24, 28:25, 38:14, 40:21, 42:20, 43:18, 43:26, 43:26, 53:2, 53:2; 2Q13 f7_8:14; 4Q11 f35:5, 4Q17 f1ii:4; 4Q26 f4:3; 4Q27 f3ii+5:13, f75_79:27; 4Q38a f5:5; 4Q51 6a_b:5, f116:5, 4Q51 f43:5, f55_57a_b+58:1, f61i+62:6; 4Q52 f6_7:14; 4Q56 f24_25:10; 4Q57 f9ii+11+12i+52:17; 4Q70 f21_22i:5; 4Q103 f7ii+11_14:6; 4Q137 f1:22; 4Q138 f1:27; 11Q5 23:10, 3:9, fEii:5; 11Q7 f4_7:14; XQ1 1:3.

2 1QIsa^a 22:7, 28:29, 36:24, 38:12, 8:17, 8:17; 4Q11 f30ii_34:7; 4Q17 f2ii:20; 4Q22 23:8; 4Q31 2:17; 4Q37 10:1; 4Q40 f1_3:7; 4Q50 f2_3:6; 4Q51 f61i+62:31, f80_83:2, 4Q56 f31i:3; 4Q60 f17:7, f17:7; 4Q72 f8i:11; 4Q76 5:6; 4Q82 f76_78i+79_81:7; 4Q128 f1:26; 4Q138 f1:8; 8Q3 f26_29:15; Mas1 f1:1, f1:2; Mas1d 2:9.

3 1QIsa^a 11:28, 11:29, 28:12, 28:14, 28:15, 28:25, 40:21, 43:18, 43:26, 53:2; 2Q13 f7_8:14; 4Q27 f3ii+5:13, 4Q38a f5:5; 4Q51 6a_b:5; 4Q57 f9ii+11+12i+52:17; 4Q137 f1:22; 4Q138 f1:27; 11Q5 3:9, 23:10, fEii:5; 11Q7 f4_7:14.

4 4Q11 f30ii_34:7; 4Q22 23:8; 4Q40 f1_3:7; 4Q60 f17:7, f17:7; 8Q3 f26_29:15; Mas1d 2:9.

Statistics, Linguistics and the 'Biblical' Dead Sea Scrolls

Scroll Name	Scroll #	לא	לוא	Directive hes	Directive he Plus	Percent Change	Directive he Minus	Percent Change	שמה	שם
2QExod^c	2Q4			0	0	0	0	0		
2QpaleoLev	2Q5			0	0	0	0	0		
2QNum^a	2Q6			0	0	0	0	0		
2QNum^b	2Q7			0	0	0	0	0		
2QNum^c	2Q8			0	0	0	0	0		
2QNum^d	2Q9			0	0	0	0	0		
2QDeut^a	2Q10			0	0	0	0	0		
2QDeut^b	2Q11			0	0	0	0	0		
2QDeut^c	2Q12			0	0	0	0	0		
2QJer	2Q13		2	1	1	1	0	0		
2QPs	2Q14			0	0	0	0	0		
2QJob	2Q15			0	0	0	0	0		
2QRuth^a *	2Q16	3		1	0	0	0	0		
2QRuth^b	2Q17			0	0	0	0	0		
3QEzek	3Q1			0	0	0	0	0		
3QPs	3Q2			0	0	0	0	0		
3QLam	3Q3			0	0	0	0	0		
4QGen-Exod^a *	4Q1	6		5	0	0	0	0		
4QGen^b *	4Q2	2		0	0	0	0	0		
4QGen^c *	4Q3			0	0	0	0	0		
4QGen^d	4Q4			0	0	0	0	0		
4QGen^e *	4Q5	2		0	0	0	0	0		
4QGen^f *	4Q6	1		0	0	0	0	0		
4QGen^g	4Q7			0	0	0	0	0		
4QGen^h *	4Q8			0	0	0	0	0		
4QGen^j *	4Q9	3		0	0	0	0	0		
4QGen^k	4Q10			0	0	0	0	0		
4QpaleoGen-Exod1 *	4Q11	10		4	1	0.20	1	0.20		1
4QpaleoGen^m	4Q12		1	0	0	0	0	0		
4QExod^b *	4Q13	3		2	0	0	0	0		
4QExod^c *	4Q14	10		3	0	0	0	0		
4QExod^d	4Q15			0	0	0	0	0		
4QExod^e	4Q16	1		0	0	0	0	0		
4QExod-Lev^f *	4Q17	1		2	1	0.33	1	0.33		
4QExod^g	4Q18			0	0	0	0	0		
4QExod^h	4Q19			0	0	0	0	0		
4QExod^j	4Q20			0	0	0	0	0		
4QExod^k	4Q21			0	0	0	0	0		
4QpaleoExod^m *	4Q22	18		7	0	0	1	0.13		1
4QLev-Num^a *	4Q23	10		8	0	0	0	0		
4QLev^b *	4Q24	18		1	0	0	0	0		

Appendix A. Pluses and Minuses of the Directive *he*:

Scroll Name	Scroll #	לא	לוא	Directive *he*s	Directive *he* Plus	Percent Change	Directive *he* Minus	Percent Change	שמה	שם
4QLev^c	4Q25	1		1	0	0	0	0		
4QLev^d	4Q26	1	3	1	1	1	0	0		
4QLev^e	4Q26a	3		0	0	0	0	0		
4QLev^g	4Q26b	1		0	0	0	0	0		
4QNum^b	4Q27		19	7	3	0.43	0	0	1	
4QDeut^a	4Q28	4		0	0	0	0	0		
4QDeut^b *	4Q29	2		0	0	0	0	0		
4QDeut^c	4Q30	13		4	0	0	0	0		
4QDeut^d *	4Q31	4		3	0	0	1	0.25		
4QDeut^e	4Q32	7		0	0	0	0	0		
4QDeut^f *	4Q33	15		0	0	0	0	0		
4QDeut^g	4Q34	4		0	0	0	0	0		
4QDeut^h *	4Q35	5		3	0	0	0	0		
4QDeutⁱ	4Q36	4		1	0	0	0	0		
4QDeut^j	4Q37	1	3	1	0	0	1	0.50		
4QDeut^k1	4Q38		1	1	0	0	0	0		
4QDeut^k2	4Q38a		2	1	1	1	0	0	1	
4QDeut^k3	4Q38b	1		0	0	0	0	0		
4QDeut^l	4Q39			0	0	0	0	0		
4QDeut^m	4Q40		1	0	0	0	1	0		1
4QDeutⁿ	4Q41	2	17	0	0	0	0	0		
4QDeut^o	4Q42	6		0	0	0	0	0		
4QDeut^p	4Q43	1		0	0	0	0	0		
4QDeut^q	4Q44			0	0	0	0	0		
4QpaleoDeut^r *	4Q45	12		0	0	0	0	0		
4QpaleoDeut^s	4Q46			0	0	0	0	0		
4QJosh^a *	4Q47	5		0	0	0	0	0		
4QJosh^b	4Q48	1		1	0	0	0	0		
4QJudg^a	4Q49			0	0	0	0	0		
4QJudg^b	4Q50			0	0	0	1	0		
4QSam^a	4Q51	9	14	14	5	0.31	2	0.13	1	
4QSam^b *	4Q52	5		5	1	0.20	0	0		
4QSam^c	4Q53		6	2	0	0	0	0		
4QKgs	4Q54	2		1	0	0	0	0		
4QIsa^a *	4Q55	6		1	0	0	0	0		
4QIsa^b *	4Q56	16		2	0	0	1	0.33		
4QIsa^c	4Q57		19	1	0	0	0	0	1	
4QIsa^d *	4Q58	17		0	0	0	0	0		
4QIsa^e *	4Q59	6		0	0	0	0	0		
4QIsa^f	4Q60	2		0	0	0	2	0		2
4QIsa^g	4Q61	3	2	0	0	0	0	0		

Statistics, Linguistics and the 'Biblical' Dead Sea Scrolls

Scroll Name	Scroll #	לא	לוא	Directive *he*s	Directive *he* Plus	Percent Change	Directive *he* Minus	Percent Change	שמה	שם
4QIsaʰ	4Q62	1		0	0	0	0	0		
4QIsaⁱ	4Q62a			0	0	0	0	0		
4QIsaʲ	4Q63	1		0	0	0	0	0		
4QIsaᵏ	4Q64	1		0	0	0	0	0		
4QIsaˡ	4Q65		2	0	0	0	0	0		
4QIsaᵐ	4Q66			0	0	0	0	0		
4QIsaⁿ	4Q67			0	0	0	0	0		
4QIsaᵒ	4Q68			0	0	0	0	0		
4QpapIsaᵖ	4Q69			0	0	0	0	0		
4QIsaᑫ	4Q69a			0	0	0	0	0		
4QIsaʳ	4Q69b			0	0	0	0	0		
4QJerᵃ	4Q70	5	5	3	1	0.33	0	0		
4QJerᵇ	4Q71			0	0	0	0	0		
4QJerᶜ *	4Q72	13		0	0	0	1	0		
4QJerᵈ	4Q72a	2		0	0	0	0	0		
4QJerᵉ	4Q72b			0	0	0	0	0		
4QEzekᵃ *	4Q73	1		1	0	0	0	0		
4QEzekᵇ	4Q74			2	0	0	0	0		
4QEzekᶜ	4Q75			0	0	0	0	0		
4QXIIᵃ *	4Q76	3		0	0	0	1	0		
4QXIIᵇ	4Q77			0	0	0	0	0		
4QXIIᶜ *	4Q78		9	1	0	0	0	0		
4QXIIᵈ	4Q79	1		0	0	0	0	0		
4QXIIᵉ	4Q80		4	0	0	0	0	0		
4QXIIᶠ	4Q81	2		0	0	0	0	0		
4QXIIᵍ *	4Q82	6	9	1	0	0	1	0.50		
4QPsᵃ *	4Q83		5	0	0	0	0	0		
4QPsᵇ *	4Q84	8		1	0	0	0	0		
4QPsᶜ *	4Q85	4		0	0	0	0	0		
4QPsᵈ	4Q86			0	0	0	0	0		
4QPsᵉ *	4Q87		3	0	0	0	0	0		
4QPsᶠ *	4Q88		1	0	0	0	0	0		
4QPsᵍ	4Q89			0	0	0	0	0		
4QGenʰ2	4Q8a			0	0	0	0	0		
4QGenʰ-para	4Q8b			0	0	0	0	0		
4QPsʰ	4Q90			0	0	0	0	0		
4QPsʲ	4Q91			0	0	0	0	0		
4QPsᵏ	4Q92			0	0	0	0	0		
4QPsˡ	4Q93			0	0	0	0	0		
4QPsᵐ	4Q94			0	0	0	0	0		
4QPsⁿ	4Q95			0	0	0	0	0		

Appendix A. Pluses and Minuses of the Directive *he*:

Scroll Name	Scroll #	לא	לוא	Directive *hes*	Directive *he* Plus	Percent Change	Directive *he* Minus	Percent Change	שמה	שם
4QPs°	4Q96		1	0	0	0	0	0		
4QPsᵖ	4Q97			0	0	0	0	0		
4QPsᑫ	4Q98			0	0	0	0	0		
4QPsʳ	4Q98a			0	0	0	0	0		
4QPsˢ	4Q98b			0	0	0	0	0		
4QPsᵗ	4Q98c			0	0	0	0	0		
4QPsᵘ	4Q98d			0	0	0	0	0		
4QPsᵛ	4Q98e			0	0	0	0	0		
4QPsʷ	4Q98f			0	0	0	0	0		
4QPsˣ	4Q98g			0	0	0	0	0		
4QJobᵃ *	4Q99	7	1	0	0	0	0	0		
4QJobᵇ	4Q100	1		0	0	0	0	0		
4QpaleoJobᶜ	4Q101	1		0	0	0	0	0		
4QProvᵃ	4Q102	3		0	0	0	0	0		
4QProvᵇ	4Q103	1		1	1	1	0	0		
4QProvᶜ	4Q103a			0	0	0	0	0		
4QRuthᵃ	4Q104			0	0	0	0	0		
4QRuthᵇ	4Q105			0	0	0	0	0		
4QCantᵃ	4Q106			0	0	0	0	0		
4QCantᵇ *	4Q107	1		0	0	0	0	0		
4QCantᶜ	4Q108			0	0	0	0	0		
4QQohᵃ	4Q109		6	0	0	0	0	0		
4QQohᵇ	4Q110		1	0	0	0	0	0		
4QLam *	4Q111		5	0	0	0	0	0		
4QDanᵃ *	4Q112	6		4	0	0	0	0		
4QDanᵇ *	4Q113		2	1	0	0	0	0		
4QDanᶜ *	4Q114	6		0	0	0	0	0		
4QDanᵈ	4Q115	2		0	0	0	0	0		
4QDanᵉ	4Q116			0	0	0	0	0		
4QEzrᵃ	4Q117			0	0	0	0	0		
4QChr	4Q118			0	0	0	0	0		
4QPhyl A *	4Q128		7	1	0	0	1	0.50		
4QPhyl B *	4Q129		10	2	0	0	0	0		
4QPhyl C *	4Q130	5		1	0	0	0	0		
4QPhyl D	4Q131			1	0	0	0	0		
4QPhyl E	4Q132			0	0	0	0	0		
4QPhyl F	4Q133			0	0	0	0	0		
4QPhyl G *	4Q134	2	8	0	0	0	0	0		
4QPhyl H *	4Q135		1	1	0	0	0	0		
4QPhyl I	4Q136	2	1	0	0	0	0	0		
4QPhyl J *	4Q137		10	2	1	0.50	0	0	1	

Statistics, Linguistics and the 'Biblical' Dead Sea Scrolls

Scroll Name	Scroll #	לא	לוא	Directive hes	Directive he Plus	Percent Change	Directive he Minus	Percent Change	שמה	שם
4QPhyl K *	4Q138		7	4	1	0.20	1	0.20	1	
4QPhyl L	4Q139		3	0	0	0	0	0		
4QPhyl M *	4Q140		5	2	0	0	0	0		
4QPhyl N	4Q141	3		0	0	0	0	0		
4QPhyl O	4Q142		0	0	0	0	0	0		
4QPhyl P	4Q143			0	0	0	0	0		
4QPhyl Q	4Q144		1	0	0	0	0	0		
4QPhyl R	4Q145	2		1	0	0	0	0		
4QPhyl S	4Q146			0	0	0	0	0		
4QPhyl T	4Q147			0	0	0	0	0		
4QPhyl U	4Q148			0	0	0	0	0		
4QMez A	4Q149			0	0	0	0	0		
4QMez B	4Q150	1		1	0	0	0	0		
4QMez C	4Q151			0	0	0	0	0		
4QMez D	4Q152			0	0	0	0	0		
4QMez E	4Q153			0	0	0	0	0		
4QMez F	4Q154			0	0	0	0	0		
4QMez G	4Q155	1		0	0	0	0	0		
4Qpap cryptA Lev^h?	4Q249j			0	0	0	0	0		
4QpapGen^o	4Q483									
4QGen^n	4Q576			0	0	0	0	0		
5QDeut	5Q1	5		0	0	0	0	0		
5QKgs	5Q2			0	0	0	0	0		
5QIsa	5Q3			0	0	0	0	0		
5QXII	5Q4		3	0	0	0	0	0		
5QPs	5Q5			0	0	0	0	0		
5QLam^a	5Q6	5	1	0	0	0	0	0		
5QLam^b	5Q7			0	0	0	0	0		
6QpaleoGen	6Q1			0	0	0	0	0		
6QpaleoLev	6Q2			0	0	0	0	0		
6QpapDeut?	6Q3			0	0	0	0	0		
6QpapKgs *	6Q4	2		0	0	0	0	0		
6QpapPs 78?	6Q5			0	0	0	0	0		
6QCant	6Q6	1		0	0	0	0	0		
6QpapDan	6Q7			1	0	0	0	0		
6QDeut?	6Q20			0	0	0	0	0		
8QGen	8Q1			0	0	0	0	0		
8QPs	8Q2			0	0	0	0	0		
8QPhyl *	8Q3	15		3	0	0	1	0.25		1
8QMez *	8Q4	5		0	0	0	0	0		
11QpaleoLev^a *	11Q1	19		0	0	0	0	0		

Appendix A. Pluses and Minuses of the Directive *he*:

Scroll Name	Scroll #	לא	לוא	Directive *he*s	Directive *he* Plus	Percent Change	Directive *he* Minus	Percent Change	שמה	שם
11QLev^b	11Q2			0	0	0	0	0		
11QDeut	11Q3			0	0	0	0	0		
11QEzek	11Q4	1		0	0	0	0	0		
11QPs^a *	11Q5		32	13	3	0.23	0	0	3	
11QPs^b	11Q6		0	0	0	0	0	0		
11QPs^c	11Q7			3	1	0.33	0	0	1	
11QPs^d	11Q8	1	1	1	0	0	0	0		
11QPs^e	11Q9			0	0	0	0	0		
34Se1	34Se1	3		1	0	0	0	0		
34Se2	34Se2			0	0	0	0	0		
5/6Hev1a	5/6Hev1a			0	0	0	0	0		
5/6Hev1b *	5/6Hev1b	9		3	0	0	0	0		
Gen	Mas1			1	0	0	2	0.67		
Lev	Mas1a			0	0	0	0	0		
Lev *	Mas1b	6		0	0	0	0	0		
Deut	Mas1c	1		0	0	0	0	0		
Ezek *	Mas1d	3		1	0	0	1	0.50		1
Psa *	Mas1e	3		0	0	0	0	0		
Psa	Mas1f			0	0	0	0	0		
Mur Gen 1 *	Mur1	4		0	0	0	0	0		
Mur Deut	Mur2	1		0	0	0	0	0		
MurIsa	Mur3	2		0	0	0	0	0		
MurEx *	Mur4	6		1	0	0	0	0		
MurXII *	Mur88	62		8	0	0	0	0		
MurGen	MurX			0	0	0	0	0		
Sdeir1	Sdeir1	16		0	0	0	0	0		
XHev/Se2	XHev/Se2			0	0	0	0	0		
XHev/Se3	XHev/Se3	1		0	0	0	0	0		
XHev/Se5 *	XHev/Se5	6		1	0	0	0	0		
XQ1 *	XQ1	11		3	1	0.33	0	0		
XQ2 *	XQ2	2		1	0	0	0	0		
XQ3 *	XQ3	16		0	0	0	0	0		
					44		27		21	7

B. מאדה

Scroll Name	Scroll Number	מאדה[1]
01QIsa^a I	1QIsaa I	1
01QIsa^a II	1QIsaa II	6
2QJer	2Q13	1
4QExod^b	4Q13	1
4QpaleoExod^m	4Q22	1
4QLev-Num^a	4Q23	1
4QNum^b	4Q27	2
4QSam^c	4Q53	1
4QXII^c	4Q78	1
4QPhyl A	4Q128	1
4QPhyl J	4Q137	1
11QPs^a	11Q5	10
11QPs^d	11Q8	1
	Total	28

---

[1] 1QIsa^a 25:24, 28:30, 32:9, 39:26, 39:29, 44:1, 51:23, 51:26; 4Q13 f3i_4:16; 4Q22 10:30; 4Q23 f60_61:1; 4Q27 f20_22:10, If1_4:4; 4Q53 f5ii_7i:6; 4Q78 f14_17:2; 4Q128 f1:19; 4Q137 f1:61; 11Q5 fEi:7, 6:14, 8:7, 10:15, 11:3, 12:11, 12:13, 20:6, 25:3, 16:10; 11Q8 f1:2.

C. Definite Articles

Scroll Name	Scroll #	לא	לוא	Definite Article	Definite Article Plus[1]	Percent Change	Definite Article Minus[2]	Percent Change
1QGen	1Q1			4	0	0.00	0	0.00
1QExo^d	1Q2	1		4	0	0.00	0	0.00
1QpaleoLev-Num^a	1Q3	1		7	0	0.00	0	0.00
1QDeut^a	1Q4		1	12	1	0.08	0	0.00
1QDeut^b *	1Q5	10		11	0	0.00	0	0.00
1QJudg	1Q6			4	0	0.00	1	0.25
1QSam	1Q7	2		9	0	0.00	0	0.00
1QIsa^b *	1Q8	89		104	3	0.03	2	0.02
1QEzek	1Q9			0	0	0	0	0
1QPs^a	1Q10			0	0	0	0	0
1QPs^b	1Q11			2	1	0.50	0	0.00
1QPs^c	1Q12			0	0	0	0	0
1QPhyl *	1Q13	8		6	0	0.00	0	0.00
1QDan^a	1Q71	1		10	0	0.00	0	0.00
1QDan^b	1Q72	2		3	0	0.00	0	0.00
1QIsa^a	1QIsa^a		443	805	52	0.06	26	0.03
1QIsa^a I	1QIsa^a I		167	592	28	0.05	16	0.03
1QIsa^a II	1QIsa^a II		276	213	24	0.11	10	0.05

1   1Q4 f9:3; 1Q8 20:29, 21:14, 26:5; 1Q11 f6:2; 1QIsa^a 1:2, 1:28, 4:1, 6:14, 6:14, 6:9, 7:13, 8:16, 8:17, 8:2, 8:24, 9:9, 10:22, 10:23, 12:14, 12:18, 12:18, 12:9, 15:10, 18:11, 18:13, 19:19, 20:23, 25:24, 26:20, 26:22, 27:12, 27:9, 28:3, 29:20, 34:1, 34:22, 34:24, 35:19, 36:13, 37:29, 38:15, 38:16, 41:22, 43:25, 44:2, 46:18, 46:25, 46:26, 46:27, 47:28, 48:20, 49:22, 51:10, 54:16, 54:18, 54:4; 4Q9 f2i:1, f5:4; 4Q13 f6ii:7; 4Q17 f1ii:6, f2ii:18, f2ii:8; 4Q22 34:8; 4Q24 f1_7:13, f20ii+22_25:16; 4Q26a f2:3; 4Q27 f1_4:2, f12:7, f24ii+27_30:13; 4Q30 f9:2; 4Q35 f5_6:5; 4Q37 10:12; 4Q45 f31_32:3; 4Q47 f9ii+13_16:10; 4Q49 f1:6; 4Q50 f2_3:10; 4Q51 10a:4, 6a_b:14, 9e_i:10, f102ii+103_106i+107_109a_b:4, f112_114:2, f26_27:3, f3_5:4, f3_5:5, f44:5, f52a_b+53:7, f61ii+63_64a_b+65_67:11, f6:6; 4Q54 f6:11; 4Q56 f10_13:1; 4Q57 f9ii+11+12i+52:33; 4Q67 f1:2; 4Q76 3:13; 4Q78 f10_12:8, f10_12:9, f18_20:10; 4Q82 f13:4, f30g+40b_43b+44:21; 4Q85 f15iii+17:26; 4Q86 3:4; 4Q111 3:2; 4Q112 f14:16, f15:17; 4Q115 f3_7:13; 4Q130 f1:3, f1:8; 4Q135 f1:1; 4Q137 f1:54; 4Q138 f1:31, f1:5; 4Q140 f1:5, f1:5; 4Q141 f1i:12; 5Q6 f1iii:6; 11Q1 3:5, 27:14, fCii:3; Mas1d 3:12; Mur88 16:12, 21:3, 22:23; XQ3 1:16.

2   1Q6 f8:1; 1Q8 21:16, f12:2; 1QIsa^a 2:8, 3:27, 6:8, 8:13, 8:4, 9:14, 10:23, 11:18, 13:14, 14:32, 15:20, 15:7, 18:1, 18:17, 18:21, 24:28, 28:19, 29:21, 29:24, 32:3, 33:21, 47:13, 52:14, 52:6, 53:5, 54:14; 2Q13 f9ii_12:8; 4Q14 1:17; 4Q14 5:40, 5:40; 4Q17 f2i:20; 4Q22 f25:5; 4Q24 f1_7:32; 4Q26 f2:4; 4Q27 f20_22:4, f20_22:4, f24ii+27_30:9; 4Q30 f32i+33:10; 4Q33 f17_19:7; 4Q37 3:1; 4Q38 f2:13; 4Q45 f33:4; 4Q51 10b_c:1, 5b_c:7, f112_114:2, f155_158:20, f40_41:3, f42a:2, f43:4, f78_79:2; 4Q54 f6:4; 4Q70 f4ii+8_10:7; 4Q72 f19_21:6; 4Q76 3:10; 4Q83 f4ii:2; 4Q84 f15iii+20_21i+22:16; 4Q86 2:13, 2:14, 3:4; 4Q87 f13:2; 4Q91 f1:4; 4Q106 f2i+3_5:13; 4Q106 f2ii:4; 4Q129 f1R:10; 4Q135 f1:3, f1:8; 4Q137 f1:25, f1:26; 4Q138 f1:33; 8Q3 f12_16:8, f12_16:8; 8Q4 f1:31; 11Q2 f3:4, f3:4; 11Q5 2:9, 23:11, 4:8, fEiii:13; Mur88 20:13, XQ2 1:1, 1:1.

Scroll Name	Scroll #	לא	לוא	Definite Article	Definite Article Plus	Percent Change	Definite Article Minus	Percent Change
2QExodᵃ	2Q1			0	0	0	0	0
2QExodᵇ	2Q2	1	1	4	0	0.00	0	0.00
2QGen	2Q3			3	0	0.00	0	0.00
2QExodᶜ	2Q4			0	0	0	0	0
2QpaleoLev	2Q5			1	0	0.00	0	0.00
2QNumᵃ	2Q6			1	0	0.00	0	0.00
2QNumᵇ	2Q7			3	0	0.00	0	0.00
2QNumᶜ	2Q8			0	0	0	0	0
2QNumᵈ	2Q9			0	0	0	0	0
2QDeutᵃ	2Q10			0	0	0	0	0
2QDeutᵇ	2Q11			0	0	0	0	0
2QDeutᶜ	2Q12			1	0	0.00	0	0.00
2QJer	2Q13		2	3	0	0.00	1	0.33
2QPs	2Q14			1	0	0.00	0	0.00
2QJob	2Q15			1	0	0.00	0	0.00
2QRuthᵃ *	2Q16	3		13	0	0.00	0	0.00
2QRuthᵇ	2Q17			3	0	0.00	0	0.00
3QEzek	3Q1			0	0	0	0	0
3QPs	3Q2			0	0	0	0	0
3QLam	3Q3			0	0	0	0	0
4QGen-Exodᵃ *	4Q1	6		43	0	0.00	0	0.00
4QGenᵇ *	4Q2	2		45	0	0.00	0	0.00
4QGenᶜ *	4Q3			13	0	0.00	0	0.00
4QGenᵈ	4Q4			15	0	0.00	0	0.00
4QGenᵉ *	4Q5	2		14	0	0.00	0	0.00
4QGenᶠ *	4Q6	1		2	0	0.00	0	0.00
4QGenᵍ	4Q7			25	0	0.00	0	0.00
4QGenʰ *	4Q8			0	0	0	0	0
4QGenʲ *	4Q9	3		20	2	0.10	0	0.00
4QGenᵏ	4Q10			10	0	0.00	0	0.00
4QpaleoGen-Exod1 *	4Q11	10		72	0	0.00	0	0.00
4QpaleoGenᵐ	4Q12		1	0	0	0	0	0
4QExodᵇ *	4Q13	3		34	1	0.03	0	0.00
4QExodᶜ *	4Q14	10		56	0	0.00	3	0.05
4QExodᵈ	4Q15			1	0	0.00	0	0.00
4QExodᵉ	4Q16	1		9	0	0.00	0	0.00
4QExod-Levᶠ *	4Q17	1		37	3	0.08	1	0.03
4QExodᵍ	4Q18			2	0	0.00	0	0.00
4QExodʰ	4Q19			0	0	0	0	0
4QExodʲ	4Q20			1	0	0.00	0	0.00
4QExodᵏ	4Q21			2	0	0.00	0	0.00

Appendix C. Definite Articles

Scroll Name	Scroll #	לא	לוא	Definite Article	Definite Article Plus	Percent Change	Definite Article Minus	Percent Change
4QpaleoExod^m *	4Q22	18		141	1	0.01	1	0.01
4QLev-Num^a *	4Q23	10		91	0	0.00	0	0.00
4QLev^b *	4Q24	18		38	2	0.05	1	0.03
4QLev^c	4Q25	1		12	0	0.00	0	0.00
4QLev^d	4Q26	1	3	10	0	0.00	1	0.10
4QLev^e	4Q26a	3		6	1	0.17	0	0.00
4QLev^g	4Q26b	1		4	0	0.00	0	0.00
4QNum^b	4Q27		19	111	3	0.03	3	0.03
4QDeut^a	4Q28	4		3	0	0.00	0	0.00
4QDeut^b *	4Q29	2		22	0	0.00	0	0.00
4QDeut^c	4Q30	13		39	1	0.03	1	0.03
4QDeut^d *	4Q31	4		33	0	0.00	0	0.00
4QDeut^e	4Q32	7		6	0	0.00	0	0.00
4QDeut^f *	4Q33	15		30	0	0.00	1	0.03
4QDeut^g	4Q34	4		4	0	0.00	0	0.00
4QDeut^h *	4Q35	5		23	1	0.04	0	0.00
4QDeut^i	4Q36	4		7	0	0.00	0	0.00
4QDeut^j	4Q37	1	3	16	1	0.06	1	0.06
4QDeut^k1	4Q38		1	10	0	0.00	1	0.10
4QDeut^k2	4Q38a		2	14	0	0.00	0	0.00
4QDeut^k3	4Q38b	1		1	0	0.00	0	0.00
4QDeut^l	4Q39			5	0	0.00	0	0.00
4QDeut^m	4Q40		1	9	0	0.00	0	0.00
4QDeut^n	4Q41	2	17	35	0	0.00	0	0.00
4QDeut^o	4Q42	6		6	0	0.00	0	0.00
4QDeut^p	4Q43	1		1	0	0.00	0	0.00
4QDeut^q	4Q44			0	0	0	0	0
4QpaleoDeut^r *	4Q45	12		28	1	0.04	1	0.04
4QpaleoDeut^s	4Q46			1	0	0.00	0	0.00
4QJosh^a *	4Q47	5		35	1	0.03	0	0.00
4QJosh^b	4Q48	1		16	0	0.00	0	0.00
4QJudg^a	4Q49			2	1	0.50	0	0.00
4QJudg^b	4Q50			5	1	0.20	0	0.00
4QSam^a	4Q51	9	14	191	12	0.06	8	0.04
4QSam^b *	4Q52	5		30	0	0.00	0	0.00
4QSam^c	4Q53		6	21	0	0.00	0	0.00
4QKgs	4Q54	2		20	1	0.05	1	0.05
4QIsa^a *	4Q55	6		21	0	0.00	0	0.00
4QIsa^b *	4Q56	16		45	1	0.02	0	0.00
4QIsa^c	4Q57		19	32	1	0.03	0	0.00
4QIsa^d *	4Q58	17		6	0	0.00	0	0.00

193

Statistics, Linguistics and the 'Biblical' Dead Sea Scrolls

Scroll Name	Scroll #	לא	לוא	Definite Article Plus	Definite Article	Percent Change	Definite Article Minus	Percent Change
4QIsa^e *	4Q59	6		14	0	0.00	0	0.00
4QIsa^f	4Q60	2		15	0	0.00	0	0.00
4QIsa^g	4Q61	3	2	0	0	0	0	0
4QIsa^h	4Q62	1		1	0	0.00	0	0.00
4QIsaⁱ	4Q62a			0	0	0	0	0
4QIsa^j	4Q63	1		0	0	0	0	0
4QIsa^k	4Q64	1		1	0	0.00	0	0.00
4QIsa^l	4Q65		2	1	0	0.00	0	0.00
4QIsa^m	4Q66			1	0	0.00	0	0.00
4QIsaⁿ	4Q67			1	1	1.00	0	0.00
4QIsa^o	4Q68			2	0	0.00	0	0.00
4QpapIsa^p	4Q69			0	0	0	0	0
4QIsa^q	4Q69a			0	0	0	0	0
4QIsa^r	4Q69b			1	0	0.00	0	0.00
4QJer^a	4Q70	5	5	29	0	0.00	1	0.03
4QJer^b	4Q71			3	0	0.00	0	0.00
4QJer^c *	4Q72	13		38	0	0.00	1	0.03
4QJer^d	4Q72a	2		6	0	0.00	0	0.00
4QJer^e	4Q72b			1	0	0.00	0	0.00
4QEzek^a *	4Q73	1		16	0	0.00	0	0.00
4QEzek^b	4Q74			9	0	0.00	0	0.00
4QEzek^c	4Q75			1	0	0.00	0	0.00
4QXII^a *	4Q76	3		19	1	0.05	1	0.05
4QXII^b	4Q77			6	0	0.00	0	0.00
4QXII^c *	4Q78		9	23	3	0.13	0	0.00
4QXII^d	4Q79	1		1	0	0.00	0	0.00
4QXII^e	4Q80		4	12	0	0.00	0	0.00
4QXII^f	4Q81	2		4	0	0.00	0	0.00
4QXII^g *	4Q82	6	9	31	2	0.06	0	0.00
4QPs^a *	4Q83		5	3	0	0.00	1	0.33
4QPs^b *	4Q84	8		11	0	0.00	1	0.09
4QPs^c *	4Q85	4		4	1	0.25	0	0.00
4QPs^d	4Q86			9	1	0.11	3	0.33
4QPs^e *	4Q87		3	7	0	0.00	1	0.14
4QPs^f *	4Q88	1		0	0	0	0	0
4QPs^g	4Q89			0	0	0	0	0
4QGen^h2	4Q8a			0	0	0	0	0
4QGen^h-para	4Q8b			0	0	0	0	0
4QPs^h	4Q90			0	0	0	0	0
4QPs^j	4Q91			0	0	0	1	0
4QPs^k	4Q92			2	0	0.00	0	0.00

Appendix C. Definite Articles

Scroll Name	Scroll #	לא	לוא	Definite Article	Definite Article Plus	Percent Change	Definite Article Minus	Percent Change
4QPs^l	4Q93			2	0	0.00	0	0.00
4QPs^m	4Q94			3	0	0.00	0	0.00
4QPs^n	4Q95			1	0	0.00	0	0.00
4QPs^o	4Q96		1	1	0	0.00	0	0.00
4QPs^p	4Q97			0	0	0	0	0
4QPs^q	4Q98			6	0	0.00	0	0.00
4QPs^r	4Q98a			0	0	0	0	0
4QPs^s	4Q98b			0	0	0	0	0
4QPs^t	4Q98c			0	0	0	0	0
4QPs^u	4Q98d			0	0	0	0	0
4QPs^v	4Q98e			0	0	0	0	0
4QPs^w	4Q98f			0	0	0	0	0
4QPs^x	4Q98g			0	0	0	0	0
4QJob^a *	4Q99	7	1	3	0	0.00	0	0.00
4QJob^b	4Q100	1		0	0	0	0	0
4QpaleoJob^c	4Q101	1		0	0	0	0	0
4QProv^a	4Q102	3		0	0	0	0	0
4QProv^b	4Q103	1		0	0	0	0	0
4QProv^c	4Q103a			0	0	0	0	0
4QRuth^a	4Q104			3	0	0.00	0	0.00
4QRuth^b	4Q105			0	0	0	0	0
4QCant^a	4Q106			8	0	0.00	2	0.25
4QCant^b *	4Q107	1		13	0	0.00	0	0.00
4QCant^c	4Q108			0	0	0	0	0
4QQoh^a	4Q109		6	9	0	0.00	0	0.00
4QQoh^b	4Q110		1	0	0	0	0	0
4QLam *	4Q111		5	2	1	0.50	0	0.00
4QDan^a *	4Q112	6		79	2	0.03	0	0.00
4QDan^b *	4Q113		2	38	0	0.00	0	0.00
4QDan^c *	4Q114	6		14	0	0.00	0	0.00
4QDan^d	4Q115	2		20	1	0.05	0	0.00
4QDan^e	4Q116			1	0	0	0	0
4QEzr^a	4Q117			9	0	0.00	0	0.00
4QChr	4Q118			1	0	0.00	0	0.00
4QPhyl A *	4Q128		7	32	0	0.00	0	0.00
4QPhyl B *	4Q129		10	15	0	0.00	1	0.07
4QPhyl C *	4Q130	5		25	2	0.08	0	0.00
4QPhyl D	4Q131			2	0	0.00	0	0.00
4QPhyl E	4Q132			0	0	0	0	0
4QPhyl F	4Q133			1	0	0.00	0	0.00
4QPhyl G *	4Q134	2	8	18	0	0.00	0	0.00

Scroll Name	Scroll #	לא	לוא	Definite Article	Definite Article Plus	Percent Change	Definite Article Minus	Percent Change
4QPhyl H *	4Q135		1	16	1	0.06	2	0.13
4QPhyl I	4Q136	2	1	13	0	0.00	0	0.00
4QPhyl J *	4Q137		10	22	1	0.05	2	0.09
4QPhyl K *	4Q138		7	37	2	0.05	1	0.03
4QPhyl L	4Q139		3	3	0	0.00	0	0.00
4QPhyl M *	4Q140		5	21	2	0.10	0	0.00
4QPhyl N	4Q141	3		1	1	1.00	0	0.00
4QPhyl O	4Q142		0	0	0	0	0	0
4QPhyl P	4Q143			0	0	0	0	0
4QPhyl Q	4Q144		1	4	0	0.00	0	0.00
4QPhyl R	4Q145	2		11	0	0.00	0	0.00
4QPhyl S	4Q146			1	0	0.00	0	0.00
4QPhyl T	4Q147			0	0	0	0	0
4QPhyl U	4Q148			0	0	0	0	0
4QMez A	4Q149			3	0	0.00	0	0.00
4QMez B	4Q150	1		4	0	0.00	0	0.00
4QMez C	4Q151			2	0	0.00	0	0.00
4QMez D	4Q152			0	0	0	0	0
4QMez E	4Q153			0	0	0	0	0
4QMez F	4Q154			2	0	0.00	0	0.00
4QMez G	4Q155	1		2	0	0.00	0	0.00
4Qpap cryptA Lev^h?	4Q249j			1	0	0.00	0	0.00
4QpapGen^o	4Q483			0	0	0	0	0
4QGen^n	4Q576			0	0	0	0	0
5QDeut	5Q1	5		12	0	0.00	0	0.00
5QKgs	5Q2			4	0	0.00	0	0.00
5QIsa	5Q3			0	0	0	0	0
5QXII	5Q4		3	2	0	0.00	0	0.00
5QPs	5Q5			0	0	0	0	0
5QLam^a	5Q6	5	1	2	1	0.50	0	0.00
5QLam^b	5Q7			0	0	0	0	0
6QpaleoGen	6Q1			0	0	0	0	0
6QpaleoLev	6Q2			0	0	0	0	0
6QpapDeut?	6Q3			0	0	0	0	0
6QpapKgs *	6Q4	2		10	0	0.00	0	0.00
6QpapPs 78?	6Q5			0	0	0	0	0
6QCant	6Q6	1		0	0	0	0	0
6QpapDan	6Q7			3	0	0.00	0	0.00
6QDeut?	6Q20			0	0	0	0	0
8QGen	8Q1			1	0	0.00	0	0.00
8QPs	8Q2			0	0	0	0	0

Appendix C. Definite Articles

Scroll Name	Scroll #	לא	לוא	Definite Article	Definite Article Plus	Percent Change	Definite Article Minus	Percent Change
8QPhyl *	8Q3	15		61	0	0.00	2	0.03
8QMez *	8Q4	5		27	0	0.00	1	0.04
11QpaleoLev[a] *	11Q1	19		86	1	0.01	0	0.00
11QLev[b]	11Q2			4	0	0.00	2	0.50
11QDeut	11Q3			2	0	0.00	0	0.00
11QEzek	11Q4	1		1	0	0.00	0	0.00
11QPs[a] *	11Q5		32	58	1	0.02	4	0.07
11QPs[b]	11Q6		0	4	0	0.00	0	0.00
11QPs[c]	11Q7			5	0	0.00	0	0.00
11QPs[d]	11Q8	1	1	2	0	0.00	0	0.00
11QPs[e]	11Q9			0	0	0	0	0
34Se1	34Se1	3		12	0	0.00	0	0.00
34Se2	34Se2			0	0	0	0	0
5/6Hev1a	5/6Hev1a			1	0	0.00	0	0.00
5/6Hev1b *	5/6Hev1b	9		7	0	0.00	0	0.00
Gen	Mas1			0	0	0	0	0
Lev	Mas1a			18	0	0.00	0	0.00
Lev *	Mas1b	6		54	0	0.00	0	0.00
Deut	Mas1c	1		0	0	0	0	0
Ezek *	Mas1d	3		23	1	0.04	0	0.00
Psa *	Mas1e	3		3	0	0.00	0	0.00
Psa	Mas1f			1	0	0.00	0	0.00
Mur Gen 1 *	Mur1	4		14	0	0.00	0	0.00
Mur Deut	Mur2	1		3	0	0.00	0	0.00
MurIsa	Mur3	2		0	0	0	0	0
MurEx *	Mur4	6		32	0	0.00	0	0.00
MurXII *	Mur88	62		212	3	0.01	1	0.00
MurGen	MurX			0	0	0	0	0
Sdeir1	Sdeir1	16		1	0	0.00	0	0.00
XHev/Se2	XHev/Se2			4	0	0.00	0	0.00
XHev/Se3	XHev/Se3	1		1	0	0.00	0	0.00
XHev/Se5 *	XHev/Se5	6		32	0	0.00	0	0.00
XQ1 *	XQ1	11		38	0	0.00	0	0.00
XQ2 *	XQ2	2		28	1	0.04	2	0.07
XQ3 *	XQ3	16		18	1	0.06	0	0.00
					123		84	

D. Direct Object Marker

Scroll Name	Scroll #	לא	לוא	Direct Object Markers	את Plus[1]	Percent Plus	את Minus[2]	Percent Minus
1QGen	1Q1			2	1	0.5	0	0
1QExod	1Q2	1		1	0	0	0	0
1QpaleoLev-Numa	1Q3	1		10	0	0	0	0
1QDeuta	1Q4		1	12	0	0	0	0
1QDeutb *	1Q5	10		3	0	0	0	0
1QJudg	1Q6			3	0	0	0	0
1QSam	1Q7	2		2	0	0	0	0
1QIsab *	1Q8	89		37	1	0.03	0	0
1QEzek	1Q9			0	0	0	0	0
1QPsa	1Q10			0	0	0	0	0
1QPsb	1Q11			0	0	0	0	0
1QPsc	1Q12			0	0	0	0	0
1QPhyl *	1Q13	8		4	0	0	0	0
1QDana	1Q71	1		2	0	0	0	0
1QDanb	1Q72	2		0	0	0	0	0
1QIsaa I	1QIsaa I		167	171	5	0.03	0	0
1QIsaa II	1QIsaa II		276	69	13	0.18	3	0.04
2QExoda	2Q1			1	0	0	0	0
2QExodb	2Q2	1	1	5	0	0	0	0
2QGen	2Q3			1	0	0	0	0
2QExodc	2Q4			0	0	0	0	0
2QpaleoLev	2Q5			0	0	0	0	0
2QNuma	2Q6			3	0	0	0	0
2QNumb	2Q7			2	0	0	0	0
2QNumc	2Q8			0	0	0	0	0
2QNumd	2Q9			0	0	0	0	0
2QDeuta	2Q10			0	0	0	0	0

---

1 1Q1 f3:2; 1Q8 24:12; 1QIsaa 2:12, 7:26, 8:10, 12:6, 22:23, 29:25, 29:25, 30:15, 31:28, 40:26, 42:29, 43:24, 44:3, 44:3, 46:18, 46:6, 53:16, 53:4; 4Q1 f34_35:6, f34_35:6; 4Q11 f20:8, f7i+8:11; 4Q13 f3i_4:15, f3i_4:19, f3i_4:2; 4Q17 f2ii:13, f2ii:8; 4Q22 17:4; 4Q23 f34ii+44_50:21; 4Q26 f4:15; 4Q27 f12:3, f12:4, f20_22:1, f55i_56:12; 4Q31 1:6; 4Q33 f32_35:1; 4Q38a f5:7; 4Q41 3:10; 4Q47 f9i_12:9; 4Q51 5b_c:3, 8a_b:1, f68_76:2; 4Q57 f13:12; 4Q76 3:13; 4Q78 f34:3; 4Q84 f25ii:1, f30ii+32i+33_34:17, f7ii+8ii+9ii+10:9; 4Q92 1:3; 4Q112 f1i+2:1; 4Q114 3:15; 4Q128 f1:29; 4Q129 f1R:6; 4Q130 f1:21; 4Q135 f1:8; 4Q137 f1:19, f1:33; 4Q138 f1:10; 4Q149 f1:3; 8Q3 f17_25:6; Mas1 f1:2; 11Q1 3:7, 6:9; 11Q5 14:10, 17:16.

2 1QIsaa 29:28, 37:26, 50:19; 4Q11 f23:8; 4Q14 2:27, 2:38; 4Q22 40:32; 4Q27 f13ii+15_17i:23; 4Q41 4:6; 4Q45 f21ii:1; 4Q51 3a_e:15, f26_27:8, f61i+62:15, f61ii+63_64a_b+65_67:4; 4Q53 f2_5i:22; 4Q72 f7:2; 4Q135 f1:9; 4Q138 f1:1; 11Q1 5:2, fK_Li:4; 11Q5 2:6; XQ2 1:19.

Appendix D. Direct Object Marker

Scroll Name	Scroll #	לא	לוא	Direct Object Markers	את Plus	Percent Plus	את Minus	Percent Minus
2QDeut^b	2Q11			0	0	0	0	0
2QDeut^c	2Q12			0	0	0	0	0
2QJer	2Q13		2	4	0	0	0	0
2QPs	2Q14			0	0	0	0	0
2QJob	2Q15			0	0	0	0	0
2QRuth^a *	2Q16	3		4	0	0	0	0
2QRuth^b	2Q17			0	0	0	0	0
3QEzek	3Q1			0	0	0	0	0
3QPs	3Q2			0	0	0	0	0
3QLam	3Q3			0	0	0	0	0
4QGen-Exod^a *	4Q1	6		45	2	0.04	0	0
4QGen^b *	4Q2	2		13	0	0	0	0
4QGen^c *	4Q3			9	0	0	0	0
4QGen^d	4Q4			5	0	0	0	0
4QGen^e *	4Q5	2		5	0	0	0	0
4QGen^f *	4Q6	1		5	0	0	0	0
4QGen^g	4Q7			8	0	0	0	0
4QGen^h *	4Q8			0	0	0	0	0
4QGen^j *	4Q9	3		8	0	0	0	0
4QGen^k	4Q10			1	0	0	0	0
4QpaleoGen-Exod1 *	4Q11	10		46	2	0.04	1	0.02
4QpaleoGen^m	4Q12		1	0	0	0	0	0
4QExod^b *	4Q13	3		18	3	0.17	0	0
4QExod^c *	4Q14	10		35	0	0	2	0.05
4QExod^d	4Q15			0	0	0	0	0
4QExod^e	4Q16	1		3	0	0	0	0
4QExod-Lev^f *	4Q17	1		46	3	0.07	0	0
4QExod^g	4Q18			1	0	0	0	0
4QExod^h	4Q19			1	0	0	0	0
4QExod^j	4Q20			2	0	0	0	0
4QExod^k	4Q21			1	0	0	0	0
4QpaleoExod^m *	4Q22	18		112	1	0.009	1	0.009
4QLev-Num^a *	4Q23	10		77	1	0.01	0	0
4QLev^b *	4Q24	18		30	0	0	0	0
4QLev^c	4Q25	1		7	0	0	0	0
4QLev^d	4Q26	1	3	4	1	0.25	0	0
4QLev^e	4Q26a	3		6	0	0	0	0
4QLev^g	4Q26b	1		0	0	0	0	0
4QNum^b	4Q27		19	66	3	0.04	1	0.02
4QDeut^a	4Q28	4		2	0	0	0	0
4QDeut^b *	4Q29	2		13	0	0	0	0

Statistics, Linguistics and the 'Biblical' Dead Sea Scrolls

Scroll Name	Scroll #	לא	לוא	Direct Object Markers	את Plus	Percent Plus	את Minus	Percent Minus
4QDeut^c	4Q30	13		18	0	0	0	0
4QDeut^d *	4Q31	4		13	1	0.08	0	0
4QDeut^e	4Q32	7		5	0	0	0	0
4QDeut^f *	4Q33	15		13	1	0.08	0	0
4QDeut^g	4Q34	4		5	0	0	0	0
4QDeut^h *	4Q35	5		16	0	0	0	0
4QDeutⁱ	4Q36	4		0	0	0	0	0
4QDeut^j	4Q37	1	3	13	0	0	0	0
4QDeut^k1	4Q38		1	6	0	0	0	0
4QDeut^k2	4Q38a		2	2	1	0.5	0	0
4QDeut^k3	4Q38b	1		0	0	0	0	0
4QDeut^l	4Q39			2	0	0	0	0
4QDeut^m	4Q40		1	2	0	0	0	0
4QDeutⁿ	4Q41	2	17	33	1	0.03	1	0.03
4QDeut^o	4Q42	6		2	0	0	0	0
4QDeut^p	4Q43	1		0	0	0	0	0
4QDeut^q	4Q44			0	0	0	0	0
4QpaleoDeut^r *	4Q45	12		14	0	0	1	0.07
4QpaleoDeut^s	4Q46			0	0	0	0	0
4QJosh^a *	4Q47	5		7	1	0.14	0	0
4QJosh^b	4Q48	1		3	0	0	0	0
4QJudg^a	4Q49			2	0	0	0	0
4QJudg^b	4Q50			1	0	0	0	0
4QSam^a	4Q51	9	14	81	3	0.04	4	0.05
4QSam^b *	4Q52	5		18	0	0	0	0
4QSam^c	4Q53		6	10	0	0	1	0.09
4QKgs	4Q54	2		6	0	0	0	0
4QIsa^a *	4Q55	6		2	0	0	0	0
4QIsa^b *	4Q56	16		8	0	0	0	0
4QIsa^c	4Q57		19	9	1	0.11	0	0
4QIsa^d *	4Q58	17		6	0	0	0	0
4QIsa^e *	4Q59	6		7	0	0	0	0
4QIsa^f	4Q60	2		6	0	0	0	0
4QIsa^g	4Q61	3	2	0	0	0	0	0
4QIsa^h	4Q62	1		1	0	0	0	0
4QIsaⁱ	4Q62a			0	0	0	0	0
4QIsa^j	4Q63	1		0	0	0	0	0
4QIsa^k	4Q64	1		0	0	0	0	0
4QIsa^l	4Q65		2	1	0	0	0	0
4QIsa^m	4Q66			1	0	0	0	0
4QIsaⁿ	4Q67			0	0	0	0	0

Appendix D. Direct Object Marker

Scroll Name	Scroll #	לא	לוא	Direct Object Markers	את Plus	Percent Plus	את Minus	Percent Minus
4QIsa^o	4Q68			0	0	0	0	0
4QpapIsa^p	4Q69			0	0	0	0	0
4QIsa^q	4Q69a			0	0	0	0	0
4QIsa^r	4Q69b			1	0	0	0	0
4QJer^a	4Q70	5	5	36	0	0	0	0
4QJer^b	4Q71			1	0	0	0	0
4QJer^c *	4Q72	13		16	0	0	1	0.06
4QJer^d	4Q72a	2		7	0	0	0	0
4QJer^e	4Q72b			1	0	0	0	0
4QEzek^a *	4Q73	1		3	0	0	0	0
4QEzek^b	4Q74			1	0	0	0	0
4QEzek^c	4Q75			1	0	0	0	0
4QXII^a *	4Q76	3		16	1	0.06	0	0
4QXII^b	4Q77			6	0	0	0	0
4QXII^c *	4Q78		9	4	1	0.25	0	0
4QXII^d	4Q79	1		0	0	0	0	0
4QXII^e	4Q80		4	3	0	0	0	0
4QXII^f	4Q81	2		0	0	0	0	0
4QXII^g *	4Q82	6	9	13	0	0	0	0
4QPs^a *	4Q83		5	0	0	0	0	0
4QPs^b *	4Q84	8		14	3	0.21	0	0
4QPs^c *	4Q85	4		0	0	0	0	0
4QPs^d	4Q86			2	0	0	0	0
4QPs^e *	4Q87		3	6	0	0	0	0
4QPs^f *	4Q88		1	0	0	0	0	0
4QPs^g	4Q89			0	0	0	0	0
4QGen^h2	4Q8a			0	0	0	0	0
4QGen^h-para	4Q8b			0	0	0	0	0
4QPs^h	4Q90			0	0	0	0	0
4QPs^j	4Q91			0	0	0	0	0
4QPs^k	4Q92			1	1	1	0	0
4QPs^l	4Q93			0	0	0	0	0
4QPs^m	4Q94			0	0	0	0	0
4QPsⁿ	4Q95			0	0	0	0	0
4QPs^o	4Q96		1	0	0	0	0	0
4QPs^p	4Q97			0	0	0	0	0
4QPs^q	4Q98			0	0	0	0	0
4QPs^r	4Q98a			0	0	0	0	0
4QPs^s	4Q98b			0	0	0	0	0
4QPs^t	4Q98c			0	0	0	0	0
4QPs^u	4Q98d			0	0	0	0	0

Statistics, Linguistics and the 'Biblical' Dead Sea Scrolls

Scroll Name	Scroll #	לא	לוא	Direct Object Markers	את Plus	Percent Plus	את Minus	Percent Minus
4QPs^v	4Q98e			0	0	0	0	0
4QPs^w	4Q98f			0	0	0	0	0
4QPs^x	4Q98g			0	0	0	0	0
4QJob^a *	4Q99	7	1	1	0	0	0	0
4QJob^b	4Q100	1		0	0	0	0	0
4QpaleoJob^c	4Q101	1		0	0	0	0	0
4QProv^a	4Q102	3		0	0	0	0	0
4QProv^b	4Q103	1		0	0	0	0	0
4QProv^c	4Q103a			0	0	0	0	0
4QRuth^a	4Q104			0	0	0	0	0
4QRuth^b	4Q105			0	0	0	0	0
4QCant^a	4Q106			1	0	0	0	0
4QCant^b *	4Q107	1		2	0	0	0	0
4QCant^c	4Q108			0	0	0	0	0
4QQoh^a	4Q109		6	0	0	0	0	0
4QQoh^b	4Q110		1	1	0	0	0	0
4QLam *	4Q111		5	0	0	0	0	0
4QDan^a *	4Q112	6		1	1	1	0	0
4QDan^b *	4Q113		2	1	0	0	0	0
4QDan^c *	4Q114	6		8	1	0.13	0	0
4QDan^d	4Q115	2		0	0	0	0	0
4QDan^e	4Q116			0	0	0	0	0
4QEzr^a	4Q117			0	0	0	0	0
4QChr	4Q118			1	0	0	0	0
4QPhyl A *	4Q128		7	20	1	0.05	0	0
4QPhyl B *	4Q129		10	11	1	0.09	0	0
4QPhyl C *	4Q130	5		11	1	0.09	0	0
4QPhyl D	4Q131			1	0	0	0	0
4QPhyl E	4Q132			0	0	0	0	0
4QPhyl F	4Q133			0	0	0	0	0
4QPhyl G *	4Q134	2	8	11	0	0	0	0
4QPhyl H *	4Q135		1	17	1	0.06	1	0.06
4QPhyl I	4Q136	2	1	6	0	0	0	0
4QPhyl J *	4Q137		10	22	2	0.09	0	0
4QPhyl K *	4Q138		7	29	1	0.03	1	0.03
4QPhyl L	4Q139		3	2	0	0	0	0
4QPhyl M *	4Q140		5	11	0	0	0	0
4QPhyl N	4Q141	3		0	0	0	0	0
4QPhyl O	4Q142		0	1	0	0	0	0
4QPhyl P	4Q143			0	0	0	0	0
4QPhyl Q	4Q144		1	1	0	0	0	0

Appendix D. Direct Object Marker

Scroll Name	Scroll #	לא	לוא	Direct Object Markers	את Plus	Percent Plus	את Minus	Percent Minus
4QPhyl R	4Q145	2		2	0	0	0	0
4QPhyl S	4Q146			0	0	0	0	0
4QPhyl T	4Q147			0	0	0	0	0
4QPhyl U	4Q148			0	0	0	0	0
4QMez A	4Q149			7	1	0.14	0	0
4QMez B	4Q150	1		1	0	0	0	0
4QMez C	4Q151			2	0	0	0	0
4QMez D	4Q152			0	0	0	0	0
4QMez E	4Q153			0	0	0	0	0
4QMez F	4Q154			0	0	0	0	0
4QMez G	4Q155	1		0	0	0	0	0
4Qpap cryptA Lev[h]?	4Q249j			1	0	0	0	0
4QpapGen[o]	4Q483			0	0	0	0	0
4QGen[n]	4Q576			1	0	0	0	0
5QDeut	5Q1	5		5	0	0	0	0
5QKgs	5Q2			3	0	0	0	0
5QIsa	5Q3			0	0	0	0	0
5QXII	5Q4		3	0	0	0	0	0
5QPs	5Q5			0	0	0	0	0
5QLam[a]	5Q6	5	1	1	0	0	0	0
5QLam[b]	5Q7			0	0	0	0	0
6QpaleoGen	6Q1			0	0	0	0	0
6QpaleoLev	6Q2			0	0	0	0	0
6QpapDeut?	6Q3			0	0	0	0	0
6QpapKgs *	6Q4	2		2	0	0	0	0
6QpapPs 78?	6Q5			0	0	0	0	0
6QCant	6Q6	1		0	0	0	0	0
6QpapDan	6Q7			0	0	0	0	0
6QDeut?	6Q20			0	0	0	0	0
8QGen	8Q1			1	0	0	0	0
8QPs	8Q2			0	0	0	0	0
8QPhyl *	8Q3	15		45	1	0.02	0	0
8QMez *	8Q4	5		19	0	0	0	0
11QpaleoLev[a] *	11Q1	19		40	2	0.05	2	0.05
11QLev[b]	11Q2			3	0	0	0	0
11QDeut	11Q3			2	0	0	0	0
11QEzek	11Q4	1		1	0	0	0	0
11QPs[a] *	11Q5		32	33	2	0.06	1	0.03
11QPs[b]	11Q6		0	1	0	0	0	0
11QPs[c]	11Q7			0	0	0	0	0
11QPs[d]	11Q8	1	1	0	0	0	0	0

Statistics, Linguistics and the 'Biblical' Dead Sea Scrolls

Scroll Name	Scroll #	לא	לוא	Direct Object Markers	את Plus	Percent Plus	את Minus	Percent Minus
11QPsᵉ	11Q9			0	0	0	0	0
34Se1	34Se1	3		3	0	0	0	0
34Se2	34Se2			0	0	0	0	0
5/6Hev1a	5/6Hev1a			3	0	0	0	0
5/6Hev1b *	5/6Hev1b	9		4	0	0	0	0
Gen	Mas1			0	1	0	0	0
Lev	Mas1a			6	0	0	0	0
Lev *	Mas1b	6		24	0	0	0	0
Deut	Mas1c	1		1	0	0	0	0
Ezek *	Mas1d	3		18	0	0	0	0
Psa *	Mas1e	3		1	0	0	0	0
Psa	Mas1f			0	0	0	0	0
Mur Gen 1 *	Mur1	4		19	0	0	0	0
Mur Deut	Mur2	1		4	0	0	0	0
MurIsa	Mur3	2		0	0	0	0	0
MurEx *	Mur4	6		14	0	0	0	0
MurXII *	Mur88	62		67	0	0	0	0
MurGen	MurX			1	0	0	0	0
Sdeir1	Sdeir1	16		9	0	0	0	0
XHev/Se2	XHev/Se2			9	0	0	0	0
XHev/Se3	XHev/Se3	1		1	0	0	0	0
XHev/Se5 *	XHev/Se5			6	13	0	0	0
XQ1 *	XQ1	11		18	0	0	0	0
XQ2 *	XQ2	2		17	0	0	1	0.06
XQ3 *	XQ3	16		12	0	0	0	0
					67		22	

E. על and אל Interchange

Scroll Name	Scroll #	לא	לוא	על	אל – על¹	Percent Towards על	אל	אל - על²	Percent Towards אל
1QGen	1Q1			1		0	3		0
1QExodᵈ	1Q2	1		3		0	4		0
1QpaleoLev-Numᵃ	1Q3	1		0		0	3		0
1QDeutᵃ	1Q4		1	0		0	1		0
1QDeutᵇ *	1Q5	10		1		0	3		0
1QJudg	1Q6			1		0	3		0
1QSam	1Q7	2		0		0	3		0
1QIsaᵇ *	1Q8	89		52	2	0.04	55	4	0.08
1QEzek	1Q9			1		0	0		0
1QPsᵃ	1Q10			0		0	1		0
1QPsᵇ	1Q11			0		0	0		0
1QPsᶜ	1Q12			0		0	1		0
1QPhyl *	1Q13	8		2		0	0		0
1QDanᵃ	1Q71	1		1		0	1		0
1QDanᵇ	1Q72	2		0		0	0		0
1QIsaᵃ I	1QIsaᵃ I		167	206	7	0.04	93	8	0.09
1QIsaᵃ II	1QIsaᵃ II		276	129	2	0.02	158	7	0.05
2QExodᵃ	2Q1			0		0	0		0
2QExodᵇ	2Q2	1	1	0		0	1		0
2QGen	2Q3			1		0	1		0
2QExodᶜ	2Q4			0		0	0		0
2QpaleoLev	2Q5			0		0	0		0
2QNumᵃ	2Q6			0		0	1		0
2QNumᵇ	2Q7			0		0	1		0
2QNumᶜ	2Q8			0		0	0		0
2QNumᵈ	2Q9			0		0	0		0
2QDeutᵃ	2Q10			0		0	0		0
2QDeutᵇ	2Q11			1		0	0		0
2QDeutᶜ	2Q12			0		0	0		0
2QJer	2Q13		2	9		0	2		0
2QPs	2Q14			2		0	0		0

---

1 1Q8 24:18, 26:12, 1QIsaᵃ 2:9, 3:12, 6:3, 6:3, 14:12, 17:15, 17:9, 29:8, 30:27; 4Q23 f5:2; 4Q51 f100_101:4, f144_146a_b:3, f3_5:6, f43:3, f61ii+63_64a_b+65_67:31, f68_76:3; 4Q52 f6_7:11, f6_7:2; 4Q53 f5ii_7i:12, f5ii_7i:12; 4Q70 f32ii_35:21; 4Q72 f44_50:14, f44_50:9; 4Q83 f19ii_20:35; 4Q99 f16ii:15; 4Q130 f1:8; 6Q4 f15:3; 11Q5 20:9; Mur88 21:3, 7:21.

2 1Q8 16:9, 23:10, 26:8, 28:11; 1QIsaᵃ 10:8, 12:2, 17:22, 23:21, 24:26, 24:27, 25:24, 25:30, 30:13, 44:5, 46:17, 49:9, 52:4, 52:7, 54:11; 4Q17 f2ii:17; 4Q22 19:5; 4Q35 f11_15:5; 4Q51 f102ii+103_106i+107_109a_b:40, f155_158:24, f61i+62:16; 4Q57 f3_5+50:6; 4Q59 f20_22:4; 4Q60 f17:3; 4Q112 f14:18; 11Q5 20:9.

Statistics, Linguistics and the 'Biblical' Dead Sea Scrolls

Scroll Name	Scroll #	לא	לוא	על	אל – על	Percent Towards על	אל	אל – על	Percent Towards אל
2QJob	2Q15			0		0	1		0
2QRuth^a *	2Q16	3		1		0	1		0
2QRuth^b	2Q17			0		0	0		0
3QEzek	3Q1			0		0	0		0
3QPs	3Q2			0		0	1		0
3QLam	3Q3			0		0	0		0
4QGen-Exod^a *	4Q1	6		7		0	39		0
4QGen^b *	4Q2	2		8		0	8		0
4QGen^c *	4Q3			3		0	0		0
4QGen^d	4Q4			3		0	0		0
4QGen^e *	4Q5	2		3		0	3		0
4QGen^f *	4Q6	1		2		0	9		0
4QGen^g	4Q7			5		0	0		0
4QGen^h *	4Q8			0		0	0		0
4QGen^j *	4Q9	3		9		0	11		0
4QGen^k	4Q10			1		0	2		0
4QpaleoGen-Exod1 *	4Q11	10		15		0	23		0
4QpaleoGen^m	4Q12		1	0		0	1		0
4QExod^b *	4Q13	3		7		0	21		0
4QExod^c *	4Q14	10		17		0	18		0
4QExod^d	4Q15			0		0	0		0
4QExod^e	4Q16	1		0		0	2		0
4QExod-Lev^f *	4Q17	1		8		0	5	1	0.2
4QExod^g	4Q18			0		0	1		0
4QExod^h	4Q19			0		0	0		0
4QExod^j	4Q20			1		0	1		0
4QExod^k	4Q21			0		0	0		0
4QpaleoExod^m *	4Q22	18		40		0	57	1	0.02
4QLev-Num^a *	4Q23	10		21	1	0.05	19		0
4QLev^b *	4Q24	18		16		0	10		0
4QLev^c	4Q25	1		4		0	3		0
4QLev^d	4Q26	1	3	5		0	3		0
4QLev^e	4Q26a	3		3		0	1		0
4QLev^g	4Q26b	1		1		0	0		0
4QNum^b	4Q27		19	28		0	52		0
4QDeut^a	4Q28	4		1		0	0		0
4QDeut^b *	4Q29	2		3		0	1		0
4QDeut^c	4Q30	13		10		0	4		0
4QDeut^d *	4Q31	4		1		0	7		0
4QDeut^e	4Q32	7		1		0	0		0
4QDeut^f *	4Q33	15		9		0	10		0
4QDeut^g	4Q34	4		1		0	2		0

Appendix E. על and אל Interchange

Scroll Name	Scroll #	לא	לוא	על	אל – על	Percent Towards על	אל	אל – על	Percent Towards אל
4QDeut^h *	4Q35	5		4		0	12	1	0.08
4QDeut^i	4Q36	4		3		0	1		0
4QDeut^j	4Q37	1	3	0		0	6		0
4QDeut^k1	4Q38		1	0		0	1		0
4QDeut^k2	4Q38a		2	4		0	6		0
4QDeut^k3	4Q38b	1		1		0	0		0
4QDeut^l	4Q39			2		0	0		0
4QDeut^m	4Q40		1	0		0	1		0
4QDeut^n	4Q41	2	17	9		0	11		0
4QDeut^o	4Q42	6		1		0	0		0
4QDeut^p	4Q43	1		0		0	1		0
4QDeut^q	4Q44			0		0	1		0
4QpaleoDeut^r *	4Q45	12		5		0	2		0
4QpaleoDeut^s	4Q46			0		0	0		0
4QJosh^a *	4Q47	5		1		0	11		0
4QJosh^b	4Q48	1		0		0	2		0
4QJudg^a	4Q49			1		0	1		0
4QJudg^b	4Q50			0		0	2		0
4QSam^a	4Q51	9	14	41	6	0.16	69	3	0.05
4QSam^b *	4Q52	5		7	2	0.29	11		0
4QSam^c	4Q53		6	5	2	0.4	19		0
4QKgs	4Q54	2		3		0	3		0
4QIsa^a *	4Q55	6		14		0	4		0
4QIsa^b *	4Q56	16		20		0	11		0
4QIsa^c	4Q57		19	21		0	9	1	0.11
4QIsa^d *	4Q58	17		2		0	3		0
4QIsa^e *	4Q59	6		8		0	10	1	0.1
4QIsa^f	4Q60	2		5		0	8	1	0.13
4QIsa^g	4Q61	3	2	2		0	1		0
4QIsa^h	4Q62	1		0		0	0		0
4QIsa^i	4Q62a			2		0	0		0
4QIsa^j	4Q63	1		0		0	0		0
4QIsa^k	4Q64	1		1		0	0		0
4QIsa^l	4Q65		2	0		0	0		0
4QIsa^m	4Q66			1		0	0		0
4QIsa^n	4Q67			1		0	0		0
4QIsa^o	4Q68			0		0	1		0
4QpapIsa^p	4Q69			0		0	0		0
4QIsa^q	4Q69a			0		0	0		0
4QIsa^r	4Q69b			0		0	0		0
4QJer^a	4Q70	5	5	20	1	0.05	14		0
4QJer^b	4Q71			0		0	2		0

Statistics, Linguistics and the 'Biblical' Dead Sea Scrolls

Scroll Name	Scroll #	לא	לוא	על	אל – על	Percent Towards על	אל	אל – על	Percent Towards אל
4QJer^c *	4Q72	13		18	2	0.11	10		0
4QJer^d	4Q72a	2		0		0	0		0
4QJer^e	4Q72b			0		0	2		0
4QEzek^a *	4Q73	1		7		0	5		0
4QEzek^b	4Q74			1		0	2		0
4QEzek^c	4Q75			0		0	0		0
4QXII^a *	4Q76	3		9		0	6		0
4QXII^b	4Q77			0		0	1		0
4QXII^c *	4Q78		9	7		0	8		0
4QXII^d	4Q79	1		0		0	0		0
4QXII^e	4Q80		4	4		0	4		0
4QXII^f	4Q81	2		2		0	1		0
4QXII^g *	4Q82	6	9	24		0	21		0
4QPs^a *	4Q83		5	8	1	0.13	14		0
4QPs^b *	4Q84	8		7		0	4		0
4QPs^c *	4Q85	4		5		0	5		0
4QPs^d	4Q86			0		0	0		0
4QPs^e *	4Q87		3	2		0	1		0
4QPs^f *	4Q88		1	0		0	3		0
4QPs^g	4Q89			0		0	1		0
4QGen^h2	4Q8a			0		0	0		0
4QGen^h-para	4Q8b			0		0	0		0
4QPs^h	4Q90			1		0	0		0
4QPs^j	4Q91			0		0	0		0
4QPs^k	4Q92			0		0	0		0
4QPs^l	4Q93			3		0	0		0
4QPs^m	4Q94			0		0	0		0
4QPsⁿ	4Q95			0		0	0		0
4QPs^o	4Q96		1	0		0	0		0
4QPs^p	4Q97			1		0	1		0
4QPs^q	4Q98			1		0	2		0
4QPs^r	4Q98a			0		0	1		0
4QPs^s	4Q98b			0		0	0		0
4QPs^t	4Q98c			1		0	0		0
4QPs^u	4Q98d			0		0	0		0
4QPs^v	4Q98e			0		0	0		0
4QPs^w	4Q98f			0		0	0		0
4QPs^x	4Q98g			0		0	0		0
4QJob^a *	4Q99	7	1	4	1	0.25	7		0
4QJob^b	4Q100	1		2		0	0		0
4QpaleoJob^c	4Q101	1		0		0	0		0
4QProv^a	4Q102	3		1		0	0		0

Appendix E. על and אל Interchange

Scroll Name	Scroll #	לא	לוא	על	אל – על	Percent Towards על	אל	אל – על	Percent Towards אל
4QProv^b	4Q103	1		0		0	0		0
4QProv^c	4Q103a			0		0	0		0
4QRuth^a	4Q104			0		0	0		0
4QRuth^b	4Q105			0		0	0		0
4QCant^a	4Q106			1		0	1		0
4QCant^b *	4Q107	1		1		0	0		0
4QCant^c	4Q108			0		0	0		0
4QQoh^a	4Q109		6	1		0	4		0
4QQoh^b	4Q110	1		1		0	0		0
4QLam *	4Q111		5	7		0	1		0
4QDan^a *	4Q112	6		11	1	0.1	3	1	0.5
4QDan^b *	4Q113		2	6		0	1		0
4QDan^c *	4Q114	6		4		0	6		0
4QDan^d	4Q115	2		1		0	0		0
4QDan^e	4Q116			0		0	0		0
4QEzr^a	4Q117			0		0	0		0
4QChr	4Q118			0		0	0		0
4QPhyl A *	4Q128		7	4		0	3		0
4QPhyl B *	4Q129		10	2		0	6		0
4QPhyl C *	4Q130	5		13		0	2		0
4QPhyl D	4Q131			1		0	0		0
4QPhyl E	4Q132			0		0	1		0
4QPhyl F	4Q133			1		0	1		0
4QPhyl G *	4Q134	2	8	5		0	5		0
4QPhyl H *	4Q135		1	1		0	8		0
4QPhyl I	4Q136	2	1	5		0	3		0
4QPhyl J *	4Q137		10	5		0	8		0
4QPhyl K *	4Q138		7	2		0	0		0
4QPhyl L	4Q139		3	3		0	0		0
4QPhyl M *	4Q140		5	2		0	1		0
4QPhyl N	4Q141	3		0		0	1		0
4QPhyl O	4Q142		0	4		0	1		0
4QPhyl P	4Q143			2		0	0		0
4QPhyl Q	4Q144		1	0		0	0		0
4QPhyl R	4Q145	2		1		0	3		0
4QPhyl S	4Q146			2		0	0		0
4QPhyl T	4Q147			0		0	0		0
4QPhyl U	4Q148			0		0	0		0
4QMez A	4Q149			0		0	0		0
4QMez B	4Q150	1		0		0	0		0
4QMez C	4Q151			0		0	0		0

Statistics, Linguistics and the 'Biblical' Dead Sea Scrolls

Scroll Name	Scroll #	לא	לוא	על	אל – על	Percent Towards על	אל	אל – על	Percent Towards אל
4QMez D	4Q152			0		0	0		0
4QMez E	4Q153			0		0	0		0
4QMez F	4Q154			0		0	2		0
4QMez G	4Q155	1		1		0	2		0
4Qpap cryptA Lev[h]?	4Q249j			0		0	0		0
4QpapGen[o]	4Q483			0		0	0		0
4QGen[n]	4Q576			0		0	0		0
5QDeut	5Q1	5		1		0	2		0
5QKgs	5Q2			1		0	1		0
5QIsa	5Q3			0		0	1		0
5QXII	5Q4		3	0		0	0		0
5QPs	5Q5			0		0	0		0
5QLam[a]	5Q6	5	1	3		0	1		0
5QLam[b]	5Q7			0		0	0		0
6QpaleoGen	6Q1			0		0	0		0
6QpaleoLev	6Q2			1		0	0		0
6QpapDeut?	6Q3			0		0	0		0
6QpapKgs *	6Q4	2		3	1	0.33	8		0
6QpapPs 78?	6Q5			0		0	0		0
6QCant	6Q6	1		1		0	1		0
6QpapDan	6Q7			5		0	0		0
6QDeut?	6Q20			0		0	0		0
8QGen	8Q1			0		0	1		0
8QPs	8Q2			1		0	0		0
8QPhyl *	8Q3	15		17		0	3		0
8QMez *	8Q4	5		3		0	1		0
11QpaleoLev[a] *	11Q1	19		22		0	21		0
11QLev[b]	11Q2			1		0	0		0
11QDeut	11Q3			0		0	1		0
11QEzek	11Q4	1		2		0	0		0
11QPs[a] *	11Q5		32	35	1	0.03	38	1	0.03
11QPs[b]	11Q6		0	4		0	0		0
11QPs[c]	11Q7			1		0	5		0
11QPs[d]	11Q8	1	1	1		0	4		0
11QPs[e]	11Q9			1		0	0		0
34Se1	34Se1	3		1		0	2		0
34Se2	34Se2			0		0	0		0
5/6Hev1a	5/6Hev1a			0		0	2		0
5/6Hev1b *	5/6Hev1b	9		8		0	7		0
Gen	Mas1			0		0	0		0
Lev	Mas1a			5		0	2		0

Appendix E. על and אל Interchange

Scroll Name	Scroll #	לא	לוא	על	אל – על	Percent Towards על	אל	אל – על	Percent Towards אל
Lev *	Mas1b	6	11			0	10		0
Deut	Mas1c	1	0			0	1		0
Ezek *	Mas1d	3	16			0	11		0
Psa *	Mas1e	3	4			0	7		0
Psa	Mas1f		0			0	1		0
Mur Gen 1 *	Mur1	4	2			0	10		0
Mur Deut	Mur2	1	1			0	0		0
MurIsa	Mur3	2	0			0	0		0
MurEx *	Mur4	6	13			0	6		0
MurXII *	Mur88	62	92	2		0.02	80		0
MurGen	MurX		0			0	1		0
Sdeir1	Sdeir1	16	0			0	2		0
XHev/Se2	XHev/Se2		1			0	5		0
XHev/Se3	XHev/Se3	1	0			0	0		0
XHev/Se5 *	XHev/Se5	6	13			0	6		0
XQ1 *	XQ1	11	2			0	5		0
XQ2 *	XQ2	2	4			0	8		0
XQ3 *	XQ3	16	8			0	5		0
				32			30		

F. Particles: ל, כ, ב

Scroll Name	Scroll #	לא	לוא	ב Plus[1]	ב Minus[2]	ל Plus[3]	ל Minus[4]	כ Plus[5]	כ Minus[6]
1QGen	1Q1								
1QExo^d	1Q2	1							
1QpaleoLev-Num^a	1Q3	1							
1QDeut^a	1Q4		1			1			
1QDeut^b *	1Q5	10							
1QJudg	1Q6								
1QSam	1Q7	2							
1QIsa^b *	1Q8	89					1		
1QEzek	1Q9								
1QPs^a	1Q10								
1QPs^b	1Q11								
1QPs^c	1Q12								
1QPhyl *	1Q13	8		1					
1QDan^a	1Q71	1					1		
1QDan^b	1Q72	2							
1QIsa^a I	1QIsa^a I		167	5		11	2	1	1
1QIsa^a II	1QIsa^a II		276	6		7	3	2	
2QExod^a	2Q1								
2QExod^b	2Q2	1	1						
2QGen	2Q3								
2QExod^c	2Q4								
2QpaleoLev	2Q5								
2QNum^a	2Q6								
2QNum^b	2Q7								

---

1   1Q13 f1_18:11; 1QIsa^a 1:23, 6:5, 9:3, 10:15, 21:30, 31:18, 37:2, 42:25, 47:15, 52:2, 53:15; 4Q23 f60_61:5; 4Q27 1f1_4:14; 4Q41 3:11; 4Q51 f85:3; 4Q56 f10_13:7; 4Q61 f1_8:33; 4Q72 f19_21:6; 4Q113 f7ii_8:15; 4Q129 f1R:6; 4Q130 f1:14, f1:9; 4Q134 f1:19, f1:29; 4Q135 f1:3; 4Q137 f1:20; 4Q155 f1:4; 8Q3 f1_11i:18, f17_25:24; 11Q5 11:13, 20:17; XQ3 1:16, 1:21.

2   4Q23 f8_14i:10; 4Q51 f44:5; 4Q87 f2ii:1; 4Q98 2:3; 4Q109 f1ii+3_6i:17; 4Q112 f3ii_6:18; 11Q5 14:14, 15:11; Mur88 15:31.

3   1Q4 f12:2; 1QIsa^a 1:15, 1:15, 3:14, 4:20, 7:22, 11:10, 22:14, 24:10, 25:23, 26:25, 26:28, 29:15, 36:5, 36:7, 37:2, 39:31, 47:20, 47:26; 2Q13 f7_8:10; 4Q1 f25ii+28_31:7; 4Q7 f1:10; 4Q10 f2:3; 4Q13 f3i_4:15; 4Q27 f20_22:30, f33ii_40:28, f33ii_40:32; 4Q33 f2_3:4; 4Q37 10:1; 4Q40 f5:6; 4Q45 f42_43:5, f7_10:5; 4Q51 f116:7, f68_76:1; 4Q52 f6_7:3; 4Q67 f1:4; 4Q72 f2_3:7; 4Q82 f30b+31aR+36_37:6; 4Q93 1:12; 4Q111 3:6; 4Q112 f3i+17:16, f3i+17:4; 11Q5 2:9, fEii:5.

4   1Q8 24:4; 1Q71 f1ii:1; 1QIsa^a 4:17, 24:16, 31:10, 42:19, 45:21; 4Q14 6:41; 4Q27 f60_64:6; 4Q28 f1:8; 4Q30 f5:3; 4Q51 f110:2, f80_83:9; 4Q53 f5ii_7i:22; 4Q72 f8i:8; 4Q92 1:3; 11Q1 fJ:4; 11Q5 12:15, 14:10, 3:1, 3:10.

5   1QIsa^a 23:23, 28:12, 53:12; 4Q13 f6ii:6; 4Q16 f1:6; 4Q37 10:13; 4Q51 f155_158:27; 4Q135 f1:11.

6   1QIsa^a 27:4; 4Q30 f9:2; 5Q6 f1iv:7.

Appendix F. Particles כ, ל, ב

Scroll Name	Scroll #	לא	לוא	ב Plus	ב Minus	ל Plus	ל Minus	כ Plus	כ Minus
2QNum^c	2Q8								
2QNum^d	2Q9								
2QDeut^a	2Q10								
2QDeut^b	2Q11								
2QDeut^c	2Q12								
2QJer	2Q13		2			1			
2QPs	2Q14								
2QJob	2Q15								
2QRuth^a *	2Q16	3							
2QRuth^b	2Q17								
3QEzek	3Q1								
3QPs	3Q2								
3QLam	3Q3								
4QGen-Exod^a *	4Q1	6				1			
4QGen^b *	4Q2	2							
4QGen^c *	4Q3								
4QGen^d	4Q4								
4QGen^e *	4Q5	2							
4QGen^f *	4Q6	1							
4QGen^g	4Q7					1			
4QGen^h *	4Q8								
4QGen^j *	4Q9	3							
4QGen^k	4Q10					1			
4QpaleoGen-Exod1 *	4Q11	10							
4QpaleoGen^m	4Q12		1						
4QExod^b *	4Q13	3				1		1	
4QExod^c *	4Q14	10					1		
4QExod^d	4Q15								
4QExod^e	4Q16	1						1	
4QExod-Lev^f *	4Q17	1							
4QExod^g	4Q18								
4QExod^h	4Q19								
4QExod^j	4Q20								
4QExod^k	4Q21								
4QpaleoExod^m *	4Q22	18							
4QLev-Num^a *	4Q23	10		1	1				
4QLev^b *	4Q24	18							
4QLev^c	4Q25	1							
4QLev^d	4Q26	1	3						
4QLev^e	4Q26a	3							
4QLev^g	4Q26b	1							
4QNum^b	4Q27		19	1		3	1		
4QDeut^a	4Q28	4				1			

213

Statistics, Linguistics and the 'Biblical' Dead Sea Scrolls

Scroll Name	Scroll #	לא	לוא	ב Plus	ב Minus	ל Plus	ל Minus	כ Plus	כ Minus
4QDeut^b *	4Q29	2							
4QDeut^c	4Q30	13				1			1
4QDeut^d *	4Q31	4							
4QDeut^e	4Q32	7							
4QDeut^f *	4Q33	15			1				
4QDeut^g	4Q34	4							
4QDeut^h *	4Q35	5							
4QDeutⁱ	4Q36	4							
4QDeut^j	4Q37	1	3		1		1		
4QDeut^k1	4Q38		1						
4QDeut^k2	4Q38a		2						
4QDeut^k3	4Q38b	1							
4QDeut^l	4Q39								
4QDeut^m	4Q40		1		1				
4QDeutⁿ	4Q41	2	17	1					
4QDeut^o	4Q42	6							
4QDeut^p	4Q43	1							
4QDeut^q	4Q44								
4QpaleoDeut^r *	4Q45	12			2				
4QpaleoDeut^s	4Q46								
4QJosh^a *	4Q47	5							
4QJosh^b	4Q48	1							
4QJudg^a	4Q49								
4QJudg^b	4Q50								
4QSam^a	4Q51	9	14	1	1	2	2	1	
4QSam^b *	4Q52	5			1				
4QSam^c	4Q53		6			1			
4QKgs	4Q54	2							
4QIsa^a *	4Q55	6							
4QIsa^b *	4Q56	16		1					
4QIsa^c	4Q57		19						
4QIsa^d *	4Q58	17							
4QIsa^e *	4Q59	6							
4QIsa^f	4Q60	2							
4QIsa^g	4Q61	3	2	1					
4QIsa^h	4Q62	1							
4QIsaⁱ	4Q62a								
4QIsa^j	4Q63	1							
4QIsa^k	4Q64	1							
4QIsa^l	4Q65		2						
4QIsa^m	4Q66								
4QIsaⁿ	4Q67					1			
4QIsa^o	4Q68								

Appendix F. Particles ב, ל, כ

Scroll Name	Scroll #	לא	לוא	ב Plus	ב Minus	ל Plus	ל Minus	כ Plus	כ Minus
4QpapIsa^p	4Q69								
4QIsa^q	4Q69a								
4QIsa^r	4Q69b								
4QJer^a	4Q70	5	5						
4QJer^b	4Q71			1					
4QJer^c *	4Q72	13				1	1		
4QJer^d	4Q72a	2							
4QJer^e	4Q72b								
4QEzek^a *	4Q73	1							
4QEzek^b	4Q74								
4QEzek^c	4Q75								
4QXII^a *	4Q76	3							
4QXII^b	4Q77								
4QXII^c *	4Q78		9						
4QXII^d	4Q79	1							
4QXII^e	4Q80		4						
4QXII^f	4Q81	2							
4QXII^g *	4Q82	6	9			1			
4QPs^a *	4Q83		5						
4QPs^b *	4Q84	8							
4QPs^c *	4Q85	4							
4QPs^d	4Q86								
4QPs^e *	4Q87		3		1				
4QPs^f *	4Q88		1						
4QPs^g	4Q89								
4QGen^h2	4Q8a								
4QGen^h-para	4Q8b								
4QPs^h	4Q90								
4QPs^j	4Q91								
4QPs^k	4Q92						1		
4QPs^l	4Q93					1			
4QPs^m	4Q94								
4QPsⁿ	4Q95								
4QPs^o	4Q96		1						
4QPs^p	4Q97								
4QPs^q	4Q98				1				
4QPs^r	4Q98a								
4QPs^s	4Q98b								
4QPs^t	4Q98c								
4QPs^u	4Q98d								
4QPs^v	4Q98e								
4QPs^w	4Q98f								
4QPs^x	4Q98g								

Statistics, Linguistics and the 'Biblical' Dead Sea Scrolls

Scroll Name	Scroll #	לא	לוא	ב Plus	ב Minus	ל Plus	ל Minus	כ Plus	כ Minus
4QJob^a *	4Q99	7	1						
4QJob^b	4Q100	1							
4QpaleoJob^c	4Q101	1							
4QProv^a	4Q102	3							
4QProv^b	4Q103	1							
4QProv^c	4Q103a								
4QRuth^a	4Q104								
4QRuth^b	4Q105								
4QCant^a	4Q106								
4QCant^b *	4Q107	1							
4QCant^c	4Q108								
4QQoh^a	4Q109			6	1				
4QQoh^b	4Q110			1					
4QLam *	4Q111			5		1			
4QDan^a *	4Q112	6			1	2			
4QDan^b *	4Q113		2	1					
4QDan^c *	4Q114	6							
4QDan^d	4Q115	2							
4QDan^e	4Q116								
4QEzr^a	4Q117								
4QChr	4Q118								
4QPhyl A *	4Q128		7						
4QPhyl B *	4Q129		10	1					
4QPhyl C *	4Q130	5		2					
4QPhyl D	4Q131								
4QPhyl E	4Q132								
4QPhyl F	4Q133								
4QPhyl G *	4Q134	2	8	2					
4QPhyl H *	4Q135		1	1				1	
4QPhyl I	4Q136	2	1						
4QPhyl J *	4Q137		10	1					
4QPhyl K *	4Q138		7						
4QPhyl L	4Q139		3						
4QPhyl M *	4Q140		5						
4QPhyl N	4Q141	3							
4QPhyl O	4Q142		0						
4QPhyl P	4Q143								
4QPhyl Q	4Q144		1						
4QPhyl R	4Q145	2							
4QPhyl S	4Q146								
4QPhyl T	4Q147								
4QPhyl U	4Q148								
4QMez A	4Q149								

Appendix F. Particles ב, ל, כ

Scroll Name	Scroll #	לא	לוא	ב Plus	ב Minus	ל Plus	ל Minus	כ Plus	כ Minus
4QMez B	4Q150	1							
4QMez C	4Q151								
4QMez D	4Q152								
4QMez E	4Q153								
4QMez F	4Q154								
4QMez G	4Q155	1		1					
4Qpap cryptA Lev[h]?	4Q249j								
4QpapGen[o]	4Q483								
4QGen[n]	4Q576								
5QDeut	5Q1	5							
5QKgs	5Q2								
5QIsa	5Q3								
5QXII	5Q4		3						
5QPs	5Q5								
5QLam[a]	5Q6	5	1						1
5QLam[b]	5Q7								
6QpaleoGen	6Q1								
6QpaleoLev	6Q2								
6QpapDeut?	6Q3								
6QpapKgs *	6Q4	2							
6QpapPs 78?	6Q5								
6QCant	6Q6	1							
6QpapDan	6Q7								
6QDeut?	6Q20								
8QGen	8Q1								
8QPs	8Q2								
8QPhyl *	8Q3	15		2					
8QMez *	8Q4	5							
11QpaleoLev[a] *	11Q1	19					1		
11QLev[b]	11Q2								
11QDeut	11Q3								
11QEzek	11Q4	1			2				
11QPs[a] *	11Q5		32	2		2	4		
11QPs[b]	11Q6		0						
11QPs[c]	11Q7								
11QPs[d]	11Q8	1	1						
11QPs[e]	11Q9								
34Se1	34Se1	3							
34Se2	34Se2								
5/6Hev1a	5/6Hev1a								
5/6Hev1b *	5/6Hev1b	9							
Gen	Mas1								
Lev	Mas1a								

217

Statistics, Linguistics and the 'Biblical' Dead Sea Scrolls

Scroll Name	Scroll #	לא	לוא	ב Plus	ב Minus	ל Plus	ל Minus	כ Plus	כ Minus
Lev *	Mas1b	6							
Deut	Mas1c	1							
Ezek *	Mas1d	3							
Psa *	Mas1e	3							
Psa	Mas1f								
Mur Gen 1 *	Mur1	4							
Mur Deut	Mur2	1							
MurIsa	Mur3	2							
MurEx *	Mur4	6							
MurXII *	Mur88	62			1				
MurGen	MurX								
Sdeir1	Sdeir1	16							
XHev/Se2	XHev/Se2								
XHev/Se3	XHev/Se3	1							
XHev/Se5 *	XHev/Se5	6							
XQ1 *	XQ1	11							
XQ2 *	XQ2	2							
XQ3 *	XQ3	16		2					
				34	9	44	21	8	3

G. Conjunction *Vav*

Scroll Name	Scroll #	לא	לוא	Number of *vavs*	*vav* Plus[1]	Percent Plus	*vav* Minus[2]	Percent Minus

1   1Q3 f5_6:10; 1Q5 f11:2; 1Q7 f4:2; 1Q8 18:8, 19:17, 20:3, 20:4, 21:18, 21:3, 22:6, 23:13, 23:15, 24:14, 25:10, 25:11, 25:17, 25:18, 25:23, 25:27, 25:5, 25:5; 1Q13 f1_18:5, f20:2; 1Q72 f1_2:11; 1QIsa^a 1:10, 1:12, 1:19, 1:19, 1:4, 2:13, 2:18, 3:10, 3:14, 3:26, 3:27, 3:28, 4:18, 5:15, 5:18, 6:17, 7:3, 8:14, 8:21, 8:9, 9:1, 9:11, 9:11, 9:12, 9:18, 10:25, 11:17, 11:24, 11:26, 11:3, 11:7, 12:10, 12:2, 13:24, 13:28, 13:6, 13:8, 13:9, 14:13, 14:19, 14:2, 14:22, 14:31, 14:8, 15:10, 15:10, 15:11, 15:6, 16:18, 16:21, 17:25, 17:7, 18:12, 19:19, 19:6, 20:23, 20:26, 21:12, 21:13, 22:1, 23:1,23:3, 23:2, 23:6, 24:27, 24:30, 25:13, 25:14, 25:21, 26:16, 26:2, 26:23, 26:31, 26:6, 27:2, 27:27, 27:27, 27:27, 27:6, 27:9, 28:10, 28:10, 28:10, 28:10, 28:12, 28:12, 28:17, 28:2, 28:25, 28:3, 29:9, 29:23, 30:18, 30:18, 31:10, 31:25, 32:10, 32:2, 32:2, 32:26, 32:3, 32:7, 32:8, 33:13, 33:15, 33:17, 33:18, 33:18, 33:19, 33:19, 33:2, 33:27, 34:1, 34:2, 34:21, 34:5, 34:5, 34:5, 34:6, 34:6, 35:10, 35:17, 35:18, 35:20, 35:21, 35:21, 35:27, 35:28, 35:3, 35:4, 35:8, 36:12, 36:18, 36:27, 36:28, 36:3, 36:5, 36:5, 37:1, 37:1, 37:15, 37:17, 37:17, 37:17, 37:19, 37:22, 37:22, 37:22, 37:22, 37:25, 37:3, 37:8, 38:10, 38:11, 38:22, 38:24, 38:26, 39:11, 39:12, 39:18, 39:19, 39:2, 39:21, 39:24, 39:25, 39:31, 39:31, 39:4, 39:7, 39:8, 40:13, 40:18, 40:19, 40:19, 40:2, 40:20, 40:20, 40:23, 40:25, 40:27, 41:15, 41:20, 41:6, 41:8, 42:27, 42:5, 42:5, 43:12, 43:14, 43:15, 43:15, 43:19, 43:24, 44:1, 44:10, 44:10, 44:17, 44:18, 44:19, 44:19, 44:23, 44:23, 44:25, 44:3, 44:7, 44:8, 44:9, 45:22, 46:22, 46:26, 46:26, 46:27, 46:28, 46:28, 46:8, 47:10, 47:13, 47:17, 47:2, 47:20, 47:23, 47:29, 48:10, 48:23, 48:25, 48:3, 48:4, 48:9, 49:10, 49:14, 49:16, 49:16, 49:21, 49:26, 49:4, 50:11, 50:14, 50:2, 50:5, 51:12, 51:15, 51:18, 51:18, 51:22, 51:7, 51:8, 53:2, 53:20; 2Q12 f1:2, f1:5; 2Q13 f6:3, f7_8:10, f9ii_12:9; 2Q14 f2:2; 4Q1 f17_18:1, f17_18:1, f19ii:11, f22ii+26:9; 4Q5 f8:1; 4Q11 f10ii:13, f39:2, f7ii:24; 4Q13 f1:5, f6ii:10, f6ii:7; 4Q14 6:38, 8:14, 8:7; 4Q22 1:30, 17:11, 18:1, 18:25, 19:1, 19:1, 38:28; 4Q23 f24_26:3, f34ii+44_50:17, f60_61:5, f8_14i:10, f8_14i:11; 4Q24 f1_7:20; 4Q26a f5:6; 4Q27 f33ii_40:14, f3ii+5:10, f42_47:4, f6_10:14, f60_64:6, f60_64:6, f60_64:8, f65_71:7; 4Q30 f5:3; 4Q33 f13_16:6; 4Q33 f4_6:10; 4Q35 f1:7, f11_15:11, f11_15:5, f11_15:6; 4Q38a f2_3:12, f2_3:5; 4Q40 f1_3:7; 4Q41 1:6, 2:9, 3:2, 4:10; 4Q44 f5ii:5; 4Q45 f13_14:5; 4Q47 f9i_12:1, f9ii+13_16:11; 4Q51 2a_d:34, 3a_e:11, 3a_e:26, 6a_b:15, 8a_b:9, f134_139:9, f149+151:5, f155_158:15, f155_158:6, f164_165:5, f17:2, f61i+62:33, f61i+62:9; 4Q53 f2_5i:23, f5ii_7i:9; 4Q54 f5:8; 4Q55 f10_11i+12_14:25, f10_11i+12_14:34, f9:8; 4Q56 f3ii:5, f31ii:5; 4Q57 f1_2+49:10, f27:40, f29:2, f31:2, f33_35+55_57:6, f9ii+11+12i+52:22, f9ii+11+12i+52:26, f9ii+11+12i+52:38, f9ii+11+12i+52:40, f9ii+11+12i+52:40; 4Q58 11:24, 3:21, 8:19, 8:20, 8:23; 4Q59 f1:3, f16:1; 4Q61 f1_8:40; 4Q63 f1:5; 4Q64 f1_5:2; 4Q67 f1:3; 4Q70 f26_28:4, f3+4i+5_7:6, f3+4i+5_7:16; 4Q72 f10_12:3, f2_3:4, f44_50:9; 4Q76 1:18, 2:7, 4:2, 6:2; 4Q78 f10_12:5, f21_23:2; 4Q82 f19b+27_32:10, f30b+31aR+36_37:8, f76_78i+79_81:15; 4Q83 f14ii:28, f14ii:34, f7_8:3, f9ii:12; 4Q84 f15iii+20_21i+22:16, f1iii+5i:14, f5ii:16; 4Q85 f13_15i:22, f15iii+17:31, f3_4i:1; 4Q86 2:2, 4:10; 4Q88 2:17, 2:17, 3:16, 3:17, 3:21, 3:21; 4Q90 f1_2:17; 4Q96 f1:1, f1:2; 4Q99 f17_18:3; 4Q107 f2ii:6; 4Q111 2:9, 3:5, 3:5; 4Q112 f1i+2:5, f3i+17:3; 4Q118 f1ii:5; 4Q129 f1R:10, f1R:18, f1R:2, f1Va:7; 4Q130 f1:13; 4Q134 f1:10, f1:13, f1:8; 4Q135 f1:1, f1:10, f1:18, f1:7, f1:9; 4Q137 f1:11, f1:15; 4Q137 f1:8; 4Q138 f1:10, f1:2, f1:3, f1:6; 4Q140 f1:21, f1:25; 4Q141 f1i:10, f1i:11, f1i:15; 5Q6 f1iv:7; 6Q7 f6_7:1; 8Q3 f12_16:16, f12_16:8, f17_25:22, f17_25:7; 8Q4 f1:10, f1:16; 11Q1 fA:3; 11Q5 3:12, 3:3, 7:3, 13:15, 14:11, 15:1, 15:1, 16:13, 22:16, 23:12, 23:15, 25:10, fCii:9, fEii:10, fEii:8, fEii:8, fEii:9; 11Q7 f3:2, f9:3; Mur88 11:36, 15:21; XHev/Se5 f1:12; XQ1 1:1, 1:20; XQ2 1:17, 1:19; XQ3 1:15, 1:24.

2   1Q8 18:13, 21:18, 23:18, 23:30, 25:6, 25:9, 25:10, 25:12, 25:12, 25:14, 25:14, 25:16, 25:30, 27:5; 1Q13 f1_18:11; 1Q71 f1ii:1; 1QIsa^a 1:26, 3:18, 5:1, 5:18, 5:18, 5:19, 5:21, 6:3, 6:5, 7:17, 8:15, 8:4, 10:2, 10:24,

Scroll Name	Scroll #	לא	לוא	Number of vavs	vav Plus	Percent Plus	vav Minus	Percent Minus
1QGen	1Q1	0	0	7	0	0	0	0
1QExod^d	1Q2	1	0	11	0	0	0	0
1QpaleoLev-Num^a	1Q3	1	0	9	1	0.11	0	0
1QDeut^a	1Q4	0	1	11	0	0	0	0
1QDeut^b *	1Q5	10	0	32	1	0.03	0	0
1QJudg	1Q6	0	0	18	0	0	0	0
1QSam	1Q7	2	0	19	1	0.05	0	0
1QIsa^b *	1Q8	89	0	487	17	0.03	14	0.03
1QEzek	1Q9	0	0	3	0	0	0	0
1QPs^a	1Q10	0	0	8	0	0	0	0
1QPs^b	1Q11	0	0	0	0	0	0	0
1QPs^c	1Q12	0	0	2	0	0	0	0
1QPhyl *	1Q13	8	0	12	2	0.15	1	0.1
1QDan^a	1Q71	1	0	13	0	0	1	0.08
1QDan^b	1Q72	2	0	12	1	0.08	0	0
1QIsa^a	1QIsa^a	0	443	2699	251	0.09	101	0.04
2QExod^a	2Q1	1	1	20	0	0	0	0
2QExod^b	2Q2	0	0	6	0	0	0	0

11:13, 11:30, 11:8, 12:15, 12:18, 12:24, 12:24, 13:17, 13:29, 14:13, 14:13, 15:1, 15:12, 15:29, 17:2, 17:25, 19:22, 22:7, 25:16, 25:28, 25:6, 26:21, 26:21, 27:14, 27:17, 27:5, 27:9, 28:24, 28:25, 31:4, 31:6, 31:6, 32:4, 33:13, 33:23, 33:25, 34:14, 34:22, 34:9, 35:21, 35:5, 35:8, 36:13, 36:17, 36:19, 36:22, 37:13, 37:15, 37:17, 37:27, 37:9, 38:10, 38:17, 38:21, 39:19, 39:4, 39:6, 39:9, 40:11, 40:12, 40:19, 40:28, 40:31, 41:20, 41:25, 41:6, 41:6, 42:2, 43:10, 43:10, 43:2, 43:2,44:13, 45:15, 46:13, 47:23, 47:27, 47:28, 48:23, 49:27, 49:6, 50:20, 51:17, 51:20, 53:18, 53:20; 4Q1 f19ii:1, f5:6, f5:7, f5:7; 4Q7 f2:3; 4Q8a f1:1; 4Q11 f1+39:5; 4Q13 f3ii+5_6i:9, f3ii+5_6i:9; 4Q16 f1:6; f1:6, f1:6, f1:6; 4Q17 f2ii:6; 4Q23 f4:9; 4Q24 f9i+10_17:27, f9ii+11ii+18_20i:12; 4Q27 f33ii_40:32, f42_47:4, f6_10:17, If1_4:14; 4Q30 f32i+33:10, f32i+33:10, f45ii:2; 4Q31 2:17, 2:2, 2:6; 4Q33 f13_16:4; 4Q35 f1:6, f11_15:3; 4Q37 10:12, 4:4; 4Q41 1:4, 3:6, 3:6, 3:12, 3:12, 3:12, 3:12, 4:10, 4:10, 4:10, 4:11, 4:11, 4:12, 4:9; 4Q45 f44:1, f5_6:6; 4Q47 f9i_12:7; 4Q49 f1:3, f1:3; 4Q51 f155_158:14, f155_158:16, f155_158:19, f55_57a_b+58:3, f61ii+63_64a_b+65_67:18, f8_10a_b+11:8; 4Q52 f6_7:18, f6_7:5; 4Q53 f5ii_7i:21, f5ii_7i:5; 4Q55 f8:4; 4Q56 f10_13:14, f10_13:3, f24_25:3, f31ii:2, f41:1; 4Q58 12:21, 12:8, 3:21; 4Q59 f4_10:7; 4Q60 f3_6:4; 4Q69 f1_2:2; 4Q70 f3+4i+5_7:6, f32ii_35:17; 4Q72 f14_18:13, f55ii:5; 4Q76 2:5; 4Q78 f4_7:11, f9:7; 4Q83 f19ii_20:25, f19ii_20:26, f19ii_20:30, f19ii_20:33, f19ii_20:35, f6:2, f9ii:11, f9ii:4, f9ii:6, f9ii:6; 4Q84 f15i+16_18i:13, f28ii_30i+31:13; 4Q85 f11:2, f15iii+17:27; 4Q87 f19:1; 4Q88 3:13, 3:20, 4:13, 4:19, 6:1, 7:8; 4Q90 f2_2:18; 4Q98g f1:1, f1:5; 4Q99 f19:1; 4Q105 f1_3:2; 4Q106 f2i+3_5:14, f2i+3_5:6, f2ii:14; 4Q109 f1i:3, f1ii+3_6i:20; 4Q112 f10_11:1, f14:16, f14:5, f3i+17:16; 4Q114 3:16; 4Q128 f1:2, f1:24, f1:55, f1:55; 4Q129 f1R:17; 4Q130 f1:10, f1:13; 4Q134 f1:20, f1:25, f1:25, f1:25, f1:26; 4Q135 f1:11, f1:8; 4Q136 f1:12, f1:8; 4Q137 f1:17, f1:20, f1:21; 4Q138 f1:2, f1:5, f1:6; 4Q139 f1:11, f1:12, f1:12, f1:12, f1:22; 4Q141 f1i:3; 4Q144 f1V:5; 4Q145 f1:5, f1:5; 4Q149 f1:3; 5Q1 1:4, 2:6; 6Q4 f10_14+72:4, 6Q7 f2_5:4; 8Q3 f12_16:12, f17_25:13, f17_25:22, f26_29:10; 8Q4 f1:16, f1:31; 11Q1 4:5, 11Q4 f3b+6:6; 11Q5 4:4, 5:13, 5:15, 5:15, 11:1, 11:4, 11:5, 11:6, 11:9, 14:4, 15:16, 16:11, 16:13, 20:11, fEiii:15, fEiii:7; 11Q7 f11:3; Mas1d 3:12; Mas1e 2:20; XHev/Se5 f1:6; 34Se2 f2i:1; XQ1 1:1, 1:4; XQ2 1:17, 1:2; XQ3 1:15, 1:16, 1:17, 1:22, 1:27, 1:27, 1:28, 1:28, 1:29, 1:29.

Appendix G. Conjunction *Vav*

Scroll Name	Scroll #	לא	לוא	Number of *vav*s	*vav* Plus	Percent Plus	*vav* Minus	Percent Minus
2QGen	2Q3	0	0	0	0	0	0	0
2QExod^c	2Q4	0	0	1	0	0	0	0
2QpaleoLev	2Q5	0	0	3	0	0	0	0
2QNum^a	2Q6	0	0	2	0	0	0	0
2QNum^b	2Q7	0	0	0	0	0	0	0
2QNum^c	2Q8	0	0	1	0	0	0	0
2QNum^d	2Q9	0	0	1	0	0	0	0
2QDeut^a	2Q10	0	0	1	0	0	0	0
2QDeut^b	2Q11	0	0	4	2	0.5	0	0
2QDeut^c	2Q12	0	2	25	3	0.12	0	0
2QJer	2Q13	0	0	3	1	0.33	0	0
2QPs	2Q14	0	0	0	0	0	0	0
2QJob	2Q15	3	0	33	0	0	0	0
2QRuth^a *	2Q16	0	0	4	0	0	0	0
2QRuth^b	2Q17	0	0	0	0	0	0	0
3QEzek	3Q1	0	0	0	0	0	0	0
3QPs	3Q2	0	0	0	0	0	0	0
3QLam	3Q3	6	0	161	4	0.02	4	0.03
4QGen-Exod^a *	4Q1	2	0	60	0	0	0	0
4QGen^b *	4Q2	0	0	21	0	0	0	0
4QGen^c *	4Q3	0	0	13	0	0	0	0
4QGen^d	4Q4	2	0	27	1	0.04	0	0
4QGen^e *	4Q5	1	0	25	0	0	0	0
4QGen^f *	4Q6	0	0	29	0	0	1	0.03
4QGen^g	4Q7	0	0	1	0	0	0	0
4QGen^h *	4Q8	3	0	32	0	0	0	0
4QGen^j *	4Q9	0	0	9	0	0	0	0
4QGen^k	4Q10	10	0	108	3	0.03	1	0.01
4QpaleoGen-Exod1 *	4Q11	0	1	5	0	0	0	0
4QpaleoGen^m	4Q12	3	0	64	3	0.05	2	0.03
4QExod^b *	4Q13	10	0	109	3	0.03	0	0
4QExod^c *	4Q14	0	0	3	0	0	0	0
4QExod^d	4Q15	1	0	2	0	0	4	2
4QExod^e	4Q16	1	0	47	0	0	1	0.02
4QExod-Lev^f *	4Q17	0	0	3	0	0	0	0
4QExod^g	4Q18	0	0	2	0	0	0	0
4QExod^h	4Q19	0	0	1	0	0	0	0
4QExod^j	4Q20	0	0	1	0	0	0	0
4QExod^k	4Q21	18	0	244	7	0.03	0	0
4QpaleoExod^m *	4Q22	10	0	150	4	0.03	1	0.01
4QLev-Num^a *	4Q23	18	0	64	1	0.02	2	0.03
4QLev^b *	4Q24	1	0	9	0	0	0	0

Statistics, Linguistics and the 'Biblical' Dead Sea Scrolls

Scroll Name	Scroll #	לא	לוא	Number of vavs	vav Plus	Percent Plus	vav Minus	Percent Minus
4QLev^c	4Q25	1	3	12	0	0	0	0
4QLev^d	4Q26	3	0	12	1	0.08	0	0
4QLev^e	4Q26a	1	0	4	0	0	0	0
4QLev^g	4Q26b	0	19	194	8	0.04	4	0.02
4QNum^b	4Q27	4	0	11	0	0	0	0
4QDeut^a	4Q28	2	0	20	0	0	0	0
4QDeut^b *	4Q29	13	0	51	1	0.02	3	0.06
4QDeut^c	4Q30	4	0	21	0	0	3	0.14
4QDeut^d *	4Q31	7	0	22	0	0	0	0
4QDeut^e	4Q32	15	0	53	2	0.04	1	0.02
4QDeut^f *	4Q33	4	0	15	0	0	0	0
4QDeut^g	4Q34	5	0	57	4	0.07	1	0.02
4QDeut^h *	4Q35	4	0	17	0	0	0	0
4QDeut^i	4Q36	1	3	38	0	0	2	0.05
4QDeut^j	4Q37	0	1	13	0	0	0	0
4QDeut^{k}1	4Q38	0	2	16	2	0.13	0	0
4QDeut^{k}2	4Q38a	1	0	1	0	0	0	0
4QDeut^{k}3	4Q38b	0	0	7	0	0	0	0
4QDeut^l	4Q39	0	1	4	1	0.25	0	0
4QDeut^m	4Q40	2	17	68	3	0.04	16	0.25
4QDeut^n	4Q41	6	0	10	0	0	0	0
4QDeut^o	4Q42	1	0	4	0	0	0	0
4QDeut^p	4Q43	0	0	5	1	0.2	0	0
4QDeut^q	4Q44	12	0	39	1	0.02	2	0.05
4QpaleoDeut^r *	4Q45	0	0	0	0	0	0	0
4QpaleoDeut^s	4Q46	5	0	27	2	0.07	1	0.04
4QJosh^a *	4Q47	1	0	14	0	0	0	0
4QJosh^b	4Q48	0	0	11	0	0	2	0.18
4QJudg^a	4Q49	0	0	9	0	0	0	0
4QJudg^b	4Q50	9	14	396	13	0.03	6	0.02
4QSam^a	4Q51	5	0	51	0	0	2	0.04
4QSam^b *	4Q52	0	6	42	2	0.05	2	0.05
4QSam^c	4Q53	2	0	19	1	0.05	0	0
4QKgs	4Q54	6	0	45	3	0.07	0	0
4QIsa^a *	4Q55	16	0	122	2	0.02	5	0.04
4QIsa^b *	4Q56	0	19	87	10	0.12	0	0
4QIsa^c	4Q57	17	0	56	4	0.07	3	0.06
4QIsa^d *	4Q58	6	0	46	2	0.04	1	0.02
4QIsa^e *	4Q59	2	0	33	0	0	1	0.03
4QIsa^f	4Q60	3	2	10	1	0.1	0	0
4QIsa^g	4Q61	1	0	6	0	0	0	0
4QIsa^h	4Q62	0	0	1	0	0	0	0

Appendix G. Conjunction *Vav*

Scroll Name	Scroll #	לא	לוא	Number of *vav*s	*vav* Plus	Percent Plus	*vav* Minus	Percent Minus
4QIsa[i]	4Q62a	1	0	3	1	0.33	0	0
4QIsa[j]	4Q63	1	0	4	1	0.25	0	0
4QIsa[k]	4Q64	0	2	4	0	0	0	0
4QIsa[l]	4Q65	0	0	1	0	0	0	0
4QIsa[m]	4Q66	0	0	3	1	0.33	0	0
4QIsa[n]	4Q67	0	0	4	0	0	0	0
4QIsa[o]	4Q68	0	0	4	0	0	1	0.25
4QpapIsa[p]	4Q69	0	0	1	0	0	0	0
4QIsa[q]	4Q69a	0	0	1	0	0	0	0
4QIsa[r]	4Q69b	5	5	85	3	0.04	2	0.02
4QJer[a]	4Q70	0	0	3	0	0	0	0
4QJer[b]	4Q71	13	0	66	3	0.04	1	0.02
4QJer[c] *	4Q72	2	0	6	0	0	0	0
4QJer[d]	4Q72a	0	0	2	0	0	0	0
4QJer[e]	4Q72b	1	0	26	0	0	0	0
4QEzek[a] *	4Q73	0	0	12	0	0	0	0
4QEzek[b]	4Q74	0	0	0	0	0	0	0
4QEzek[c]	4Q75	3	0	58	4	0.07	1	0.02
4QXII[a] *	4Q76	0	0	5	0	0	0	0
4QXII[b]	4Q77	0	9	46	2	0.04	2	0.05
4QXII[c] *	4Q78	1	0	5	0	0	0	0
4QXII[d]	4Q79	0	4	19	0	0	0	0
4QXII[e]	4Q80	2	0	6	0	0	0	0
4QXII[f]	4Q81	6	9	98	3	0.03	0	0
4QXII[g] *	4Q82	0	5	28	4	0.11	10	0.42
4QPs[a] *	4Q83	8	0	34	3	0.08	2	0.07
4QPs[b] *	4Q84	4	0	41	3	0.07	2	0.05
4QPs[c] *	4Q85	0	0	10	2	0.2	0	0
4QPs[d]	4Q86	0	3	10	0	0	1	0.1
4QPs[e] *	4Q87	0	1	26	6	0.19	6	0.3
4QPs[f] *	4Q88	0	0	5	0	0	0	0
4QPs[g]	4Q89	0	0	0	0	0	1	0
4QGen[h]2	4Q8a	0	0	0	0	0	0	0
4QGen[h]-para	4Q8b	0	0	2	1	0.33	1	1
4QPs[h]	4Q90	0	0	2	0	0	0	0
4QPs[j]	4Q91	0	0	0	0	0	0	0
4QPs[k]	4Q92	0	0	1	0	0	0	0
4QPs[l]	4Q93	0	0	3	0	0	0	0
4QPs[m]	4Q94	0	0	1	0	0	0	0
4QPs[n]	4Q95	0	1	4	2	0.5	0	0
4QPs[o]	4Q96	0	0	0	0	0	0	0
4QPs[p]	4Q97	0	0	7	0	0	0	0

Statistics, Linguistics and the 'Biblical' Dead Sea Scrolls

Scroll Name	Scroll #	לא	לוא	Number of vavs	vav Plus	Percent Plus	vav Minus	Percent Minus
4QPs^q	4Q98	0	0	4	0	0	0	0
4QPs^r	4Q98a	0	0	0	0	0	0	0
4QPs^s	4Q98b	0	0	0	0	0	0	0
4QPs^t	4Q98c	0	0	1	0	0	0	0
4QPs^u	4Q98d	0	0	0	0	0	0	0
4QPs^v	4Q98e	0	0	1	0	0	0	0
4QPs^w	4Q98f	0	0	1	0	0	2	2
4QPs^x	4Q98g	7	1	20	1	0.05	1	0.05
4QJob^a *	4Q99	1	0	2	0	0	0	0
4QJob^b	4Q100	1	0	2	0	0	0	0
4QpaleoJob^c	4Q101	3	0	9	0	0	0	0
4QProv^a	4Q102	1	0	15	0	0	0	0
4QProv^b	4Q103	0	0	0	0	0	0	0
4QProv^c	4Q103a	0	0	18	0	0	0	0
4QRuth^a	4Q104	0	0	5	0	0	1	0.2
4QRuth^b	4Q105	0	0	1	0	0	3	3
4QCant^a	4Q106	1	0	11	0	0	0	0
4QCant^b *	4Q107	0	0	0	0	0	0	0
4QCant^c	4Q108	0	6	9	0	0	2	0.22
4QQoh^a	4Q109	0	1	0	0	0	0	0
4QQoh^b	4Q110	0	5	8	3	0.38	0	0
4QLam *	4Q111	6	0	83	2	0.02	4	0.05
4QDan^a *	4Q112	0	2	28	0	0	0	0
4QDan^b *	4Q113	6	0	39	0	0	1	0.03
4QDan^c *	4Q114	2	0	15	0	0	0	0
4QDan^d	4Q115	0	0	1	0	0	0	0
4QDan^e	4Q116	0	0	7	0	0	0	0
4QEzr^a	4Q117	0	0	5	1	0.2	0	0
4QChr	4Q118	0	7	42	0	0	4	0.10
4QPhyl A *	4Q128	0	10	42	4	0.09	1	0.03
4QPhyl B *	4Q129	5	0	56	1	0.02	2	0.02
4QPhyl C *	4Q130	0	0	2	0	0	0	0
4QPhyl D	4Q131	0	0	1	0	0	0	0
4QPhyl E	4Q132	0	0	11	0	0	0	0
4QPhyl F	4Q133	2	8	31	3	0.08	5	0.18
4QPhyl G *	4Q134	0	1	39	5	0.12	2	0.06
4QPhyl H *	4Q135	2	1	16	0	0	2	0.13
4QPhyl I	4Q136	0	10	49	3	0.06	3	0.07
4QPhyl J *	4Q137	0	7	55	4	0.07	3	0.06
4QPhyl K *	4Q138	0	3	9	0	0	1	0.11
4QPhyl L	4Q139	0	5	29	2	0.06	4	0.15
4QPhyl M *	4Q140	3	0	10	3	0.27	1	0.14

Appendix G. Conjunction *Vav*

Scroll Name	Scroll #	לא	לוא	Number of *vav*s	*vav* Plus	Percent Plus	*vav* Minus	Percent Minus
4QPhyl N	4Q141	0	0	5	0	0	0	0
4QPhyl O	4Q142	0	0	7	0	0	0	0
4QPhyl P	4Q143	0	1	2	0	0	1	0.5
4QPhyl Q	4Q144	2	0	8	0	0	2	0.25
4QPhyl R	4Q145	0	0	2	0	0	0	0
4QMez A	4Q149	0	0	4	0	0	1	0.25
4QMez B	4Q150	1	0	6	0	0	0	0
4QMez C	4Q151	0	0	4	0	0	0	0
4QMez D	4Q152	0	0	3	0	0	0	0
4QMez E	4Q153	0	0	0	0	0	0	0
4QMez F	4Q154	0	0	1	0	0	0	0
4QMez G	4Q155	1	0	11	0	0	0	0
4Qpap cryptA Lev[h]?	4Q249j	0	0	0	0	0	0	0
4QpapGen[o]	4Q483	0	0	0	0	0	0	0
4QGen[n]	4Q576	0	0	0	0	0	0	0
5QDeut	5Q1	5	0	14	0	0	2	0.14
5QKgs	5Q2	0	0	10	0	0	0	0
5QIsa	5Q3	0	0	1	0	0	0	0
5QXII	5Q4	0	3	1	0	0	0	0
5QPs	5Q5	0	0	3	0	0	0	0
5QLam[a]	5Q6	5	1	4	1	0.25	0	0
5QLam[b]	5Q7	0	0	0	0	0	0	0
6QpaleoGen	6Q1	0	0	5	0	0	0	0
6QpaleoLev	6Q2	0	0	2	0	0	0	0
6QpapDeut?	6Q3	0	0	1	0	0	0	0
6QpapKgs *	6Q4	2	0	25	0	0	1	0.04
6QpapPs 78?	6Q5	0	0	0	0	0	0	0
6QCant	6Q6	1	0	0	0	0	0	0
6QpapDan	6Q7	0	0	7	1	0.13	1	0.17
6QDeut?	6Q20	0	0	0	0	0	0	0
8QGen	8Q1	0	0	3	0	0	0	0
8QPs	8Q2	0	0	2	0	0	0	0
8QPhyl *	8Q3	15	0	107	4	0.04	4	0.04
8QMez *	8Q4	5	0	41	2	0.05	2	0.05
11QpaleoLev[a] *	11Q1	19	0	136	1	0.01	1	0.01
11QLev[b]	11Q2	0	0	10	0	0	0	0
11QDeut	11Q3	0	0	2	0	0	0	0
11QEzek	11Q4	1	0	8	0	0	1	0.125
11QPs[a] *	11Q5	0	32	242	17	0.07	16	0.07
11QPs[b]	11Q6	0	0	2	0	0	0	0
11QPs[c]	11Q7	0	0	12	2	0.15	1	0.1
11QPs[d]	11Q8	1	1	10	0	0	0	0

Statistics, Linguistics and the 'Biblical' Dead Sea Scrolls

Scroll Name	Scroll #	לא	לוא	Number of vavs	vav Plus	Percent Plus	vav Minus	Percent Minus
11QPs^e	11Q9	0	0	0	0	0	0	0
34Se1	34Se1	3	0	17	0	0	0	0
34Se2	34Se2	0	0	0	0	0	0	0
5/6Hev1a	5/6Hev1a	0	0	1	0	0	0	0
5/6Hev1b *	5/6Hev1b	9	0	49	0	0	0	0
Gen	Mas1	0	0	3	0	0	2	0.67
Lev	Mas1a	0	0	8	0	0	0	0
Lev *	Mas1b	6	0	66	0	0	0	0
Deut	Mas1c	1	0	10	0	0	0	0
Ezek *	Mas1d	3	0	71	0	0	0	0
Psa *	Mas1e	3	0	27	0	0	0	0
Psa	Mas1f	0	0	2	0	0	0	0
Mur Gen 1 *	Mur1	4	0	35	0	0	0	0
Mur Deut	Mur2	1	0	3	0	0	0	0
MurIsa	Mur3	2	0	2	0	0	0	0
MurEx *	Mur4	6	0	78	0	0	0	0
MurXII *	Mur88	62	0	448	2	0.004	0	0
MurGen	MurX	0	0	1	0	0	0	0
Sdeir1	Sdeir1	16	0	16	0	0	0	0
XHev/Se2	XHev/Se2	0	0	13	0	0	1	0.08
XHev/Se3	XHev/Se3	1	0	3	0	0	0	0
XHev/Se5 *	XHev/Se5	6	0	75	1	0.01	1	0.01
XQ1 *	XQ1	11	0	50	2	0.04	2	0.04
XQ2 *	XQ2	2	0	56	2	0.03	2	0.04
XQ3 *	XQ3	16	0	45	2	0.04	11	0.26
					478		312	

226

H. Shifts to *Vav* Plus Imperfect

Scroll Name	Scroll #	לא	לוא	Number of Verbs	Shifts to *Vav*+Imperfect[1]	Ratio Verbal System Variants to Number of Verbs
1QGen	1Q1			17		0
1QExod^d	1Q2	1		16		0
1QpaleoLev-Num^a	1Q3	1		15		0
1QDeut^a	1Q4		1	27		0
1QDeut^b *	1Q5	10		54		0
1QJudg	1Q6			22		0
1QSam	1Q7	2		28		0
1QIsa^b *	1Q8	89		1130	3	0.003
1QEzek	1Q9			2		0
1QPs^a	1Q10			22		0
1QPs^b	1Q11			6		0
1QPs^c	1Q12			5		0
1QPhyl *	1Q13	8		43		0
1QDan^a	1Q71	1		16		0
1QDan^b	1Q72	2		20		0
1QIsa^a I	1QIsa^a I		167	2265	28	0.01
1QIsa^a II	1QIsa^a II		276	2678	49	0.02
2QExod^a	2Q1			0		0
2QExod^b	2Q2	1	1	28		0
2QGen	2Q3			13		0
2QExod^c	2Q4			2		0
2QpaleoLev	2Q5			6		0
2QNum^a	2Q6			3		0
2QNum^b	2Q7			5		0
2QNum^c	2Q8			0		0
2QNum^d	2Q9			1		0
2QDeut^a	2Q10			3		0
2QDeut^b	2Q11			4		0

---

1 1Q8 20:3, 20:4, f10:8, 1QIsa^a 2:19, 3:10, 4:7, 4:17, 4:17, 7:3, 8:7, 9:11, 10:12, 10:25, 11:24, 14:21, 16:10, 16:21, 17:25, 17:7, 19:6, 20:23, 21:1, 21:12, 21:13, 21:15, 23:20, 23:21, 23:25, 23:3, 27:12, 27:16, 31:5, 32:27, 32:7, 33:15, 33:18, 33:6, 34:2, 34:5, 34:5, 34:6, 34:6, 35:21, 35:3, 35:4, 36:18, 36:3, 36:5, 36:5, 37:17, 37:22, 37:22, 37:25, 38:24, 39:11, 39:12, 39:4, 40:18, 40:18, 40:18, 40:19, 42:5, 42:5, 43:14, 44:1, 44:18, 44:19, 46:15, 46:26, 46:26, 46:28, 46:28, 47:13, 47:14, 47:17, 49:10, 50:21, 52:8, 53:23; 4Q1 f22ii+26:9; 4Q7 f2:3; 4Q9 f3_4:2; 4Q13 f6ii:7; 4Q14 6:38; 4Q44 f5ii:11; 4Q51 f17:2; 4Q55 f11ii+15:18; 4Q56 f3ii:5; 4Q57 f29:2, f30:2; 4Q58 11:24, 3:21; 4Q64 f1_5:5; 4Q72 f44_50:7; 4Q76 4:4; 4Q78 f18_20:9; 4Q83 f14ii:34, f9ii:12; 4Q85 f15iii+17:31; 4Q86 4:10; 4Q88 2:17, 3:17; 4Q90 f1_2:17; 4Q98a f2ii:3; 4Q111 3:5; 4Q141 f1i:15; 11Q5 7:3, 25:1, 25:10, fEii:8, fEii:8, fEii:9, fEii:10; 11Q7 f9:3; XHev/Se5 f1:5.

Statistics, Linguistics and the 'Biblical' Dead Sea Scrolls

Scroll Name	Scroll #	לא	לוא	Number of Verbs	Shifts to Vav+Imperfect	Ratio Verbal System Variants to Number of Verbs
2QDeut^c	2Q12			2		0
2QJer	2Q13		2	56		0
2QPs	2Q14			6		0
2QJob	2Q15			1		0
2QRuth^a *	2Q16	3		56		0
2QRuth^b	2Q17			10		0
3QEzek	3Q1			2		0
3QPs	3Q2			1		0
3QLam	3Q3			4		0
4QGen-Exod^a *	4Q1	6		229	1	0.004
4QGen^b *	4Q2	2		96		0
4QGen^c *	4Q3			25		0
4QGen^d	4Q4			17		0
4QGen^e *	4Q5	2		46		0
4QGen^f *	4Q6	1		37		0
4QGen^g	4Q7			31	1	0.03
4QGen^h *	4Q8			4		0
4QGen^j *	4Q9	3		60	1	0.02
4QGen^k	4Q10			12		0
4QpaleoGen-Exod1 *	4Q11	10		173		0
4QpaleoGen^m	4Q12		1	5		0
4QExod^b *	4Q13	3		117	1	0.01
4QExod^c *	4Q14	10		6	1	0.17
4QExod^d	4Q15			7		0
4QExod^e	4Q16	1		56		0
4QExod-Lev^f *	4Q17	1				0
4QExod^g	4Q18			4		0
4QExod^h	4Q19			4		0
4QExod^j	4Q20			2		0
4QExod^k	4Q21			1		0
4QpaleoExod^m *	4Q22	18		421		0
4QLev-Num^a *	4Q23	10		224		0
4QLev^b *	4Q24	18		123		0
4QLev^c	4Q25	1		27		0
4QLev^d	4Q26	1	3	19		0
4QLev^e	4Q26a	3		20		0
4QLev^g	4Q26b	1		8		0
4QNum^b	4Q27		19	336		0
4QDeut^a	4Q28	4		33		0
4QDeut^b *	4Q29	2		38		0
4QDeut^c	4Q30	13		143		0

Appendix H. Shifts to *Vav* Plus Imperfect

Scroll Name	Scroll #	לא	לוא	Number of Verbs	Shifts to *Vav*+Imperfect	Ratio Verbal System Variants to Number of Verbs
4QDeut^d *	4Q31	4		54		0
4QDeut^e	4Q32	7		45		0
4QDeut^f *	4Q33	15		116		0
4QDeut^g	4Q34	4		41		0
4QDeut^h *	4Q35	5		93		0
4QDeutⁱ	4Q36	4		31		0
4QDeut^j	4Q37	1	3	70		0
4QDeut^k1	4Q38		1	32		0
4QDeut^k2	4Q38a		2	31		0
4QDeut^k3	4Q38b	1		2		0
4QDeut^l	4Q39			10		0
4QDeut^m	4Q40		1	17		0
4QDeutⁿ	4Q41	2	17	113		0
4QDeut^o	4Q42	6		20		0
4QDeut^p	4Q43	1		4		0
4QDeut^q	4Q44			18	1	0.06
4QpaleoDeut^r *	4Q45	12		99		0
4QpaleoDeut^s	4Q46			3		0
4QJosh^a *	4Q47	5		67		0
4QJosh^b	4Q48	1		27		0
4QJudg^a	4Q49			8		0
4QJudg^b	4Q50			21		0
4QSam^a	4Q51	9	14	748	1	0.001
4QSam^b *	4Q52	5		94		0
4QSam^c	4Q53		6	78		0
4QKgs	4Q54	2		12		0
4QIsa^a *	4Q55	6		112	1	0.01
4QIsa^b *	4Q56	16		287	1	0.004
4QIsa^c	4Q57		19	268	2	0.007
4QIsa^d *	4Q58	17		170	2	0.01
4QIsa^e *	4Q59	6		93		0
4QIsa^f	4Q60	2		104		0
4QIsa^g	4Q61	3	2	18		0
4QIsa^h	4Q62	1		13		0
4QIsaⁱ	4Q62a			4		0
4QIsa^j	4Q63	1		4		0
4QIsa^k	4Q64	1		13	1	0.08
4QIsa^l	4Q65		2	5		0
4QIsa^m	4Q66			9		0
4QIsaⁿ	4Q67			10		0
4QIsa^o	4Q68			10		0

Statistics, Linguistics and the 'Biblical' Dead Sea Scrolls

Scroll Name	Scroll #	לא	לוא	Number of Verbs	Shifts to Vav+Imperfect	Ratio Verbal System Variants to Number of Verbs
4QpapIsa^p	4Q69			6		0
4QIsa^q	4Q69a			0		0
4QIsa^r	4Q69b			0		0
4QJer^a	4Q70	5	5	209		0
4QJer^b	4Q71			9		0
4QJer^c *	4Q72	13		156	1	0.006
4QJer^d	4Q72a	2		9		0
4QJer^e	4Q72b			0		0
4QEzek^a *	4Q73	1		37		0
4QEzek^b	4Q74			12		0
4QEzek^c	4Q75			1		0
4QXII^a *	4Q76	3		93	1	0.01
4QXII^b	4Q77			13		0
4QXII^c *	4Q78		9	106	1	0.01
4QXII^d	4Q79	1		4		0
4QXII^e	4Q80		4	37		0
4QXII^f	4Q81	2		14		0
4QXII^g *	4Q82	6	9	262		0
4QPs^a *	4Q83		5	130	2	0.02
4QPs^b *	4Q84	8		142		0
4QPs^c *	4Q85	4		102	1	0.01
4QPs^d	4Q86			47	1	0.02
4QPs^e *	4Q87		3	62		0
4QPs^f *	4Q88		1	55	2	0.04
4QPs^g	4Q89			24		0
4QGen^h2	4Q8a			2	1	0.5
4QGen^h-para	4Q8b					0
4QPs^h	4Q90					0
4QPs^j	4Q91			10		0
4QPs^k	4Q92			14		0
4QPs^l	4Q93			6		0
4QPs^m	4Q94			6		0
4QPsⁿ	4Q95			6		0
4QPs^o	4Q96		1	32		0
4QPs^p	4Q97			6	1	0.17
4QPs^q	4Q98			5		0
4QPs^r	4Q98a			2		0
4QPs^s	4Q98b			0		0
4QPs^t	4Q98c			2		0
4QPs^u	4Q98d			7		0
4QPs^v	4Q98e			11		0

Appendix H. Shifts to *Vav* Plus Imperfect

Scroll Name	Scroll #	לא	לוא	Number of Verbs	Shifts to *Vav*+Imperfect	Ratio Verbal System Variants to Number of Verbs
4QPs^w	4Q98f			60		0
4QPs^x	4Q98g			5		0
4QJob^a *	4Q99	7	1	12		0
4QJob^b	4Q100	1		16		0
4QpaleoJob^c	4Q101	1		41		0
4QProv^a	4Q102	3		18		0
4QProv^b	4Q103	1		5		0
4QProv^c	4Q103a			17		0
4QRuth^a	4Q104					0
4QRuth^b	4Q105			35		0
4QCant^a	4Q106			1		0
4QCant^b *	4Q107	1		23		0
4QCant^c	4Q108			7		0
4QQoh^a	4Q109		6	66	1	0.02
4QQoh^b	4Q110		1	130		0
4QLam *	4Q111		5	73		0
4QDan^a *	4Q112	6		51		0
4QDan^b *	4Q113		2	30		0
4QDan^c *	4Q114	6		3		0
4QDan^d	4Q115	2		7		0
4QDan^e	4Q116			4		0
4QEzr^a	4Q117			68		0
4QChr	4Q118			69		0
4QPhyl A *	4Q128		7	80		0
4QPhyl B *	4Q129		10	7		0
4QPhyl C *	4Q130	5		5		0
4QPhyl D	4Q131			19		0
4QPhyl E	4Q132			42		0
4QPhyl F	4Q133			71		0
4QPhyl G *	4Q134	2	8	28		0
4QPhyl H *	4Q135		1	84		0
4QPhyl I	4Q136	2	1	64		0
4QPhyl J *	4Q137		10	9		0
4QPhyl K *	4Q138		7	51		0
4QPhyl L	4Q139		3	20	1	0.05
4QPhyl M *	4Q140		5	13		0
4QPhyl N	4Q141	3		6		0
4QPhyl O	4Q142		0	7		0
4QPhyl P	4Q143			20		0
4QPhyl Q	4Q144		1	6		0
4QPhyl R	4Q145	2		3		0

Scroll Name	Scroll #	לא	לוא	Number of Verbs	Shifts to *Vav*+Imperfect	Ratio Verbal System Variants to Number of Verbs
4QPhyl S	4Q146			1		0
4QMez A	4Q149			0		0
4QMez B	4Q150	1		3		0
4QMez C	4Q151			21		0
4QMez D	4Q152			4		0
4QMez E	4Q153			2		0
4QMez F	4Q154			35		0
4QMez G	4Q155	1		3		0
4Qpap cryptA Lev^h?	4Q249j					0
4QpapGen^o	4Q483					0
4QGen^n	4Q576					0
5QDeut	5Q1	5		5		0
5QKgs	5Q2			10		0
5QIsa	5Q3			43		0
5QXII	5Q4		3	2		0
5QPs	5Q5			2		0
5QLam^a	5Q6	5	1	3		0
5QLam^b	5Q7			1		0
6QpaleoGen	6Q1			32		0
6QpaleoLev	6Q2			0		0
6QpapDeut?	6Q3			14		0
6QpapKgs *	6Q4	2		17		0
6QpapPs 78?	6Q5					0
6QCant	6Q6	1		5		0
6QpapDan	6Q7			9		0
6QDeut?	6Q20			162		0
8QGen	8Q1			53		0
8QPs	8Q2			227		0
8QPhyl *	8Q3	15		11		0
8QMez *	8Q4	5		4		0
11QpaleoLev^a *	11Q1	19		21		0
11QLev^b	11Q2			748	7	0.01
11QDeut	11Q3			11		0
11QEzek	11Q4	1		72	1	0.01
11QPs^a *	11Q5		32	35		0
11QPs^b	11Q6		0	2		0
11QPs^c	11Q7			23		0
11QPs^d	11Q8	1	1	0		0
11QPs^e	11Q9			3		0
34Se1	34Se1	3		204		0
34Se2	34Se2			0		0

Appendix H. Shifts to *Vav* Plus Imperfect

Scroll Name	Scroll #	לא	לוא	Number of Verbs	Shifts to *Vav*+Imperfect	Ratio Verbal System Variants to Number of Verbs
5/6Hev1a	5/6Hev1a			9		0
5/6Hev1b *	5/6Hev1b	9		93		0
Gen	Mas1			19		0
Lev	Mas1a			137		0
Lev *	Mas1b	6		84		0
Deut	Mas1c	1		8		0
Ezek *	Mas1d	3		59		0
Psa *	Mas1e	3		3		0
Psa	Mas1f			3		0
Mur Gen 1 *	Mur1	4		98		0
Mur Deut	Mur2	1		1048		0
MurIsa	Mur3	2		2		0
MurEx *	Mur4	6		6		0
MurXII *	Mur88	62		3		0
MurGen	MurX			13		0
Sdeir1	Sdeir1	16		96	1	0.01
XHev/Se2	XHev/Se2					0
XHev/Se3	XHev/Se3	1				0
XHev/Se5 *	XHev/Se5	6				0
XQ1 *	XQ1	11		69		0
XQ2 *	XQ2	2		89		0
XQ3 *	XQ3	16		74		0
					116	

233

I. Preterite

Scroll Name	Scroll #	לא	לוא	Number of Preterites	Preterite Plus[1]	Percent Decrease	Preterite Minus[2]	Percent Decrease
1QGen	1Q1					0		0
1QExod^d	1Q2	1				0		0
1QpaleoLev-Num^a	1Q3	1				0		0
1QDeut^a	1Q4		1			0		0
1QDeut^b *	1Q5	10		2		0	1	0.5
1QJudg	1Q6					0		0
1QSam	1Q7	2				0		0
1QIsa^b *	1Q8	89				0		0
1QEzek	1Q9					0		0
1QPs^a	1Q10					0		0
1QPs^b	1Q11					0		0
1QPs^c	1Q12					0		0
1QPhyl *	1Q13	8				0		0
1QDan^a	1Q71	1				0		0
1QDan^b	1Q72	2				0		0
1QIsa^a I	1QIsa^a I		167	88	1	0.01	7	0.08
1QIsa^a II	1QIsa^a II		276	151	4	0.03	5	0.03
2QExod^a	2Q1					0		0
2QExod^b	2Q2	1	1			0		0
2QGen	2Q3					0		0
2QExod^c	2Q4					0		0
2QpaleoLev	2Q5					0		0
2QNum^a	2Q6					0		0
2QNum^b	2Q7					0		0
2QNum^c	2Q8					0		0
2QNum^d	2Q9					0		0
2QDeut^a	2Q10					0		0
2QDeut^b	2Q11					0		0
2QDeut^c	2Q12					0		0
2QJer	2Q13		2			0		0
2QPs	2Q14					0		0
2QJob	2Q15					0		0
2QRuth^a *	2Q16	3				0		0

1 1QIsa^a 24:21, 30:24, 40:19, 44:17, 44:8; 4Q51 2a_d:34, 3a_e:11, f155_158:15, f61i+62:33, f68_76:21; 4Q88 2:17, 3:21, 3:21;11Q5 22:16.
2 1Q5 f13ii:4, 1QIsa^a 11:8, 17:10, 30:1, 34:8, 37:18, 40:23, 41:6, 43:2, 5:1, 5:21, 53:11, 8:24; 4Q41 4:7; 4Q51 f112_114:2, f112_114:3, f112_114:9, f120:4, f155_158:14, f155_158:16, f68_76:11, f68_76:18, f80_83:2; 4Q52 f6_7:18; 4Q53 f5ii_7i:21, f5ii_7i:23, f7ii_11:12; 4Q56 f24_25:3; 4Q88 6:1; 4Q98 1:7; 4Q98g f1:1; 6Q7 f2_5:4; 8Q3 f17_25:13; Mas1d 3:12.

Appendix I. Preterite

Scroll Name	Scroll #	לא	לוא	Number of Preterites	Preterite Plus	Percent Decrease	Preterite Minus	Percent Decrease
2QRuth[b]	2Q17					0		0
3QEzek	3Q1					0		0
3QPs	3Q2					0		0
3QLam	3Q3					0		0
4QGen-Exod[a] *	4Q1	6				0		0
4QGen[b] *	4Q2	2				0		0
4QGen[c] *	4Q3					0		0
4QGen[d]	4Q4					0		0
4QGen[e] *	4Q5	2				0		0
4QGen[f] *	4Q6	1				0		0
4QGen[g]	4Q7					0		0
4QGen[h] *	4Q8					0		0
4QGen[j] *	4Q9	3				0		0
4QGen[k]	4Q10					0		0
4QpaleoGen-Exod1 *	4Q11	10				0		0
4QpaleoGen[m]	4Q12		1			0		0
4QExod[b] *	4Q13	3				0		0
4QExod[c] *	4Q14	10				0		0
4QExod[d]	4Q15					0		0
4QExod[e]	4Q16	1				0		0
4QExod-Lev[f] *	4Q17	1				0		0
4QExod[g]	4Q18					0		0
4QExod[h]	4Q19					0		0
4QExod[j]	4Q20					0		0
4QExod[k]	4Q21					0		0
4QpaleoExod[m] *	4Q22	18				0		0
4QLev-Num[a] *	4Q23	10				0		0
4QLev[b] *	4Q24	18				0		0
4QLev[c]	4Q25	1				0		0
4QLev[d]	4Q26	1	3			0		0
4QLev[e]	4Q26a	3				0		0
4QLev[g]	4Q26b	1				0		0
4QNum[b]	4Q27		19			0		0
4QDeut[a]	4Q28	4				0		0
4QDeut[b] *	4Q29	2				0		0
4QDeut[c]	4Q30	13				0		0
4QDeut[d] *	4Q31	4				0		0
4QDeut[e]	4Q32	7				0		0
4QDeut[f] *	4Q33	15				0		0
4QDeut[g]	4Q34	4				0		0
4QDeut[h] *	4Q35	5				0		0
4QDeut[i]	4Q36	4				0		0

235

Statistics, Linguistics and the 'Biblical' Dead Sea Scrolls

Scroll Name	Scroll #	לא	לוא	Number of Preterites	Preterite Plus	Percent Decrease	Preterite Minus	Percent Decrease
4QDeut^j	4Q37	1	3			0		0
4QDeut^k1	4Q38		1			0		0
4QDeut^k2	4Q38a		2			0		0
4QDeut^k3	4Q38b	1				0		0
4QDeut^l	4Q39					0		0
4QDeut^m	4Q40		1			0		0
4QDeutⁿ	4Q41	2	17	12		0	1	0.08
4QDeut^o	4Q42	6				0		0
4QDeut^p	4Q43	1				0		0
4QDeut^q	4Q44					0		0
4QpaleoDeut^r *	4Q45	12				0		0
4QpaleoDeut^s	4Q46					0		0
4QJosh^a *	4Q47	5				0		0
4QJosh^b	4Q48	1				0		0
4QJudg^a	4Q49					0		0
4QJudg^b	4Q50				5	0		0
4QSam^a	4Q51	9	14	261		0	9	0.03
4QSam^b *	4Q52	5		40		0	1	0.03
4QSam^c	4Q53		6	23		0	3	0.13
4QKgs	4Q54	2				0		0
4QIsa^a *	4Q55	6				0		0
4QIsa^b *	4Q56	16		12		0	1	0.08
4QIsa^c	4Q57		19			0		0
4QIsa^d *	4Q58	17				0		0
4QIsa^e *	4Q59	6				0		0
4QIsa^f	4Q60	2				0		0
4QIsa^g	4Q61	3	2			0		0
4QIsa^h	4Q62	1				0		0
4QIsaⁱ	4Q62a					0		0
4QIsa^j	4Q63	1				0		0
4QIsa^k	4Q64	1				0		0
4QIsa^l	4Q65		2			0		0
4QIsa^m	4Q66					0		0
4QIsaⁿ	4Q67					0		0
4QIsa^o	4Q68					0		0
4QpapIsa^p	4Q69					0		0
4QIsa^q	4Q69a					0		0
4QIsa^r	4Q69b					0		0
4QJer^a	4Q70	5	5			0		0
4QJer^b	4Q71					0		0
4QJer^c *	4Q72	13				0		0
4QJer^d	4Q72a	2				0		0

Appendix I. Preterite

Scroll Name	Scroll #	לא	לוא	Number of Preterites	Preterite Plus	Percent Decrease	Preterite Minus	Percent Decrease
4QJer^e	4Q72b					0		0
4QEzek^a *	4Q73	1				0		0
4QEzek^b	4Q74					0		0
4QEzek^c	4Q75					0		0
4QXII^a *	4Q76	3				0		0
4QXII^b	4Q77					0		0
4QXII^c *	4Q78		9			0		0
4QXII^d	4Q79	1				0		0
4QXII^e	4Q80		4			0		0
4QXII^f	4Q81	2				0		0
4QXII^g *	4Q82	6	9			0		0
4QPs^a *	4Q83		5			0		0
4QPs^b *	4Q84	8				0		0
4QPs^c *	4Q85	4				0		0
4QPs^d	4Q86					0		0
4QPs^e *	4Q87		3		3	0		0
4QPs^f *	4Q88		1	14		0	1	0.07
4QPs^g	4Q89					0		0
4QGen^h2	4Q8a					0		0
4QGen^h-para	4Q8b					0		0
4QPs^h	4Q90					0		0
4QPs^j	4Q91					0		0
4QPs^k	4Q92					0		0
4QPs^l	4Q93					0		0
4QPs^m	4Q94					0		0
4QPs^n	4Q95					0		0
4QPs^o	4Q96		1	1		0	1	1
4QPs^p	4Q97					0		0
4QPs^q	4Q98					0		0
4QPs^r	4Q98a					0		0
4QPs^s	4Q98b					0		0
4QPs^t	4Q98c					0		0
4QPs^u	4Q98d					0		0
4QPs^v	4Q98e			1		0	1	1
4QPs^w	4Q98f					0		0
4QPs^x	4Q98g					0		0
4QJob^a *	4Q99	7	1			0		0
4QJob^b	4Q100	1				0		0
4QpaleoJob^c	4Q101	1				0		0
4QProv^a	4Q102	3				0		0
4QProv^b	4Q103	1				0		0
4QProv^c	4Q103a					0		0

Statistics, Linguistics and the 'Biblical' Dead Sea Scrolls

Scroll Name	Scroll #	לא	לוא	Number of Preterites	Preterite Plus	Percent Decrease	Preterite Minus	Percent Decrease
4QRuth^a	4Q104					0		0
4QRuth^b	4Q105					0		0
4QCant^a	4Q106					0		0
4QCant^b *	4Q107	1				0		0
4QCant^c	4Q108					0		0
4QQoh^a	4Q109		6			0		0
4QQoh^b	4Q110		1			0		0
4QLam *	4Q111		5			0		0
4QDan^a *	4Q112	6				0		0
4QDan^b *	4Q113		2			0		0
4QDan^c *	4Q114	6				0		0
4QDan^d	4Q115	2				0		0
4QDan^e	4Q116					0		0
4QEzr^a	4Q117					0		0
4QChr	4Q118					0		0
4QPhyl A *	4Q128		7			0		0
4QPhyl B *	4Q129		10			0		0
4QPhyl C *	4Q130	5				0		0
4QPhyl D	4Q131					0		0
4QPhyl E	4Q132					0		0
4QPhyl F	4Q133					0		0
4QPhyl G *	4Q134	2	8			0		0
4QPhyl H *	4Q135		1			0		0
4QPhyl I	4Q136	2	1			0		0
4QPhyl J *	4Q137		10			0		0
4QPhyl K *	4Q138		7			0		0
4QPhyl L	4Q139		3			0		0
4QPhyl M *	4Q140		5			0		0
4QPhyl N	4Q141	3				0		0
4QPhyl O	4Q142		0			0		0
4QPhyl P	4Q143					0		0
4QPhyl Q	4Q144		1			0		0
4QPhyl R	4Q145	2				0		0
4QPhyl S	4Q146					0		0
4QMez A	4Q149					0		0
4QMez B	4Q150	1				0		0
4QMez C	4Q151					0		0
4QMez D	4Q152					0		0
4QMez E	4Q153					0		0
4QMez F	4Q154					0		0
4QMez G	4Q155	1				0		0
4Qpap cryptA Lev^h?	4Q249j					0		0

Appendix I. Preterite

Scroll Name	Scroll #	לא	לוא	Number of Preterites	Preterite Plus	Percent Decrease	Preterite Minus	Percent Decrease
4QpapGenᵒ	4Q483					0		0
4QGenⁿ	4Q576					0		0
5QDeut	5Q1	5				0		0
5QKgs	5Q2					0		0
5QIsa	5Q3					0		0
5QXII	5Q4		3			0		0
5QPs	5Q5					0		0
5QLamᵃ	5Q6	5	1			0		0
5QLamᵇ	5Q7					0		0
6QpaleoGen	6Q1					0		0
6QpaleoLev	6Q2					0		0
6QpapDeut?	6Q3					0		0
6QpapKgs *	6Q4	2		1		0	1	1
6QpapPs 78?	6Q5					0		0
6QCant	6Q6	1				0		0
6QpapDan	6Q7					0		0
6QDeut?	6Q20			7		0	1	0.14
8QGen	8Q1					0		0
8QPs	8Q2					0		0
8QPhyl *	8Q3	15				0		0
8QMez *	8Q4	5				0		0
11QpaleoLevᵃ *	11Q1	19				0		0
11QLevᵇ	11Q2				1	0		0
11QDeut	11Q3					0		0
11QEzek	11Q4	1				0		0
11QPsᵃ *	11Q5		32			0		0
11QPsᵇ	11Q6		0			0		0
11QPsᶜ	11Q7					0		0
11QPsᵈ	11Q8	1	1			0		0
11QPsᵉ	11Q9					0		0
34Se1	34Se1	3				0		0
34Se2	34Se2					0		0
5/6Hev1a	5/6Hev1a					0		0
5/6Hev1b *	5/6Hev1b	9				0		0
Gen	Mas1					0		0
Lev	Mas1a			17		0	1	0.06
Lev *	Mas1b	6				0		0
Deut	Mas1c	1				0		0
Ezek *	Mas1d	3				0		0
Psa *	Mas1e	3				0		0
Psa	Mas1f					0		0
Mur Gen 1 *	Mur1	4				0		0

Statistics, Linguistics and the 'Biblical' Dead Sea Scrolls

Scroll Name	Scroll #	לא	לוא	Number of Preterites	Preterite Plus	Percent Decrease	Preterite Minus	Percent Decrease
Mur Deut	Mur2	1				0		0
MurIsa	Mur3	2				0		0
MurEx *	Mur4	6				0		0
MurXII *	Mur88	62				0		0
MurGen	MurX					0		0
Sdeir1	Sdeir1	16				0		0
XHev/Se2	XHev/Se2					0		0
XHev/Se3	XHev/Se3	1				0		0
XHev/Se5 *	XHev/Se5	6				0		0
XQ1 *	XQ1	11				0		0
XQ2 *	XQ2	2				0		0
XQ3 *	XQ3	16				0		0
					14		34	

J. Infinitive Absolute

Scroll Name	Scroll #	לא	לוא	Number of Infinitives Absolute	Away Infinitives Absolute[1]	Ratio Verbal System Variations to Number of Verbs
1QGen	1Q1					0
1QExod	1Q2	1				0
1QpaleoLev-Numᵃ	1Q3	1				0
1QDeutᵃ	1Q4		1			0
1QDeutᵇ *	1Q5	10				0
1QJudg	1Q6					0
1QSam	1Q7	2				0
1QIsaᵇ *	1Q8	89		13	4	0.31
1QEzek	1Q9					0
1QPsᵃ	1Q10					0
1QPsᵇ	1Q11					0
1QPsᶜ	1Q12					0
1QPhyl *	1Q13	8				0
1QDanᵃ	1Q71	1				0
1QDanᵇ	1Q72	2				0
1QIsaᵃ I	1QIsaᵃ I		167	39	4	0.10
1QIsaᵃ II	1QIsaᵃ II		276	24	11	0.46
2QExodᵃ	2Q1					0
2QExodᵇ	2Q2	1	1			0
2QGen	2Q3					0
2QExodᶜ	2Q4					0
2QpaleoLev	2Q5					0
2QNumᵃ	2Q6					0
2QNumᵇ	2Q7					0
2QNumᶜ	2Q8					0
2QNumᵈ	2Q9					0
2QDeutᵃ	2Q10					0
2QDeutᵇ	2Q11					0
2QDeutᶜ	2Q12					0
2QJer	2Q13		2			0
2QPs	2Q14					0
2QJob	2Q15					0
2QRuthᵃ *	2Q16	3				0
2QRuthᵇ	2Q17					0

---

1 1Q8 25:30, 25:30, 25:31, 25:31; 1QIsaᵃ 4:17, 15:30, 16:19, 17:25, 30:24, 31:8, 36:2, 36:7, 47:17, 47:20, 47:29, 48:15, 48:15, 48:24, 48:25; 4Q51 f61ii+63_64a_b+65_67:21, f80_83:13, 3a_e:28; 4Q52 f10_23:13; 4Q56 f22_23:3; 4Q58 11:24; 4Q83 f6:3; 11Q5 5:15, 6:8.

Statistics, Linguistics and the 'Biblical' Dead Sea Scrolls

Scroll Name	Scroll #	לא	לוא	Number of Infinitives Absolute	Away Infinitives Absolute	Ratio Verbal System Variations to Number of Verbs
3QEzek	3Q1					0
3QPs	3Q2					0
3QLam	3Q3					0
4QGen-Exod^a *	4Q1	6				0
4QGen^b *	4Q2	2				0
4QGen^c *	4Q3					0
4QGen^d	4Q4					0
4QGen^e *	4Q5	2				0
4QGen^f *	4Q6	1				0
4QGen^g	4Q7					0
4QGen^h *	4Q8					0
4QGen^j *	4Q9	3				0
4QGen^k	4Q10					0
4QpaleoGen-Exod1 *	4Q11	10				0
4QpaleoGen^m	4Q12		1			0
4QExod^b *	4Q13	3				0
4QExod^c *	4Q14	10				0
4QExod^d	4Q15					0
4QExod^e	4Q16	1				0
4QExod-Lev^f *	4Q17	1				0
4QExod^g	4Q18					0
4QExod^h	4Q19					0
4QExod^j	4Q20					0
4QExod^k	4Q21					0
4QpaleoExod^m *	4Q22	18				0
4QLev-Num^a *	4Q23	10				0
4QLev^b *	4Q24	18				0
4QLev^c	4Q25	1				0
4QLev^d	4Q26	1	3			0
4QLev^e	4Q26a	3				0
4QLev^g	4Q26b	1				0
4QNum^b	4Q27		19			0
4QDeut^a	4Q28	4				0
4QDeut^b *	4Q29	2				0
4QDeut^c	4Q30	13				0
4QDeut^d *	4Q31	4				0
4QDeut^e	4Q32	7				0
4QDeut^f *	4Q33	15				0
4QDeut^g	4Q34	4				0
4QDeut^h *	4Q35	5				0
4QDeut^i	4Q36	4				0

Appendix J. Infinitive Absolute

Scroll Name	Scroll #	לא	לוא	Number of Infinitives Absolute	Away Infinitives Absolute	Ratio Verbal System Variations to Number of Verbs
4QDeut^j	4Q37	1	3			0
4QDeut^k1	4Q38		1			0
4QDeut^k2	4Q38a		2			0
4QDeut^k3	4Q38b	1				0
4QDeut^l	4Q39					0
4QDeut^m	4Q40		1			0
4QDeut^n	4Q41	2	17			0
4QDeut^o	4Q42	6				0
4QDeut^p	4Q43	1				0
4QDeut^q	4Q44					0
4QpaleoDeut^r *	4Q45	12				0
4QpaleoDeut^s	4Q46					0
4QJosh^a *	4Q47	5				0
4QJosh^b	4Q48	1				0
4QJudg^a	4Q49					0
4QJudg^b	4Q50					0
4QSam^a	4Q51	9	14	14	3	0.21
4QSam^b *	4Q52	5		1	1	1
4QSam^c	4Q53		6			0
4QKgs	4Q54	2				0
4QIsa^a *	4Q55	6				0
4QIsa^b *	4Q56	16		3	1	0.33
4QIsa^c	4Q57		19			0
4QIsa^d *	4Q58	17		3	1	0.33
4QIsa^e *	4Q59	6				0
4QIsa^f	4Q60	2				0
4QIsa^g	4Q61	3	2			0
4QIsa^h	4Q62	1				0
4QIsa^i	4Q62a					0
4QIsa^j	4Q63	1				0
4QIsa^k	4Q64	1				0
4QIsa^l	4Q65		2			0
4QIsa^m	4Q66					0
4QIsa^n	4Q67					0
4QIsa^o	4Q68					0
4QpapIsa^p	4Q69					0
4QIsa^q	4Q69a					0
4QIsa^r	4Q69b					0
4QJer^a	4Q70	5	5			0
4QJer^b	4Q71					0
4QJer^c *	4Q72	13				0

243

Statistics, Linguistics and the 'Biblical' Dead Sea Scrolls

Scroll Name	Scroll #	לא	לוא	Number of Infinitives Absolute	Away Infinitives Absolute	Ratio Verbal System Variations to Number of Verbs
4QJer^d	4Q72a	2				0
4QJer^e	4Q72b					0
4QEzek^a *	4Q73	1				0
4QEzek^b	4Q74					0
4QEzek^c	4Q75					0
4QXII^a *	4Q76	3				0
4QXII^b	4Q77					0
4QXII^c *	4Q78		9			0
4QXII^d	4Q79	1				0
4QXII^e	4Q80		4			0
4QXII^f	4Q81	2				0
4QXII^g *	4Q82	6	9			0
4QPs^a *	4Q83		5	1	1	1
4QPs^b *	4Q84	8				0
4QPs^c *	4Q85	4				0
4QPs^d	4Q86					0
4QPs^e *	4Q87		3			0
4QPs^f *	4Q88		1			0
4QPs^g	4Q89					0
4QGen^{h}2	4Q8a					0
4QGen^h-para	4Q8b					0
4QPs^h	4Q90					0
4QPs^j	4Q91					0
4QPs^k	4Q92					0
4QPs^l	4Q93					0
4QPs^m	4Q94					0
4QPs^n	4Q95					0
4QPs^o	4Q96		1			0
4QPs^p	4Q97					0
4QPs^q	4Q98					0
4QPs^r	4Q98a					0
4QPs^s	4Q98b					0
4QPs^t	4Q98c					0
4QPs^u	4Q98d					0
4QPs^v	4Q98e					0
4QPs^w	4Q98f					0
4QPs^x	4Q98g					0
4QJob^a *	4Q99	7	1			0
4QJob^b	4Q100	1				0
4QpaleoJob^c	4Q101	1				0
4QProv^a	4Q102	3				0

Appendix J. Infinitive Absolute

Scroll Name	Scroll #	לא	לוא	Number of Infinitives Absolute	Away Infinitives Absolute	Ratio Verbal System Variations to Number of Verbs
4QProv^b	4Q103	1				0
4QProv^c	4Q103a					0
4QRuth^a	4Q104					0
4QRuth^b	4Q105					0
4QCant^a	4Q106					0
4QCant^b *	4Q107	1				0
4QCant^c	4Q108					0
4QQoh^a	4Q109		6			0
4QQoh^b	4Q110		1			0
4QLam *	4Q111		5			0
4QDan^a *	4Q112	6				0
4QDan^b *	4Q113		2			0
4QDan^c *	4Q114	6				0
4QDan^d	4Q115	2				0
4QDan^e	4Q116					0
4QEzr^a	4Q117					0
4QChr	4Q118					0
4QPhyl A *	4Q128		7			0
4QPhyl B *	4Q129		10			0
4QPhyl C *	4Q130	5				0
4QPhyl D	4Q131					0
4QPhyl E	4Q132					0
4QPhyl F	4Q133					0
4QPhyl G *	4Q134	2	8			0
4QPhyl H *	4Q135		1			0
4QPhyl I	4Q136	2	1			0
4QPhyl J *	4Q137		10			0
4QPhyl K *	4Q138		7			0
4QPhyl L	4Q139		3			0
4QPhyl M *	4Q140		5			0
4QPhyl N	4Q141	3				0
4QPhyl O	4Q142		0			0
4QPhyl P	4Q143					0
4QPhyl Q	4Q144		1			0
4QPhyl R	4Q145	2				0
4QPhyl S	4Q146					0
4QMez A	4Q149					0
4QMez B	4Q150	1				0
4QMez C	4Q151					0
4QMez D	4Q152					0
4QMez E	4Q153					0

Statistics, Linguistics and the 'Biblical' Dead Sea Scrolls

Scroll Name	Scroll #	לא	לוא?	Number of Infinitives Absolute	Away Infinitives Absolute	Ratio Verbal System Variations to Number of Verbs
4QMez F	4Q154					0
4QMez G	4Q155	1				0
4Qpap cryptA Lev[h]?	4Q249j					0
4QpapGen[o]	4Q483					0
4QGen[n]	4Q576					0
5QDeut	5Q1	5				0
5QKgs	5Q2					0
5QIsa	5Q3					0
5QXII	5Q4		3			0
5QPs	5Q5					0
5QLam[a]	5Q6	5	1			0
5QLam[b]	5Q7					0
6QpaleoGen	6Q1					0
6QpaleoLev	6Q2					0
6QpapDeut?	6Q3					0
6QpapKgs *	6Q4	2				0
6QpapPs 78?	6Q5					0
6QCant	6Q6	1				0
6QpapDan	6Q7					0
6QDeut?	6Q20					0
8QGen	8Q1					0
8QPs	8Q2					0
8QPhyl *	8Q3	15		0	2	0
8QMez *	8Q4	5				0
11QpaleoLev[a] *	11Q1	19				0
11QLev[b]	11Q2					0
11QDeut	11Q3					0
11QEzek	11Q4	1				0
11QPs[a] *	11Q5		32			0
11QPs[b]	11Q6		0			0
11QPs[c]	11Q7					0
11QPs[d]	11Q8	1	1			0
11QPs[e]	11Q9					0
34Se1	34Se1	3				0
34Se2	34Se2					0
5/6Hev1a	5/6Hev1a					0
5/6Hev1b *	5/6Hev1b	9				0
Gen	Mas1					0
Lev	Mas1a					0
Lev *	Mas1b	6				0
Deut	Mas1c	1				0

Appendix J. Infinitive Absolute

Scroll Name	Scroll #	לא	לוא	Number of Infinitives Absolute	Away Infinitives Absolute	Ratio Verbal System Variations to Number of Verbs
Ezek *	Mas1d	3				0
Psa *	Mas1e	3				0
Psa	Mas1f					0
Mur Gen 1 *	Mur1	4				0
Mur Deut	Mur2	1				0
MurIsa	Mur3	2				0
MurEx *	Mur4	6				0
MurXII *	Mur88	62				0
MurGen	MurX					0
Sdeir1	Sdeir1	16				0
XHev/Se2	XHev/Se2					0
XHev/Se3	XHev/Se3	1				0
XHev/Se5 *	XHev/Se5	6				0
XQ1 *	XQ1	11				0
XQ2 *	XQ2	2				0
XQ3 *	XQ3	16				0
					28	

K. Suffix - Plus

Scroll Name	Scroll #	לא	לוא	Number of Suffix Plus[1]
1QGen	1Q1			
1QExod	1Q2	1		
1QpaleoLev-Numª	1Q3	1		
1QDeutª	1Q4		1	
1QDeutᵇ *	1Q5	10		
1QJudg	1Q6			
1QSam	1Q7	2		
1QIsaᵇ *	1Q8	89		2
1QEzek	1Q9			
1QPsª	1Q10			
1QPsᵇ	1Q11			
1QPsᶜ	1Q12			
1QPhyl *	1Q13	8		
1QDanª	1Q71	1		
1QDanᵇ	1Q72	2		
1QIsaª I	1QIsaª I		167	12
1QIsaª II	1QIsaª II		276	19
2QExodª	2Q1			
2QExodᵇ	2Q2	1	1	
2QGen	2Q3			
2QExodᶜ	2Q4			
2QpaleoLev	2Q5			
2QNumª	2Q6			
2QNumᵇ	2Q7			
2QNumᶜ	2Q8			
2QNumᵈ	2Q9			
2QDeutª	2Q10			
2QDeutᵇ	2Q11			
2QDeutᶜ	2Q12			
2QJer	2Q13		2	2
2QPs	2Q14			
2QJob	2Q15			
2QRuthª *	2Q16	3		

---

1 1Q8 23:25, f3ii+5i:3; 1QIsaª 1:16, 5:21, 11:30, 11:30, 11:8, 13:22, 14:10, 20:14, 20:29, 20:31, 22:26, 25:19, 30:28, 30:29, 33:12, 33:23, 33:26, 35:10, 36:3, 37:18, 39:16, 43:22, 44:17, 44:22, 44:8, 46:28, 47:10, 47:20, 50:29, 51:27, 54:10; 2Q13 f9ii_12:3, f9ii_12:4; 4Q14 8:31; 4Q17 f4:3; 4Q22 38:9; 4Q23 f31_32i+33:6; 4Q26 f4:16, f4:5; 4Q27 f51_54:28; 4Q35 f9:1; 4Q45 f7_10:6; 4Q51 f102ii+103_106i+107_109a_b:29, f40_41:3; 4Q57 f12ii+14_15+53:28, f12ii+14_15+53:28, f9ii+11+12i+52:38; 4Q58 8:22; 4Q74 f6ii:4; 4Q82 f19b+27_32:5; 4Q83 f19ii_20:33, f9ii:4; 4Q89 f1i:8; 4Q107 f2ii:8; 4Q111 3:3, 3:3; 5Q6 f1ii:7; 8Q3 f26_29:19; 11Q1 3:7, fD:1; 11Q2 f7:3; 11Q5 8:13.

Appendix K. Suffix - Plus

Scroll Name	Scroll #	לא	לוא	Number of Suffix Plus
2QRuth[b]	2Q17			
3QEzek	3Q1			
3QPs	3Q2			
3QLam	3Q3			
4QGen-Exod[a] *	4Q1	6		
4QGen[b] *	4Q2	2		
4QGen[c] *	4Q3			
4QGen[d]	4Q4			
4QGen[e] *	4Q5	2		
4QGen[f] *	4Q6	1		
4QGen[g]	4Q7			
4QGen[h] *	4Q8			
4QGen[j] *	4Q9			
4QGen[k]	4Q10			
4QpaleoGen-Exod1 *	4Q11	3		
4QpaleoGen[m]	4Q12			
4QExod[b] *	4Q13	10		
4QExod[c] *	4Q14		1	
4QExod[d]	4Q15	3		
4QExod[e]	4Q16	10		1
4QExod-Lev[f] *	4Q17			
4QExod[g]	4Q18	1		
4QExod[h]	4Q19	1		1
4QExod[j]	4Q20			
4QExod[k]	4Q21			
4QpaleoExod[m] *	4Q22			
4QLev-Num[a] *	4Q23			
4QLev[b] *	4Q24	18		1
4QLev[c]	4Q25	10		1
4QLev[d]	4Q26	18		
4QLev[e]	4Q26a	1		
4QLev[g]	4Q26b	1	3	2
4QNum[b]	4Q27	3		
4QDeut[a]	4Q28	1		
4QDeut[b] *	4Q29		19	1
4QDeut[c]	4Q30	4		
4QDeut[d] *	4Q31	2		
4QDeut[e]	4Q32	13		
4QDeut[f] *	4Q33	4		
4QDeut[g]	4Q34	7		
4QDeut[h] *	4Q35	15		
4QDeut[i]	4Q36	4		
4QDeut[j]	4Q37	5		1

Statistics, Linguistics and the 'Biblical' Dead Sea Scrolls

Scroll Name	Scroll #	לא	לוא	Number of Suffix Plus
4QDeut^k1	4Q38	4		
4QDeut^k2	4Q38a	1	3	
4QDeut^k3	4Q38b		1	
4QDeut^l	4Q39		2	
4QDeut^m	4Q40	1		
4QDeutⁿ	4Q41			
4QDeut^o	4Q42		1	
4QDeut^p	4Q43	2	17	
4QDeut^q	4Q44	6		
4QpaleoDeut^r *	4Q45	1		
4QpaleoDeut^s	4Q46			
4QJosh^a *	4Q47	12		1
4QJosh^b	4Q48			
4QJudg^a	4Q49	5		
4QJudg^b	4Q50	1		
4QSam^a	4Q51			
4QSam^b *	4Q52			
4QSam^c	4Q53	9	14	2
4QKgs	4Q54	5		
4QIsa^a *	4Q55		6	
4QIsa^b *	4Q56	2		
4QIsa^c	4Q57	6		
4QIsa^d *	4Q58	16		
4QIsa^e *	4Q59		19	3
4QIsa^f	4Q60	17		1
4QIsa^g	4Q61	6		
4QIsa^h	4Q62	2		
4QIsaⁱ	4Q62a	3	2	
4QIsa^j	4Q63	1		
4QIsa^k	4Q64			
4QIsa^l	4Q65	1		
4QIsa^m	4Q66	1		
4QIsaⁿ	4Q67		2	
4QIsa^o	4Q68			
4QpapIsa^p	4Q69			
4QIsa^q	4Q69a			
4QIsa^r	4Q69b			
4QJer^a	4Q70			
4QJer^b	4Q71			
4QJer^c *	4Q72	5	5	
4QJer^d	4Q72a			
4QJer^e	4Q72b	13		
4QEzek^a *	4Q73	2		

Appendix K. Suffix - Plus

Scroll Name	Scroll #	לֹא	לוֹא	Number of Suffix Plus
4QEzek^b	4Q74			
4QEzek^c	4Q75	1		
4QXII^a *	4Q76			1
4QXII^b	4Q77			
4QXII^c *	4Q78	3		
4QXII^d	4Q79			
4QXII^e	4Q80		9	
4QXII^f	4Q81	1		
4QXII^g *	4Q82		4	
4QPs^a *	4Q83	2		
4QPs^b *	4Q84	6	9	1
4QPs^c *	4Q85		5	2
4QPs^d	4Q86	8		
4QPs^e *	4Q87	4		
4QPs^f *	4Q88			
4QPs^g	4Q89		3	
4QGen^h2	4Q8a		1	
4QGen^h-para	4Q8b			1
4QPs^h	4Q90			
4QPs^j	4Q91			
4QPs^k	4Q92			
4QPs^l	4Q93			
4QPs^m	4Q94			
4QPsⁿ	4Q95			
4QPs^o	4Q96		1	
4QPs^p	4Q97			
4QPs^q	4Q98			
4QPs^r	4Q98a			
4QPs^s	4Q98b			
4QPs^t	4Q98c			
4QPs^u	4Q98d			
4QPs^v	4Q98e			
4QPs^w	4Q98f			
4QPs^x	4Q98g			
4QJob^a *	4Q99	7	1	
4QJob^b	4Q100	1		
4QpaleoJob^c	4Q101	1		
4QProv^a	4Q102	3		
4QProv^b	4Q103	1		
4QProv^c	4Q103a			
4QRuth^a	4Q104			
4QRuth^b	4Q105			
4QCant^a	4Q106			

Statistics, Linguistics and the 'Biblical' Dead Sea Scrolls

Scroll Name	Scroll #	לא	לוא	Number of Suffix Plus
4QCant^b *	4Q107	1		1
4QCant^c	4Q108			
4QQoh^a	4Q109		6	
4QQoh^b	4Q110		1	
4QLam *	4Q111		5	2
4QDan^a *	4Q112	6		
4QDan^b *	4Q113		2	
4QDan^c *	4Q114	6		
4QDan^d	4Q115	2		
4QDan^e	4Q116			
4QEzr^a	4Q117			
4QChr	4Q118			
4QPhyl A *	4Q128		7	
4QPhyl B *	4Q129		10	
4QPhyl C *	4Q130	5		
4QPhyl D	4Q131			
4QPhyl E	4Q132			
4QPhyl F	4Q133			
4QPhyl G *	4Q134	2	8	
4QPhyl H *	4Q135		1	
4QPhyl I	4Q136	2	1	
4QPhyl J *	4Q137		10	
4QPhyl K *	4Q138		7	
4QPhyl L	4Q139		3	
4QPhyl M *	4Q140		5	
4QPhyl N	4Q141	3		
4QPhyl O	4Q142		0	
4QPhyl P	4Q143			
4QPhyl Q	4Q144		1	
4QPhyl R	4Q145	2		
4QPhyl U	4Q148			
4QMez A	4Q149			
4QMez B	4Q150	1		
4QMez C	4Q151			
4QMez D	4Q152			
4QMez E	4Q153			
4QMez F	4Q154			
4QMez G	4Q155	1		
4Qpap cryptA Lev^h?	4Q249j			
4QpapGen^o	4Q483			
4QGenⁿ	4Q576			
5QDeut	5Q1	5		
5QKgs	5Q2			

Appendix K. Suffix - Plus

Scroll Name	Scroll #	לא	לוא	Number of Suffix Plus
5QIsa	5Q3			
5QXII	5Q4		3	
5QPs	5Q5			
5QLam^a	5Q6	5	1	1
5QLam^b	5Q7			
6QpaleoGen	6Q1			
6QpaleoLev	6Q2			
6QpapDeut?	6Q3			
6QpapKgs *	6Q4	2		
6QpapPs 78?	6Q5			
6QCant	6Q6	1		
6QpapDan	6Q7			
6QDeut?	6Q20			
8QGen	8Q1			
8QPs	8Q2			
8QPhyl *	8Q3	15		1
8QMez *	8Q4	5		
11QpaleoLev^a *	11Q1	19		2
11QLev^b	11Q2			1
11QDeut	11Q3			
11QEzek	11Q4	1		
11QPs^a *	11Q5		32	1
11QPs^b	11Q6		0	
11QPs^c	11Q7			
11QPs^d	11Q8	1	1	
11QPs^e	11Q9			
34Se1	34Se1	3		
34Se2	34Se2			
5/6Hev1a	5/6Hev1a			
5/6Hev1b *	5/6Hev1b	9		
Gen	Mas1			
Lev	Mas1a			
Lev *	Mas1b	6		
Deut	Mas1c	1		
Ezek *	Mas1d	3		
Psa *	Mas1e	3		
Psa	Mas1f			
Mur Gen 1 *	Mur1	4		
Mur Deut	Mur2	1		
MurIsa	Mur3	2		
MurEx *	Mur4	6		
MurXII *	Mur88	62		
MurGen	MurX			

Scroll Name	Scroll #	לא	לוא	Number of Suffix Plus
Sdeir1	Sdeir1	16		
XHev/Se2	XHev/Se2			
XHev/Se3	XHev/Se3	1		
XHev/Se5 *	XHev/Se5	6		
XQ1 *	XQ1	11		
XQ2 *	XQ2	2		
XQ3 *	XQ3	16		
				64

Index of Authors

Abegg, M.G., Jr., 6, 8, 14, 19, 22, 26–8, 41, 60, 73, 92, 95–7, 106–9, 112, 126–7, 13–4, 143, 164–5
Altman, D.G., 66
Andersen, F.I., 116
Auer, A., 37–8, 70
Baden, J., 108
Berger, P.L., 161, 165–6
Biber, D., 11–13, 40–1, 44, 46–8, 50–55, 60–1
Brooke, G.J., 11, 165
Brown, F., 45, 96
Browner, W.S., 64
Burrows, M., 18–22
Cantos Gómez, P., 42, 61
Collins, J.J., 8–9
Conrad, S., 11–13, 40, 41, 46, 55, 60
Cook, J.A., 2-3, 164–5
Cross, F.M., 4, 10, 12, 25, 38, 69, 116, 145, 153, 155, 159
Crystal, D., 4–5
Fassberg, S.E., 8, 19, 28–9, 49, 92, 141
Feagin, C., 45
Fischer, O., 4
Forbes, A.D., 3, 116
Geiger, G., 10, 35
Goshen-Gottstein, M., 22–4, 26, 98, 116
Grintz, J.M., 12
Grossman, M.L., 161
Halliday, M.A.K., 161–3
Hernández-Campoy, J.M., 45
Holmstedt, R.D., 2–3, 4, 42–4
Hurvitz, A., 1–3, 12, 24, 96, 155
Jacobs, J., 73
Joosten, J., 8–9, 27–9, 108–9
Kim, D.-H., 13
Kutscher, E.Y., 7–8, 12, 18–24, 26–33, 41, 85–6, 96–7, 101, 103, 126, 128, 132–3, 140–1, 172
Labov, W., 3, 47, 55
Lamb, D.A., 161
Longacre, D., 130

Luckmann, T., 161, 165–6
Lumley, T., 65
Mansoor, M., 20–1
Marantz, A., 34
Milik, J.T., 14, 97
Morag, S., 9
Muraoka, T., 7–8, 19, 26–8, 32, 41, 79, 80, 87–9, 92, 97, 101, 109, 111, 116, 123, 132–4, 159
Neuman, W.L., 48–54
Newsom, C., 161, 166
Oakes, M.P, 102
Polzin, R., 2, 3, 111, 155
Pulikottil, P., 19
Qimron, E., 24, 26–30, 80, 82, 96, 111, 116, 132–3, 141–2, 150, 158
Quintana-Domeque, C., 69
Rabin, C., 161
Rendsburg, G.A., 11–12, 161, 163
Renouf, A., 45
Reppen, R., 4, 47, 55, 60
Reymond, E.D., 3, 9–10, 29–30, 70
Rezetko, R., 1-5, 13, 30–6, 55, 80
Romaine, S., 45, 65
Rubinstein, A., 55
Sáenz-Badillos, A., 96, 139, 158
Schilling, N., 45
Schniedewind, W.M., 161, 163, 165
Screnock, J., 4
Talmon, S., 10, 12
Tigchelaar, E.J.C., 25, 161, 163, 167–70
Tov, E., 6, 16, 24–6, 33, 49, 82, 91, 128, 152, 160, 167, 170
Ulrich, E., 14, 23, 61, 126–8, 143, 145, 153
Voeste, A., 37–8, 70
Weitzman, S., 163–5
Wise, M. O., 164–5
Yadin, Y., 82, 161
Young, I., 1–5, 30–6, 55, 116, 155

Index of Biblical Texts

Genesis, 1, 15, 145
Exodus, 1, 10, 53
Leviticus, 1
Numbers, 1, 76, 146–9
Deuteronomy, 1, 76
Joshua, 1
Judges, 80
1 Samuel, 154–9
2 Samuel, 2, 154–9
2 Kings, 1
1 Chronicles, 1
2 Chronicles, 1–2

Ezra, 1
Nehemiah, 1
Esther, 1, 4
Psalms, 52, 53, 54, 81
Song of Songs, 11
Isaiah, 6, 47–55, 103, 120, 130, 136, 140, 141
Jeremiah, 167
Ezekiel, 167
Daniel, 1, 48
Zephaniah, 164–5

Index of Dead Sea Scroll Texts

1QIsa^a, 7, 10, 11, 18–26, 29, 32, 43, 48–54, 59, 79, 81, 85–9, 93, 97, 101, 103–4, 120, 125–45
1QIsa^b, 23, 47–8, 52–4, 93–5, 125, 142–4
4QGen-Exod^a, 139
4QExod^b, 81
4QExod^c, 142
4QExod-Lev^f, 88
4QLev-Num^a, 81
4QNum^b, 76, 125, 145–52
4QpaleoExod^m, 48, 53–4, 81, 88, 137, 139
4QDeut^c, 111, 142
4QDeut^j, 88
4QJudg^b, 89
4QKgs, 88

4QSam^a, 44, 93, 101, 121, 125, 139, 152–60, 168
4QIsa^b, 111
4QIsa^c, 101
4QXII^a, 111
4QXII^c, 81
4QPs^a, 81
4QPs^d, 142
4QPhyl A, 14, 76, 179
4QPhyl K, 88
4QPhyl M, 88
11QPs^a, 48, 52–4, 81, 101, 120, 142
11QPs^c, 58, 79